In this revised and updated edition of his 1989 book, Peter Dorrell provides a comprehensive guide to the uses of photography in archaeology. Drawing on nearly forty years of experience, he examines the use of photography in conservation, in surveys, in field archaeology, and in archaeological laboratories. He offers a clear and well-illustrated explanation of the techniques involved, with sections on equipment and materials, survey and site photography, architectural photography, the recording of different types of artifacts, registration and storage, the use of ultra-violet and infra-red, and photography for publication. He also covers the growing use of video and electronic recording systems.

This book will be essential reading for students of archaeology and conservation, for professional and amateur archaeologists with only a little knowledge of photography, and also for competent photographers who would like to use their skills in the field of archaeology.

PHOTOGRAPHY IN ARCHAEOLOGY
AND CONSERVATION

CAMBRIDGE MANUALS IN ARCHAEOLOGY

Series editors

Don Brothwell, *University of York*
Graeme Barker, *University of Leicester*
Dena Dincauze, *University of Massachusetts, Amherst*
Ann Stahl, *State University of New York, Binghamton*

Already published

J. D. Richards and N. S. Ryan, DATA PROCESSING IN ARCHAEOLOGY
Simon Hillson, TEETH
Alwyne Wheeler and Andrew K. G. Jones, FISHES
Lesley Adkins and Roy Adkins, ARCHAEOLOGICAL ILLUSTRATION
Marie-Agnès Courty, Paul Goldberg and Richard MacPhail, SOILS AND
MICROMORPHOLOGY IN ARCHAEOLOGY
Clive Orton, Paul Tyers and Alan Vince, POTTERY IN ARCHAEOLOGY
R. Lee Lyman, VERTEBRATE TAPHONOMY

Cambridge Manuals in Archaeology are reference handbooks designed for an international audience of professional archaeologists and archaeological scientists in universities, museums, research laboratories, field units, and the public service. Each book includes a survey of current archaeological practice alongside essential reference material on contemporary techniques and methodology.

PHOTOGRAPHY IN ARCHAEOLOGY AND CONSERVATION

SECOND EDITION

Peter G. Dorrell

Institute of Archaeology
University College London

Published by the Press Syndicate of the University of Cambridge
The Pitt Building, Trumpington Street, Cambridge CB2 1RP
40 West 20th Street, New York, NY 10011–4211, USA
10 Stamford Road, Oakleigh, Melbourne 3166, Australia

First published 1989
Second edition 1994

Printed in Great Britain at the University Press, Cambridge

A catalogue record for this book is available from the British Library

Library of Congress cataloguing in publication data

Dorrell, Peter G.
Photography in archaeology and conservation / Peter G. Dorrell. – 2nd edn.
   p. cm. – (Cambridge manuals in archaeology)
Includes bibliographical references and index.
ISBN 0 521 45534 0 (hc) – ISBN 0 521 45554 5 (pb)
1. Photography in archaeology.   I. Title.   II. Series.
CC79.P46D67   1994
930.1′028–dc20   93-46903 CIP

ISBN 0 521 45534 0 hardback (second edition)
ISBN 0 521 32797 0 hardback (first edition)
ISBN 0 521 45554 5 paperback

CE

To Sheila

CONTENTS

ILLUSTRATIONS

Figures

PREFACE

This book is based on courses in archaeological and conservation photography given to students at the Institute of Archaeology, University College London, and on the experience of some years of facing, and sometimes solving, archaeological and photographic problems in Britain, the Mediterranean and the Levant.

A number of books have been published on the subject of archaeological photography, although none of them very recently (Cookson (1954), Matthews (1968), Simmons (1969), Conlon (1973), Chéné et Réveillac (1975), Harp (1975), Nassau (1976)). There are also several books on general archaeological techniques which include substantial sections on photography, e.g. Dever and Lance (1978), Joukowsky (1980), Barker (1982). However, there have been considerable changes in archaeology and conservation, and in photography, in recent years. The other disciplines that are so rapidly becoming involved in the traditional field of archaeology frequently call for special photographic techniques; and the new materials and equipment available to photography are bewildering in their diversity. Most important of all, perhaps, the funding that either field or laboratory work can command has by no means kept pace with rising costs, and recommendations of photographic materials and equipment must constantly take such costs into account. In the same way, any suggestions about methods of working must consider the most economical use of time and personnel.

Partly because of these economic pressures, many archaeologists and conservators now take their own photographs, even on major sites, as they have always done on smaller sites and surveys. This book seeks to provide them with a guide through the complexities of modern photography. Its second purpose is to give a background of archaeological and conservation practice for the many competent photographers, whether professional or amateur, who, caught up in the fascination of the subject, want to use their skills to record the evidence of man's past.

Archaeology is fast becoming a strange amalgam of hand tools and high technology, and photography stands somewhere mid-way between the two. Rather like the English language, it is easy to learn and even easier to use badly. Its prime function is to record, but that record is often incomplete, and all sorts of errors can render it deceiving. By the nature of archaeology, once the structure or artifact is photographed it will probably be altered or

xiii

destroyed, and, for better or worse, the photograph will stand as a true image, along with other records. The photographer has a duty to ensure that the record is clear, correct and complete.

I am grateful for the assistance of many colleagues in the Institute of Archaeology in the writing of this book, and in particular for the practical help of Stuart Laidlaw, Demonstrator in the Photography Department.

PREFACE TO THE SECOND EDITION

Since the first edition of this book was published in 1989, more and more information has emerged from digs, surveys and conservation programmes, themselves proliferating, while techniques and theories have become more complex if not always more informative. A few more books and papers have appeared on one or other aspect of archaeological photography, e.g. Reiss (1990), and Howell and Blanc (1992), although none that sets out to be comprehensive.

For the future, there are two important challenges, as yet unresolved. One is how the mass of information, visual, textual and mathematical, resulting from excavation and post-excavation work on a site, or from a survey, can be made accessible quickly, coherently, and reasonably economically. At present, information, the results of analyses, and statements and interpretations of underlying theories are apt to arrive piecemeal through interim reports, conference papers, monographs, and articles in different journals, culminating perhaps years or even decades later in a final report which, because of sheer bulk, cannot contain all the accrued information and is thus necessarily selective – a selectivity which in the nature of such things is bound to reflect the opinions and preoccupations of the editor or the director.

The second challenge, equally intractable but in a different way, concerns the new techniques that are rapidly encroaching on the field of silver-based photography. The recording, storage, manipulation and retrieval of images through computer-based systems has already transformed large areas of commercial photography. Undoubtedly within a decade or so these innovations will affect the management of archaeological information, although the form that the changes will take is not yet at all clear. A minor, but worrying, offshoot of this process is the ease with which digitally stored images can be manipulated and changed. This facility is already causing problems in other fields of photography, and one can foresee the dangers that might arise if the photographic record of sites or artifacts could no longer be regarded as objective and reliable.

Perhaps there are no short-term solutions to these problems – and certainly no easy ones – but at least they should be borne in mind by anyone concerned with the future of the discipline.

ACKNOWLEDGEMENTS

Plate 45 is reproduced by kind permission of Professor David Oates, and Plates 49 to 52 by that of Mr Jonathan Tubb.

xvi

THE EARLY DAYS OF ARCHAEOLOGICAL PHOTOGRAPHY

As with many scientific advances, photography was the result of the coming together of discoveries in several countries and the application of principles of physics and chemistry long known but not previously put to practical use.

The history of photography is well documented (e.g. Jeffrey (1981); a comprehensive account of early archaeological photography, especially in France, is given in Feyler (1987)), and there is no need to recount it in any detail here, nor to try to assess the claims that have been made for national priorities. Briefly, by 1838 L. J. Daguerre in France had developed a workable process for recording an image on silver-plated copper sheets; and by 1841 W. H. Fox Talbot in England had patented his 'Calotype' process whereby a negative image on silver chloride-impregnated paper was contact printed to give a positive image on a sheet of similar paper. In 1851 F. Scott Archer published an account of his invention of the collodion process, which made possible the use of a glass plate rather than a paper or metal base, thus increasing the effective speed and the range of tones of negatives. The plates had to be coated and used immediately, while still wet, a great inconvenience in field photography, and it was not until the 1870s that a reliable system of using bromide–gelatine emulsions – the dry plate – became available.

Photography began to be used for the recording of antiquities surprisingly early. In this country, Fox Talbot – himself an antiquarian, among many other things – took photographs of manuscripts, engravings and busts.

At this time archaeology was still very much influenced by antiquarianism, and there was little interest in the context or in the sequence of objects and buildings. Sites, and particularly classical sites, were regarded largely as a source of suitable exhibits for public and private collections, and the travellers, diplomats and soldiers who described, drew and, later, photographed them were rarely concerned with anything beyond the visible, standing remains. In the latter part of the century photography played a major role in the development of a more scientific, analytical approach to recording and excavation of sites. By its nature, photography was, and is, unselective; it records the background as well as the building, the deposit in which an object is found as well as the object itself. In addition, it was seen to be objective. Draughtsmen and scholars, in Europe at any rate, were trained in and were familiar with the classical tradition and when they moved beyond the Mediterranean they were apt still to consider and record artifacts –

particularly statuary – according to the classical canon. Photography did much to counteract this understandable bias.

By the 1850s archaeologists had begun to regard photography as a panacea, rather as their descendants a hundred years later were to regard C14 (radioactive carbon) dating, and much the same sort of disillusion followed when it was realised that such innovations were capable of distorting evidence. In 1852 the Trustees of the British Museum consulted Fox Talbot, Brooke (the Superintendent of the Photographic Department of the Royal Observatory) and Wheatstone (physicist and father of electro-telegraphy) regarding the possibility of photographing cuneiform tablets in the museum; and in 1853 Roger Fenton, at the invitation of the Trustees, submitted a report on the costs of building a glass-house and darkroom in the Museum grounds for the photography of artifacts by the Calotype process. The Museum's action had been prompted by the great number of artifacts, and especially tablets and inscriptions, that had arrived from Sir Henry Layard's excavations at Nineveh (Nimrud). These, it was felt, could be adequately studied only if photographs were distributed to a wide circle of scholars. Like so many subsequent schemes, this grand plan of recording and distribution ran out of funds part-way through, and was never completed.[1] Layard's books on Nineveh (e.g. Layard (1849)) had in fact been illustrated by engravings based on field drawings.

In 1854 the Society of Antiquaries appointed, at his own suggestion, Dr H. W. Diamond as Honorary Photographer to the Society, but he seems to have undertaken little photography on the Society's behalf thereafter (Evans (1956): 290–3). Also in 1854 the Society wrote to the Lieutenant General of the Ordnance of the British Army, then on its way to the Crimea, asking that 'the photographer who accompanies the army in the East may be instructed to take and transmit photographic views of any antiquities which he may observe'. Lord Raglan agreed to the request, although doubting that there were many ancient remains to be seen in Bulgaria, where the headquarters then was. No photographs materialised, although the photographer – the same Roger Fenton who had earlier been in correspondence with the British Museum – will always be remembered for his classic photographs of the battlefields of the Crimea, producing more than 350 negatives, the first ever to be taken in war conditions.

During the same period in France public interest in the new medium was intense, and public funding for its use in recording monuments and ancient sites was considerably greater and better organised than in this country. Baron Gros made daguerrotypes of the monuments of North Africa, and the first of the photographs of French architecture that formed the nucleus of the Archives Photographiques at Paris date from 1850. In 1851 the administra-

[1] I am indebted to Dr Julian Reade of the Western Asiatic Department of the British Museum for information on these transactions.

tion of the Beaux Arts sent photographers out to 'constitute the basis of a
pictorial and archaeological museum' of the principal monuments (Philibert
(1975)). An outstanding contribution to the early recording of ancient sites
was the series of photographs of monuments in Egypt, Nubia, Palestine and
Syria made by M. du Camp during his travels with Flaubert from 1849 to
1851. In 1851, L. D. Blanquart-Evrard opened a photographic printing
works in Lille, using (without acknowledgement) a modification of Fox

Plate 1   Gate at Khorsabad. Taken by M. Tranchand during Place's
excavations, 1852–1855.

Talbot's Calotype process. He produced a folio of 125 of du Camp's photographs, which enjoyed a huge popular success and did much to make accessible the monuments of the East both to scholars and to the general public.

Probably the first archaeological expedition to use photography in the field was that of R. Lepsius in Egypt in 1842–45. Perhaps the most significant French work, however, from the standpoint of archaeological photography, was the series of photographs made by M. Tranchand during the excavations of V. Place in Assyria from 1852 to 1855 (Pillet (1962)). Place, the French Consul in Mosul, followed the discoveries of his predecessor in the post, P. E. Botta, by conducting the first excavations at Khorsabad, and recording the rock-cut figures at Maltai and Bavian. Place and Tranchand also travelled through Armenia and Kurdestan and photographed the more picturesque sites. The first records were made by daguerrotype, but later the Calotype process was used. Although the original negatives seem to have disappeared after the Second World War, most of them were reprinted or copied in the

Plate 2   The Cnidus Lion. Lithograph based on a photograph taken during C. T. Newton's excavations, 1860.

1920s, and they had already been used as the basis for the engravings that illustrated Place's publications (Place (1867)). As can be seen (Plate 1), they compare well with many modern site photographs; there is sufficient raking light to record the detail of the brickwork and of the statues, the viewpoint has been chosen to show the depth of the arch, the level of the foreground and the top of the wall, and the photograph includes a figure to serve as a scale.

Plate 3   Archway at Samothrace. Albumen print from Conze's report on the excavations, 1880.

Photography also played a part in the expansion of interest in the Biblical sites of Palestine, starting with the work of A. Salzmann in 1854 and Captain Wilson's survey of Jerusalem in the 1860s. In Egypt in 1855 J. B. Greene made calotype photographs of his excavations at Thebes, and in 1865 C. P. Smith was the first to use magnesium flash lighting, in the interior chambers of the Great Pyramid (Feyler (1987)).

At about the same time, C. T. Newton was excavating in Greece and Turkey, and in his magnificent report (Newton (1862)), published within a year of the end of the excavation, many of the litho illustrations were directly based on photographs taken on site (Plate 2). Many of the plates were simpler and less cluttered than the one shown here, although most seem to include several pipe-smoking seamen and nonchalant midshipmen.

Probably the first report to use actual photographs and not lithographs or engravings derived from photographs (and it has also been called 'perhaps the first modern archaeological excavation account we have' (Daniel (1967, p. 143)), was that of Conze (Conze *et al.* (1880)) of his work at Samothrace. The publication includes gold-toned albumen paper prints tipped-in to the pages (Plate 3). They appear not to have faded in a hundred years, and the standard of photography is excellent. Certainly they equal, or surpass, the photographs in many present-day reports. Publications continued to be illustrated in this way, or by derived engravings or lithographs, for some years, and effective methods of photomechanical reproduction did not become widespread until the last decades of the century, although 'heliotypes' printed from collodion surfaces appeared some years earlier (e.g. Plate 4 from Pattison, (1872)).

In America, W. H. Jackson, the great photographer of the American West, made the first records of the Mesa Verde and other Pueblo sites of the South-western States in the years following 1870. In the 1880s, A. P. Maudslay, E. H. Thompson, T. Maler and others made extensive records of the buildings and monuments of Mexico; some of these photographs were of a very high standard, contributing to the great archive of the Peabody Museum. But systematic, scientific excavation was slow to start in the New World. During this period the looting and destruction of sites in the continent equalled that in Europe and the Middle East; and because the sites of North America in particular were generally smaller and more vulnerable than those in the Middle East, the process was even more destructive. It was really only with the excavations of F. W. Putnam in Ohio from 1890 onwards that photography in America became a tool of field archaeology rather than simply a way to illustrate the monuments.

During the last years of the nineteenth century and the first quarter of the twentieth, photography took its place as one of the standard techniques of excavation and of the recording of artifacts.

Although photographs of ancient sites had been taken from captive balloons as far back as the 1880s, the full potentialities of aerial photography in the study of ancient settlement in the Middle East were realised only just before, and during, the First World War. The development of these potentialities in the interpretation of the less evident traces of sites in Europe in the 1920s was due largely to the work of O. G. S. Crawford in Wessex (a brief account of the development of aerial photography in archaeology is given in Daniel (1967), pp. 285–290).

The idea that site photographs should reveal every detail of the excavations as they proceeded, with sections precisely cut and meticulously cleaned, was, characteristically, propounded and insisted on by Mortimer Wheeler, and carried out by his photographer, M. B. Cookson, during their long association. However rarely achieved, this ideal remains central to the practice of archaeological photography today.

Plate 4   Handle of bronze vessel from Buitron. Heliotype illustration from *Archaeologia* 1872.

2

BASIC PRINCIPLES AND PRACTICE

A book of this nature must assume a certain knowledge of the basic principles of photography. There are many reliable books that can be consulted (Langford (1986) is one of the most comprehensive), and all that is attempted in this chapter is a resumé of the terms and concepts most often used, and a brief explanation of how the principles are applied in archaeological photography.

Forming an image

Visible light, the section of the electromagnetic spectrum from about 400 to 700 nanometres (1 nanometre, nm, = 10^{-9} metres, or one-millionth of a millimetre) that is reflected from an object or scene, can be focussed through a lens by 'bending' or refraction of the light rays to form a sharp image behind the lens. Sections of the total spectrum of wavelengths shorter or longer than visible light can also be recorded photographically by the special techniques of ultra-violet and infra-red photography.

Light reflected from a very distant object – more or less at infinity – will reach the lens as parallel beams, and the distance between the lens and the point at which such light is focussed constitutes the *focal length* of the lens. This is always expressed in millimetres. Since the focal length of a lens determines the size of the image, i.e. for an object the same distance away from the lens a long focal length lens will give a larger image than one of short focal length, it also determines the *angle of view*, the amount of the scene in front of the camera taken in by the lens.[1] For each format of camera (i.e. the size of film for which the camera is designed) one particular focal length of lens is taken as 'standard'. By convention, the *standard lens* is of a focal length about the same as the diagonal of the film format, but, more important, the angle of view accepted by the standard lens is approximately the same – about 45° – as that taken in by the relaxed human eye, disregarding the area of peripheral vision. Thus, if the whole of a negative taken with a standard lens were enlarged, or if a transparency were thrown on a screen, the observers would see much the same amount of the scene or object, and objects at different distances within the picture would be in roughly the same propor-

---

[1] This is not completely true, since the angle taken in by a lens focussed to infinity is not the same as that taken in when it is focussed on a closer object, but the difference is small enough to be unimportant in this context.

tions, as if they were looking at the scene themselves.[2] For a 35 mm format, the standard lens is of focal length 50 or 55 mm, for 6 × 6 or 6 × 4.5 cm format, 75 or 80 mm, for 6 × 9 cm, 100 mm, and for 5 × 4 in, 150 mm.

A term similar to angle of view, though not identical, is *covering power* or coverage. The covering power of a lens is the maximum area at the film plane over which the lens will give a sharp and evenly illuminated image. This varies with the lens construction and the format for which the lens was designed. Ideally, for a 35 mm format lens, of whatever length, the covering power should be just enough to cover the diagonal of the format at all magnifications and no more, so that there is no surplus light projected through the lens and not falling on the film. Within the body of a small-format camera, which for reasons of compactness is always as small as possible, any surplus light is likely to reflect in some degree from the walls of the body and to reach the film as '*flare*', overall unfocussed light that degrades the image. For a large-format camera with movements (see next chapter), on the other hand, the covering power needs to be considerably greater than the size of the film, otherwise camera movements cannot be used without immediately running out of image. Since the dimensions of a large-format camera are not judged to be so important, the body can be proportionately larger, and the bellows act as a baffle to intercept and absorb surplus light. Because of differences in covering power, a lens designed for one format is not usually suitable for use in a camera of a larger format, no matter what the focal length.

Lenses are available in other focal lengths, apart from the standard one, but the range of choice is widely different between one format and another. For most makes of 35 mm camera, fifteen or more different lengths of lens are available, ranging from 'fish-eye' lenses of 6 or 8 mm focal length, giving an angle of 180° or more, to extremely long lenses with a focal length of 1200 mm and an angle of only 2°. Only a few of these would be useful in archaeology; suitable sets are suggested in Chapters 8 and 9. The range is more restricted for other formats; perhaps six or eight on average for medium-format cameras, and no more than three or four for large format. Both short (*wide-angle*) lenses and long lenses (often referred to as *telephoto* lenses, although telephoto implies a certain type of design in which the focal length is greater than the actual physical length of the lens, and not all long lenses are therefore telephoto) have certain characteristics arising from their angles of view which affect the appearance of the image.

Perspective and distortion
Perspective, taken here to mean simply the apparent difference in the relative sizes of near and far objects, is a function of the distance away of the observer

---

[2] This again needs to be qualified. To achieve this viewpoint, strictly speaking, the observer should be at a distance from the image of the focal length of the lens × the degree of enlargement. But except in extreme cases – looking at a wall-size enlargement from a distance of 50 cm for instance – the viewing distance is not critical.

– or of the camera – and nothing else. If three cameras with short, standard and long focal-length lenses were lined up side by side, focussed on, say, a building 100 m away, each viewfinder would show a different amount of the building and its background, but the perspective effect – the apparent difference in size between the nearest and the farthest parts of the building – would be the same in each case (Plates 5, 6 and 7). If, however, the cameras were so positioned that each showed the leading corner of the building as the same size on the viewfinder, the camera with the short lens being therefore closest to the building and that with the long lens farthest away, then the perspective effect would be different in each case; steeper with the short lens and flatter with the long (Plates 8 and 9). Although there cannot be a question of 'correct' or 'incorrect' perspective as such in a photograph, undoubtedly the perspective that seems most natural is that presented by a standard lens because of the correspondence of the angle of view of this lens with the eye.

Short lenses are subject to so-called *wide-angle distortion*. This arises from the obliqueness of the rays at the edge of the field and gives a radial distortion of objects at the sides, and especially in the corners, of the photograph (Plates 10, 11, 12 and 13). This effect increases the shorter the focal length, and for the purposes of accurate record becomes unacceptable with a lens whose angle of view is wider than about 75 to 80°, i.e. 28 mm lenses on 35 mm format cameras, 40 mm on 6 × 6 cm, 80 mm on 5 × 4 in. Older wide-angle lenses suffered, as cheap ones still do, from *barrel distortion* (the convex curvature of lines towards the edge of the field) and fall-off of definition and illumination in the corners of the field. These problems have largely been overcome in modern lenses, but such faults as still occur are, again, greater the wider the angle.

Long lenses are less subject to such aberrations, since the chief cause, obliqueness of the rays entering the lens, does not apply. They do suffer very often from a slight lowering of the contrast range of the image compared with shorter lenses, and from a slight loss of resolution. This is due simply to the fact that most photographs using long lenses are taken at considerable distances, within which there may be air turbulence and scattering of blue light and ultra-violet. This can be partly overcome by using a UV barrier filter for both colour and black and white. Perspective often appears to be very much flattened in photographs taken with a long lens, distant objects appearing to be of much the same size as those in the middle distance, giving a 'stacked-up' appearance to successive planes of the photograph. This effect, and at least some of the effect of wide-angle distortion, is made more apparent because photographs, if they are of a similar size, are normally viewed from about the same distance from the eye. For someone reading a book or journal, this would be about 30 or 40 cm; but using the formula of focal length × enlargement, for a photograph taken with a 24 mm lens and enlarged five times, the distance should be 12 cm, while for one taken with a

Plate 5

Plate 6

Plate 7

Focal length and perspective. Plate 5 was taken with a 35 mm camera fitted with a 100 mm lens, Plate 6 from the same position with a 50 mm lens and Plate 7 with a 28 mm lens. The angle of view, and thus the sizes of objects in the frame, is different in each case, but the perspective effect is identical.

Plate 8

Plate 9

Focal length and perspective. Plate 8 was taken with a 35 mm camera fitted with a 28 mm lens, and Plate 9 from farther away but on approximately the same line. The perspective effect, and particularly the amount of roof revealed, is quite different.

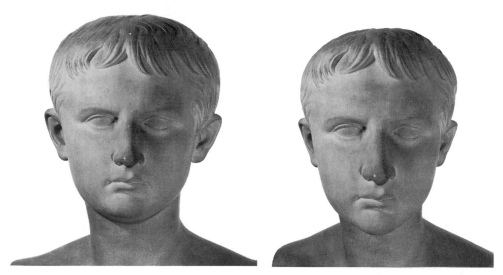

Plate 10, Plate 11   Wide-angle lens and perspective. Plate 10 was taken with a 5 × 4 in camera fitted with a 240 mm lens from a distance of about 3 m, Plate 11 with the same camera with a 90 mm lens from about 50 cm. The distorted appearance given by the wider angle lens is due to the steeper perspective.

Plate 12, Plate 13   Distortion due to viewpoint. Both were taken with a 5 × 4 in camera fitted with a 150 cm lens, Plate 12 from about 2 m and Plate 13 from about 40 cm. The difference in the proportions of the figures is due partly to the steeper perspective of the near viewpoint, and partly to the steeper angle of view. The more distant view also 'sees' farther round the pot.

500 mm lens and enlarged to the same extent, it should be 2.5 m. Some distortion is therefore inevitable.

Focussing and exposure
On nearly all lenses the amount of light passing through the lens is controlled by an *iris diaphragm*, a device of overlapping metal leaves within the lens, itself controlled by the *aperture ring* on the lens barrel. The *stops* or *f-numbers*

marked on this ring are *relative apertures*, i.e. they are calculated from the ratio of the diameter of the opening and the focal length of the lens, so that the amount of light passed by a lens set to a particular f-number will be the same, in theory, as that passed by any other lens, no matter what its focal length, at the same setting. There is, as usual, a slight reservation about this, since different lenses have rather different light-passing qualities, depending on the density of the glass, the number of elements and the lens coating, but these differences are usually small enough to be ignored. The rather arcane series of numbers shown on the aperture ring, a series which all manufacturers now follow (f2, f2.8, f4, f5.6, f8, f11, f16, f22, f32) is related to area and not diameter, so an adjustment of the aperture ring from one position to the next will halve or double the amount of light admitted through the lens. Fast lenses, i.e. lenses of large diameter in relation to their focal length, often have maximum apertures larger than f2, e.g. f1.8, 1.4, or 1.2; f1.4 is roughly twice the area of f2, and f1.8 is intermediate between the two.

Apart from its importance in determining the exposure (the total dosage of light reaching the film, calculated from aperture × shutter speed), the aperture is one of the factors affecting the *depth of field* and *depth of focus*.

Depth of field

When a camera is focussed at any distance, a point reflected from that distance should be reproduced as a point on the film, so far as the resolution of the emulsion and the aberrations of the lens allow. Points in front of and beyond that distance become successively less well-defined discs the farther they are from the focussed distance. There is a zone, however, which extends in front of and behind the focussed distance within which points will appear to be acceptably sharp in the print or transparency, since the eye has a limited resolving power. This is the depth of field, and it varies with focal length, with the distance at which the lens is focussed, with the aperture and with the size of the disc deemed acceptable (known as the *circle of confusion*). The first three of these factors are associated with the apex angle of the cone of light subtended at the lens, and thus with the diameter of the disc of light reaching the film. The geometry in this context is unimportant, but the practical considerations are considerable.

Firstly, the shorter the focal length, the greater the depth of field. This applies if two photographs are taken from the same position with lenses of different focal length. In the wider-angle photograph, each object within the viewfinder will appear smaller, and components of each object smaller down to the point level, and therefore the depth of field will take in more of them, front to back. If an object is focussed to the same size with the two lenses, however, that is if the shorter lens is closer to the object than the longer one, the depth of field will be virtually the same. There is another consideration, however; the standard lens for a 35 mm camera is 50 mm, while that for a

5 × 4 in format is 150 mm. Both take in roughly the same angle, but when both are set to f8, for instance, the shorter lens will give a depth of field about four times as great as that of the longer lens.

Secondly, the farther away the object, the greater the depth of field. The more distant the object, the smaller will its image be, the closer behind the lens will it be focussed, and the greater will be the depth of field. If an object in the middle distance is focussed upon, objects and spaces behind it will appear smaller than those in front of it, and thus the depth of field extends farther behind an object at this distance than it does in front. For any focal length of lens, at any aperture, it is possible to calculate a distance at which the depth of field will just extend back to infinity. This is known as the *hyperfocal distance*, and at this distance sharp focus will extend from the object back to infinity, and forward half as far as the hyperfocal distance. Thus for a photograph to show the most distant detail in sharp focus and as much as possible of the foreground sharply, it is unnecessary to focus on the distant detail; if the lens is set to the hyperfocal distance, the distance will appear sharply focussed but much more of the foreground will also be sharp. Unlike most depth of field calculations, which are rather complicated, the formula for hyperfocal distance is fairly simple:

$$\frac{\text{Focal length}^2}{\text{f-no.} \times \text{diameter of circle of confusion}} = \text{hyperfocal distance}$$

The size of the circle of confusion is discussed below, but taking it for the moment to be 0.03 mm, then for a 50 mm lens set at f8:

$$\frac{2500}{8 \times 0.03} = 10.4 \text{ m}$$

So if the lens were set at this distance, detail would be acceptably sharp from half this distance, 5.2 m, to infinity. The disparity between the two parts of the depth of field has led to the general precept 'focus one third of the way back'. This certainly holds good for distant objects, and to focus, for instance, one third back in the visible depth of a building will give the best chance of having the whole building in focus; but the difference between the two depths becomes less the closer the object, and at 'same size' the two are the same depth and the system is symmetrical. For close-up work, therefore, and for distances up to about 1 m (with a standard lens), it is better to focus one half of the way back.

The third consideration involving depth of field is that the smaller the aperture the greater the depth of field. As the lens is closed down the cone of light reflected from any point and reaching the lens is similarly narrowed, and an acceptable circle of confusion will be farther from the apex of the cone; points nearer and farther from the point of focus will therefore be rendered sharply and the depth of field will be increased. The effect is fairly straightforward: as the aperture is decreased the depth of field increases (Plates 14, 15, 16 and 17). This applies with all focal lengths and at all distances, but the amount of increase is not constant, nor can it be plotted on a straight line. The increase, for instance, between f22 and f32 is much greater than the increase between f2 and f2.8.

Plate 14

Plate 15

Aperture and depth of field. All were taken with a 6 × 6 cm camera fitted with an 80 mm lens, at a distance of 1 m from the central figurine.

Finally, the larger the acceptable circle of confusion, the greater the depth of field. On the face of it, this means no more than saying, 'if it is acceptable for the nearest and farthest parts of the object to appear slightly out of focus, then the depth of field can be said to cover the object', a fairly meaningless provision. But there are two other considerations; one, which has already

Plate 16

Plate 17

The depth, front to back, of the group was 50 cm. In Plate 14 the aperture was f2.8, in Plate 15, f5.6, in Plate 16, f 11, and in Plate 17, f 22.

been mentioned in connection with perspective, is viewing distance. A photograph published in a book will probably be looked at from ordinary reading distance. The same photograph enlarged to cover a wall might look equally sharp if the viewing distance were similarly increased, perhaps to three or four metres, but if it were viewed from, say, one metre, the resolution would have to be much finer. In other words, the acceptable circle of confusion would be smaller. The other consideration is the degree of enlargement necessitated by the format. A 5 × 4 in negative would have to be enlarged about two and a half times to make an A4 print from the whole frame, while a 35 mm negative would have to be enlarged about eight and a half times to make a print of similar size. Thus the smaller the negative, the more critical must the resolution be, and the smaller the acceptable circle of confusion. If both cameras were fitted with their respective standard lenses, or with other lenses of similar angles of view, this difference would go some way to compensate for the shorter depth of field of the longer lens. Because of this need for greater resolution on small formats, good lenses for 35 mm cameras are designed to yield a circle of confusion of a maximum size of 0.03 or 0.025 mm (this, though, is the 'circle of least confusion' i.e. the maximum size of disc corresponding to a point on the plane of focus, not on the edge of the depth of field). For larger formats, an acceptable circle is often taken to be $\frac{1}{1000}$ of the focal length, i.e. 0.15 mm for a 150 mm lens on 5 × 4 in, or 0.1 mm for a 100 mm lens on 6 × 9 cm format.

So, in practice, to achieve a maximum depth of field, a short lens should be used on a small-format camera, with as small an aperture as possible, and if sharpness is needed right to the horizon, focussed to the hyperfocal distance; while for a minimum depth of field, the ideal is a long lens on a large-format camera, with a large aperture, and focussed from one half to one third of the way back in the visible depth of the object (if this gives too short an exposure to be practicable, light can be reduced with a neutral density filter without affecting the depth of field).

In general, in archaeological site photography a considerable, if not the theoretical maximum, depth of field is desirable. Almost everything in the picture is sharply focussed and all detail is clear. There are times, however, when a much shallower depth is preferable; for showing some architectural detail clearly against a jumbled background, for instance, or for selecting one artifact from among several in a museum showcase, it is effective for the detail or artifact to be sharply focussed and the background to be out of focus. The problem of depth of field in close-up photography is discussed in Chapter 10.

Depth of focus
A concept in some ways parallel with that of depth of field, and often confused with it, is depth of focus. While depth of field is concerned with how deep a zone in front of the lens can be brought into acceptable focus, depth of

focus describes the distance through which the film plane can be moved, backwards and forwards, while retaining the image of an object or point in sharp focus. This adjustment, and its deliberate use, are of much less frequent concern than is the depth of field, and the factors that affect it need be discussed only briefly. It is chiefly of importance in the use of camera movements; when the back or front of the camera is swung or tilted so that the lens axis no longer meets the film plane at right angles, the edges of the image will become unsharp unless they fall within the depth of focus. (The use of camera movements is discussed in Chapter 3.)

The controlling factors are the same as those affecting depth of field, focal length, focussed distance, aperture and the acceptable size of the circle of confusion; and they are similarly based on the narrowing of cones of light from the lens, but the effects are different.

Firstly, in this case the longer the focal length, the greater the depth of focus. Thus a large-format camera with a relatively long standard lens has an inherently greater depth of focus than has a smaller format with a shorter standard lens. This is why the fullest camera movements can be achieved only with large-format cameras, and why the plane of the film in 35 mm cameras has to be so exactly positioned with pressure plate and guide rails – the shallowness of the depth of focus leaves no room for manoeuvre. Secondly, again unlike depth of field, the closer the camera is focussed, the greater the depth of focus, and this depth extends equally on both sides of the film plane. For this reason, it can be difficult to focus a large-format camera used for close-up photography; the back of the camera can be moved backwards and forwards by a centimetre or more without apparently affecting greatly the sharpness of the image. It often helps to focus with a magnifying glass in these circumstances.

Thirdly, as with the depth of field, the smaller the aperture the greater the depth of focus. For this reason, when the use of swing or tilt movements throws the edges of the image out of focus, sharpness can, within limits, be restored by stopping down the aperture. This is also the reason why a camera, or an enlarger, should always be focussed with the lens wide open, especially when the camera is being used for close-up work, or the enlarger for low magnification. The reduced depth of focus makes it easier to judge when the image is sharp. Finally, as with depth of field, obviously the lower the permissible standard of sharpness, the larger the acceptable circle of confusion, and thus the greater the depth of focus.

The practical points arising from these considerations of depth of focus can be summed up thus: the greatest correction of convergence can be achieved only with a large-format camera; any misalignment of the film in a small-format camera will result in unsharp photographs; cameras and enlargers should always be focussed with the aperture wide open; and, for close-up work with a large-format camera, the sharpness of the image should be checked with a magnifying glass.

3

EQUIPMENT

This chapter does not represent a complete catalogue and description of photographic equipment of all kinds, nor anything approaching it. It is concerned only with the types of cameras and lenses employed in archaeology and conservation, and with darkslides, shutters, light meters and light filters, some of which may be unfamiliar to archaeologists and conservators whose experience has been limited to 35 mm cameras. The use of camera movements is also discussed, since an understanding of them can be of value in all the aspects of photography discussed in the chapters that follow. For the same reason, some general points are made about the purpose and use of scales. Later chapters deal with the special requirements for equipment used in different fields, such as site photography and the photography of objects in the laboratory or studio.

Cameras and lenses

Cameras

There are two types of *large-format cameras* in general use: *monorail cameras* (Plate 18), in which a lens panel and a film (focussing) panel move along a central rail, the two panels connected by bellows; and *baseboard* or *technical cameras* (Plate 19), in which a hinged flap which carries the lens panel folds down from a box-like body to the back of which is attached a focussing screen. Both types are also known as *view cameras*.

Monorail cameras are the most widely used large-format cameras for architecture and for studio use. The commonest format is 5×4 in (12.5×10 cm, but known universally as 5×4 cameras), although larger sizes (23×18 cm (9×7 in) and 25×20 cm (10×8 in)) are also made. For both site and conservation photography, the advantages of using a size any larger than 5×4 would be minimal, and the larger sizes are more expensive, more unwieldy and higher in film cost.

Because so few are produced, all monorail cameras are relatively expensive (between twice and six times the cost of an average 35 mm camera), and they remain so on the secondhand market. The front panel (or '*standard*') can take different lenses, each in its own panel, and the rear standard houses the focussing screen, which is usually engraved with a grid for accurate alignment of verticals and horizontals. The screen is held on spring arms so that when the film-holder (or *darkslide*) is slotted into position in front of it, the film should be in exactly the same plane as was the focussing screen while the image was being focussed. To give sufficient lens-to-film extension to accommodate very long lenses and for close-up work, an extra bellows unit can be fitted, and for short lenses, when the ordinary accordion bellows would hold the two standards too far apart, they can be replaced by 'bag' bellows

Plate 18   Typical monorail camera with all movements at zero.

Plate 19   Typical baseboard camera with all movements at zero.

which are much less bulky. The camera is focussed by moving either the rear or the front standard along the rail, to which they are attached by bearings with focussing knobs and locking mechanisms. Both standards are so designed that the lens panel and the film panel can be moved vertically and horizontally and can be swung about vertical and horizontal axes. The use of these adjustments is discussed in the following section on camera movements.

The advantages of the monorail camera are its modular design, which enables its various parts to be rearranged or replaced, and its flexibility, which allows of the fullest use of camera movements. For precision work it cannot be bettered, and as with other large-format cameras the size of the film can yield the best possible resolution, while the use of single-sheet films means that adjustments can be made at the processing stage which are impossible with roll film. On the other hand, monorail cameras are rather heavy and unwieldy for use in the field; they must be used with a tripod; film is relatively expensive (one sheet of 5 × 4 costs about six times as much as one frame of 35 mm); and processing equipment costs more and takes up more space than does that for smaller formats. The number of exposures that can be made at one session is restricted by the number of darkslides available, unless a changing bag is used.

Technical cameras are less flexible than monorail; they have the same size advantage but a limited range of movements. Since they can be folded they are less bulky to carry but just about as heavy. They can be hand-held, given a strong left wrist, which monorail cameras cannot. Their new price is in the same range as monorails, but they can be bought more cheaply secondhand (presumably because most professionals prefer monorail in this format). Before the advent of medium-format SLR (single lens reflex) cameras there was a type of camera known as a *'press camera'*, and these still turn up from time to time on the secondhand market. They should be avoided, however cheap, because while having the appearance of technical cameras, they have no movements at all, and there is little point in buying a large-format camera without this facility. Restriction of darkslide numbers and processing are the same for all technical cameras as for monorail cameras.

Field cameras were the forerunners of technical cameras. Made of brass and mahogany, the few that are still made are expensive to buy new, and they are almost equally expensive secondhand. They are beautiful pieces of crafts-manship and dealers buy them up to resell as *objets d'art*. They are rather awkward to use but if one is available – and there are still plenty about at the back of museum cupboards – they are not at all to be despised. They can do all that a technical camera can, and they have one unique and considerable advantage: if broken, they can be easily repaired on site. Even if a field camera were dropped down a deep trench, the chances are that, using glue and string, it could be made serviceable again, which is more than can be said for virtually any other camera.

As well as the 5 × 4 in format, a few manufacturers make both monorail and technical cameras in a smaller size – 2 ½ × 3 ½ in (6.5 × 9 cm). These are rather rare, and they are not proportionately cheaper than the larger size, but for site work they have great advantages. Lighter and more compact, they can still produce a negative of high quality, and they can moreover be fitted with roll-film backs, so that single negatives can be taken and processed separately, or eight or ten negatives, depending on format, taken on roll film. Roll-film backs can also be fitted on to some larger-format cameras, but at the cost of being able to use only the centre of the screen. One disadvantage of the 2 ½ × 3 ½ in format is that only a restricted range of sheet films are made in this size. In particular, lith film is not, so they can be used for line copying only by the tedious method of cutting up larger sheets of film in the darkroom. It is possible, just, to cut two sheets of 2 ½ × 3 ½ in from one sheet of 5 × 4 in, but it is a finicky business.

As well as these smaller monorail and technical cameras, there is a considerable, and growing, range of *medium-format cameras* available, both twin and single-lens reflex. They are all based on 120 roll film, so all have the same film width – 6 cm – but different models divide the length of the film differently, giving 8, 10, 12 or 15 exposures along the roll. Some can also be used with 220 film, giving twice the number of exposures. Twin-lens reflex cameras are being replaced in professional use by single-lens reflex, and are therefore obtainable relatively cheaply on the secondhand market. Only one manufacturer, Mamiya, makes a twin-lens reflex with interchangcable lenses. Although heavy, these cameras are quite suitable for use in the field. They suffer from parallax error (i.e. the viewing lens does not frame exactly the same image as the taking lens), but this is relatively unimportant in all but close-up work, and they have the advantage of a large viewfinder, the same size as the format, at right angles to the lens axis, so that the camera can be held at arm's length, looking vertically down into a trench, or sideways hard against the wall of a tomb, for focussing. There is a wide range of medium-format single-lens reflex cameras available, and the prices range from twice up to five or six times that of an average 35 mm camera. They are still expensive when secondhand, and caution should be used here, as it should when buying good secondhand 35 mm cameras. Such cameras may have been used only by amateurs and sold when still unworn, but more of them are likely to be ex-professional, and professionals are apt to have given the camera very heavy use indeed before selling it. They can give excellent results, and to a large extent combine the advantages of a larger format with the ease of handling of 35 mm cameras, but a good part of their price is accounted for by features such as speed of reloading, focussing screen information displays and wide-aperture lenses which are of no particular value on a dig. It would be difficult to justify the cost of such a camera to an excavation, although of course if one became available without cost it should be welcomed. Some have a very limited range of lens movements, and some manufacturers supply shift lenses for them – again, at a considerable cost.

Of the two types of *35 mm camera* available – SLR and rangefinder – the commoner, SLR, type is preferable. The only advantages of rangefinder cameras – a relatively silent shutter, and the image being visible throughout the exposure – are of little value for site photography and are more than outweighed by the lack of parallax error and the ready availability of SLR cameras. There are, of course, a great variety of makes and models available, at a considerable range of prices. Most of them are thoroughly reliable, and fierce competition ensures that price is more or less matched by value, although there are a few prestigious names which command disproportionately high prices. It is always worthwhile comparing the prices from different dealers, since discounts and special offers are constantly being promoted and, for secondhand equipment, looking through the private advertisements in photographic magazines. With such a field to choose from, selection becomes a matter of the money available and of personal preference. One can list, however, the features that are necessary for site and laboratory work, those that are desirable but not vital, and those that are positively undesirable.

The important features are:

> interchangeable lens mounts;
> built-in meter with centre weighting or, better still, spot facility;
> depth of field pre-view facility;
> manual operating mode and, if the camera is automatic, aperture priority mode.

Desirable though not vital:

> self-timer;
> exposure lock;
> interchangeable screen and viewfinder (if there is a choice, the most useful type of screen is one engraved with grid lines; upright and inclined viewfinders might occasionally be desirable);
> long exposure facility (up to 4 or 6 seconds);
> LED display in viewfinder (much more visible in dim conditions);
> under- and over-exposure, or 'backlight' facility;
> dedicated or automatic flash facility;
> facility for self-winder, if the camera is to be used on a tower, kite or balloon;
> facility for remote control, similarly;
> black body.

Positively undesirable:

> self-focus and auto-zoom;
> DX coding setting only (useless if bulk film is used);
> fully automatic mode only;
> shutter-priority mode only.

There are a few other facilities available, for example data back and automatic exposure bracketing, which are never likely to be very useful but which can do no harm, if they cost no more.

In general, metal bodies are tougher than plastic, and popular makes and models are more easily serviced than exotic ones. Ease of handling is a personal matter, depending largely on how big the photographer's hands are and on his or her eyesight, and this can only be decided by handling various models.

The past few years have seen a proliferation of *compact* cameras: small 35 mm bodies, usually plastic, with non-interchangeable lenses, and with all or many of their functions automatic. Such cameras are a pleasure to use: light, well designed and extremely simple in operation; but although they might well be useful on a dig for informal photographs, or as a back-up, they should not be relied upon as the sole camera. Their range of facilities is too restricted, particularly for close-up work, and many are not strongly enough built.

Lenses

A standard lens, a moderately wide-angle lens (75–85°), and more occasionally, a moderately long-focal-length lens (18–12°) should deal with most situations on a dig. For 35 mm and roll-film cameras a macro lens is useful and more convenient than using extension tubes. Although there are many occasions on a dig when a lens of wider angle of view than 85° would seem useful, such lenses inevitably produce such distortion at the edge of the field, through both steepened perspective and curvature of straight lines, as to outweigh their advantage of wider coverage. 85° seems to be about the limit at which an acceptable image can be produced. Lenses are designed for one particular format, and are not usually interchangeable between formats.

The normal lens for *large-format*, 5 × 4 in, cameras is 150 mm focal length with a maximum aperture of f5.6. This is quite large enough for normal purposes, and anything bigger, at this focal length, would be inconveniently heavy. The usual wide-angle lens is 90 mm, although wider lenses are available, with a maximum aperture of f8. A longer-than-standard lens is useful but rarely essential with large-format cameras. The quality of the negative should be such that a small part of it can be enlarged if need be.

Lenses for *medium-format*, 6 × 9 cm monorail and technical cameras, like those for 5 × 4 format, are mounted in removable lens panels and any suitable lens can be used in any camera. Lenses for roll-film cameras, however, are normally in mounts very like those of 35 mm cameras, and are usually supplied by the camera manufacturer, and these cannot be used with other models. Standard lenses are 80–100 mm, wide-angle 50–60 mm and long lenses 150–180 mm. Aperture sizes are normally larger than those of lenses for monorail and technical cameras – f2.8–f4 – partly because they are used for action photographs and partly because they are reflex cameras and more light is needed for focussing. Macro-zoom and shift lenses can be obtained for some makes of roll-film cameras.

For *35 mm cameras* the choice is wide indeed, and both the camera makers and independent lens manufacturers advertise a quite bewildering array of lenses of different lengths, apertures and qualities. The standard lens has a focal length of 50 or 55 mm, although many photographers prefer to use a slightly wider lens – 35 or 40 mm – as the normal, giving a rather wider view without undue perspective distortion. The most useful wide-angle lens is probably the 28 mm, giving an angle of 75° (this is also a relatively cheap lens) or the 24 mm with an angle of 85° (which has the advantage that a 2 m long grave, for example, can be photographed from head height, given a tall photographer). A lens longer than 135 mm (18°) or 200 mm (12°) is very rarely needed. For artifacts *in situ*, a macro lens of 50 or 100 mm is useful, and for sites with standing walls etc., a 28 mm shift lens. Some or all of the lenses from 28 to 200 mm can be replaced by a zoom lens, some models of which include a macro facility, and many 35 mm cameras are now sold with a zoom lens as standard. The advantages are obvious: one lens instead of two or three; the ability, particularly useful with colour transparencies, to frame the structure or object exactly; and the fact that the lens need never be changed or the camera body interior exposed – this is important, especially in dusty environments. On the debit side, the resolution of a zoom at any particular focal length is rarely, except with the most expensive models, as good as is that of a prime lens of that length; most zooms exhibit some slight distortion of straight lines at the extreme ends of their travel; and compared with prime lenses, they are rather heavy and unwieldy. A possible compromise is to use a short-travel zoom, say 40–80 mm, to replace the standard lens, which will probably deal with more than half the photographs needed, with minimal aberrations, and to carry prime wide-angle and long lenses.

The price of lenses covers a wide range, both between manufacturers and between dealers. To some extent this reflects the quality of the lens, but with most focal lengths there are two, or sometimes three different sizes of lens made by each manufacturer, and the largest, naturally, is the most expensive. Thus, standard 50 mm lenses are on offer with f1.2, f1.4, f1.7 and f2 maximum aperture. The dealer may well recommend the largest and most expensive, but for use in archaeology f2, the cheapest, is just as good as f1.2, which may cost three times as much. There is a large market in secondhand lenses, both through dealers and through private sales, and this should always be checked before buying a lens (except for standard lenses, which are normally supplied with new bodies, making it scarcely worthwhile trying to buy them more cheaply). They are, fortunately, easy to check: so long as the exposed glass faces are unscratched and unabraded, the lens barrel undented, and the focussing movement and aperture ring free-moving, they should be quite as good as new lenses.

These, then, are the main types of cameras and lenses likely to be used on digs and in conservation. Polaroid cameras are sometimes used for reference photographs (and to placate photograph-hungry locals) and, much less commonly, circuit cameras for taking panoramic views, sub-miniature cameras for tomb boreholes, and aerial cameras. These, however, are not often seen on digs.

Camera movements
The normal zero position for any camera is with the line of the lens axis in the centre of, and at right angles to, the film plane. In other words, the back and the front of the camera are parallel, and the lens is lined up with the centre of the film. This simple geometry can be changed in a number of ways, either

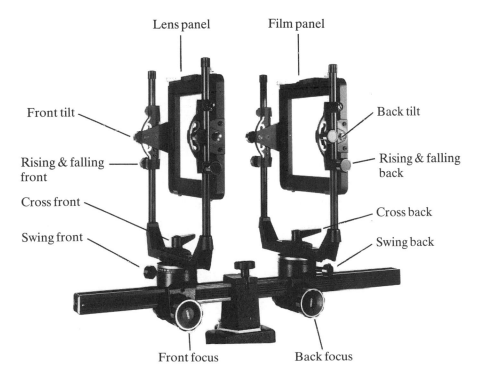

Plate 20   Monorail camera, skeleton view, showing the controls of the various movements.

displacing the lens axis above, below or to one side of the centre of the film plane without changing the right angle at which the two meet, or altering the angle so that the film plane and the lens panel are no longer parallel, or both.

The full range of these movements can be achieved only on a large-format monorail camera. Most technical cameras incorporate a somewhat smaller range of movements, as do some roll-film cameras. A limited degree of displacement of the image is possible on 35 mm and some medium-format cameras by means of a Perspective Control (PC) or *shift* lens.

Monorail cameras

Monorail cameras are so arranged that the film and lens panels can be moved laterally and vertically, independently of each other. The movements are referred to as rising and drop front, rising and drop back, cross front and cross back. Similarly, both panels can be swung about vertical and horizontal axes which should, ideally, run through the centre of the panels. The movements about the vertical axis are known as swing front and back, and those about the horizontal axis as tilt front and back (Plates 20, 21, 22, 23 and 24). Apart from the focussing controls, which on monorail cameras can be adjusted by moving either the front or the back panel, the only other movement – although not of the same order – is the so-called revolving back, whereby the film holder can be inserted either vertically or horizontally.

Technical cameras

Technical cameras normally incorporate rising and cross front, and a drop front can be contrived by tipping back the lens panel and hingeing down the baseboard. This hingeing movement also provides a degree of back tilt. Most do not have a swing front, nor can the front panel be tilted forward. The back panel has limited swing and tilt movements, but not lateral or vertical ones.

Use of movements

These movements, either alone or in combination, are used for two purposes: to alter the shape of the image, and to alter the plane of sharp focus imaged.

If the focussing screen of a camera were replaced by a larger sheet of ground glass, it would be seen that the image was, of course, circular, since it comes through a circular lens. The extent of the image is also a good deal larger than the format of the film: for a standard, large-format lens, about 30% larger, although far less for wide-angle and the process lenses used only for flat copy. This larger circle, indicative of the covering power of the lens, is not uniform right out to its rim: its outer edge will give a darker and less well-defined image than will its central area. The loss of light and definition result from various lens aberrations and are far less in a lens of good quality than in a poor (which usually means a cheap) lens. Within the limits of the

Plate 21   Camera movements: rising front and drop back.

Plate 22   Camera movements: cross front and back (from above).

lens covering power, it is therefore possible to use a part of the total image above, below or to one side of the centre of the circle.

If a camera is aligned with a rectangular object or structure so that it is square-on to its face – whether the face is of a soap-flake packet or a building – the verticals and horizontals of the image will be parallel and, if the lens has no serious aberrations, straight. The proportions of the rectangle will also be correct. When the camera angle is changed, however, so that it is looking up at the rectangle, or down, or from one side, parallels in the direction of

Plate 23   Camera movements: tilt front and back.

Plate 24   Camera movements: swing front and back (from above).

viewing appear to converge. This of course is no different from the effect on the eye of looking up at a tall building, or down into a hole in the ground. There are, however, two effects of this common phenomenon that have to be taken into account in photographing any object. Firstly, when we look up at a tall building or along a set of railway lines, we know very well that the parallels do not really converge, and our minds automatically compensate for the illusion; but if we are looking not at a tall building but at a two-dimensional image of a tall building, then the convergence can be distracting, especially if it is only slight. If the picture is of a skyscraper, viewed from close by, we may find the image acceptable and even pleasing and dramatic; but if the sides of the building are only slightly out of alignment with the sides of the print, the effect is disturbing; there is also the optical illusion that seems to show the building leaning back. The second consideration is of greater importance. Unless there are strong points of reference within the picture – scales or something of the sort – we cannot determine the proportions of the object. This is the more important when the object is of irregular shape. The foreshortened image given in a photograph looking down at a packet of soap-flakes can be, to a certain degree, discounted in our minds; we know that it is in reality rectangular. But if the photograph is looking down at a pot, or up at a column, we have no such aid, and when the foreshortening is not very steep, our minds assume that the proportions are correct – that the base of the pot really is that much smaller than the rim (Plates 25, 26, 27 and 28).

This effect can be minimised, though not entirely eliminated, by increasing the distance between camera and object while keeping it at the same angle. The difference in proportion between the base and the rim, that is the steepness of perspective, is entirely a matter of the relative distances from the lens (or for that matter from the eye of the beholder) of the two points. Thus, if the photograph were taken at such a distance and at such an angle that the lens was 50 cm from the rim and 60 cm from the base, the ratio between the two would be 60:50 or 1.2:1; so, if the negative were enlarged so that the base measured 10 cm across, assuming that the rim were actually of the same diameter it would appear to be 12 cm across. Move the camera back by 100 cm, and the ratio becomes 160:150, or 1.07:1, so if the base were enlarged to 10 cm, the rim would measure 10.7 cm. If it were moved back 5 m, the relative sizes would be 10 cm and 10.2 cm, roughly.

Since the perspective effect is entirely a matter of relative distances, it is not affected by focal length, and a long lens, giving a large image at a distance, will yield the same ratios as if a shorter lens were used at that distance and the negative enlarged. Obviously the degree of distortion judged acceptable will vary from case to case, and it might be argued that no one is going to base any system of pottery analysis or comparison on measuring the rims and bases of photographed pottery – for that sort of exercise accurately drawn profiles would be sought. Nevertheless, perhaps the commonest use of published

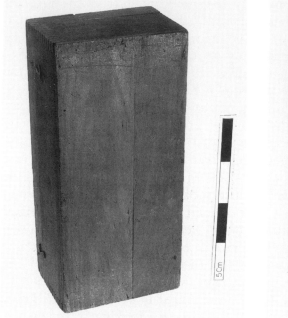

Plate 25

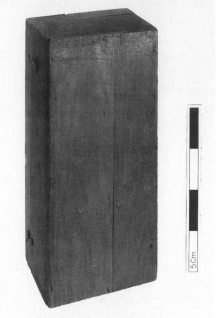

Plate 27

Plate 26

Plate 28

Plates 25 and 26 were taken looking down slightly and without correction, while in Plates 27 and 28, taken from the same positions, the back of the camera was adjusted to vertical. The slight foreshortening of the uncorrected photographs is more apparent with the box than with the pot, but both appear more squat than do the corrected versions.

photographs of pots is by excavators looking for parallels, and by students and research workers studying the artifacts of certain periods or regions. For these purposes artifact records that incorporate a systematic error can be very misleading. Much the same considerations apply to architectural photographs (as is discussed in Chapter 6) and again, especially to non-right-angled shapes. A foreshortened photograph, for instance, of a church steeple might give an accurate idea of building style and materials, but very little of proportions, the more so if, as is not uncommon, the steeple were tiled or slated and the sizes of the tiles or slates and of the crockets diminished from bottom to top. The effect of great but indeterminate height would be considerable. Again, the effect is greatly reduced by distance but, unlike artifacts that can usually be placed to suit the photographer, it may not be possible to find a viewpoint which gives a reasonably proportioned record of the height but from which the rest of the building is visible.

To return to the use of camera movements, the important relationship is that between the back of the camera – the film plane – and the front of the object or structure being photographed. If these two are parallel, and disregarding for the moment such things as pyramids and the Tower of Pisa, the proportions and angles will be reproduced faithfully. Thus, if a camera is set up on flat ground in front of a building and levelled, so that the lens axis is

Plate 29, Plate 30   Foreshortening. In Plate 29 the camera was pointing both up at the building and along its facade. In Plate 30, taken from the same position, the back of the camera was made parallel with the front of the building in both dimensions. Notice also the drawback often met in photographing buildings in towns – the line of parked cars.

horizontal, the centre point in the photograph will be about the same distance above the ground as the lens – 1.5 to 2 m in ordinary circumstances. The top of the building might well therefore be out of the frame. Tilt the camera up, and the building is foreshortened, but if the lens panel alone is raised, keeping it parallel with the back, more of the top of the building will show in the focussing screen, and less of the foreground (Plates 29 and 30). It might be thought that the same effect could be achieved by raising the whole camera, but the extra height so revealed would be no more than the amount by which the camera is raised. By using the rising front, however, the amount gained would be in the ratio of lens-to-object distance:lens-to-image distance, a very much greater gain.

So long as the top of the building is not out of the circle of coverage of the lens, resolution and evenness of illumination will be maintained. Similarly, if the camera is recording an excavation from the top of a trench and is pointed downward, the sides of the trench will appear to converge, but if the film panel is vertical, parallel with the back wall of the trench, and the lens lowered, the sides of the trench will not. If the trench is of considerable depth, it is rarely possible to correct the verticals completely, unless the trench is also very wide; the angles are simply too extreme. What can be particularly disconcerting is if there are standing walls at the bottom of the trench which, viewed from above, appear to splay out from their bases. The same arrangement of vertical back and dropped lens panel can be used to restore vertical proportions to the photograph of a pot or other artifact. Whether used above or below the lens axis, a greater mechanical movement can be obtained by tipping the whole camera up or down and using the swing back and front to restore the panels to the vertical. Care must be taken when using the drop front not to include the end of the rail in the photograph. The solution is simply to move the front panel to the extreme end of the rail and focus by the back.

Another serious limitation is that the circle of coverage is limited, and on most monorails the mechanical movements possible go well beyond the optical potential of any lens. If the lens is raised too far, dark and unsharp areas will appear at the lower corners of the focussing screen, i.e. the upper corners of the image, since the image is inverted (Plate 31); if on the other hand the lens is lowered, the effect will be seen in the upper corners, and if moved too far sideways, in the corners opposite to the direction of movement. Within limits, this '*cut-off*' is curable. If, when the lens panel is raised beyond its limit of coverage, it is tipped slightly back (i.e. the top of the panel is moved back towards the film plane) (Plate 32) the axis of the lens will be moved down nearer to the centre of the film, and the coverage will be restored, at the expense of having the plane of sharp focus no longer coinciding with the film plane, but lying across it at an angle. If the top and bottom limits of this plane of sharp focus fall within the depth of focus of the lens, the image will still be acceptably sharp and the verticals still corrected. This procedure sounds complex, but in practice it is quite simple. Set up the camera with all movements at zero; level it both along and across the lens axis by using a spirit level (many monorail cameras have spirit levels built into their front and rear panels), focus the image and, if the top of the building or structure is not visible, move the lens panel up until it is; look carefully at the bottom corners of the screen for signs of cut-off (this is often difficult to see, particularly in bright sunlight, and it may be necessary to cover the camera and the photographer's head with a black cloth). If there is cut-off, tilt the lens panel back while watching the effect, tilting it only as much as is needed to restore coverage. Check the focus – some cameras need readjustment at this stage – and ensure that the centre of the image is quite sharp; check the

Plate 31   Cut-off occurring at the top of the frame when the rising front is raised to its fullest extent.

focus at the top and bottom, and if both appear unsharp close the lens aperture down, which extends the depth of focus, and re-check (this is best done with a magnifying glass). The procedure is similar if the lens panel is moved downward. The easiest way to determine which way to tilt or swing the lens panel is to envisage the lens axis extended running along the centre-line of the lens. In each case coverage is restored by moving that imaginary line towards the centre of the film.

Occasionally it is desirable to restore the parallelism of horizontal lines – looking along the façade of a building, for example – although converging horizontal lines are not so disturbing to the eye as vertical ones. Just the same rules apply: set up the camera with the film plane parallel with the façade and move the front to take in the whole building, swinging the front panel if the lens coverage is incomplete.

One special use of such a movement is in the photography of wall paintings or something similar in a space insufficient to allow the camera to be set squarely in front. If the camera is set diagonally to the face of the wall, and the back and front swung to be parallel with the painting, by crossing the front more distance can be found while maintaining the square-on view of the painting. This method is also normally used in order to photograph mirrors or other highly reflective surfaces without also recording a reflection of the camera.

Plate 32   Correction for cut-off: the lens panel is tilted back so as to bring the lens axis closer to the centre of the negative.

Horizontal and vertical movements may be used together if it is desirable to obtain cornerwise view, as it were, of a façade. Corrected coverage can be restored in both planes. Again, start from a zero position and adjust for, and correct for, each plane in turn.

Controlling the plane of sharp focus

When a camera is set up with the movements in the zero position, the focussed lens will render sharply a plane coinciding with that of the film and at right angles to the lens axis. In most circumstances this arrangement is adequate to deal with whatever structure or artifact is being photographed; detail in front of or behind this plane of sharp focus being rendered sharply enough within the depth of field. Occasionally, however, even with the smallest aperture the depth of field is not sufficient, especially if what is being photographed is an inclined plane. Consider, for instance, the problem of photographing a pavement or roadway. Ideally, of course, if the pavement is to be recorded in its true proportions, the camera should be elevated with its back horizontal and pointing down at the pavement; there is no need for the camera to be directly over the central part of the pavement – it could well be positioned above one edge and the image centred by using the rising front and drop back. But elevating the camera may not be possible, or not desirable, if for example the photograph is also intended to show standing walls. So the camera has to be inclined from tripod height and looking along the pavement, and it could well be that, even with the lens focussed a third of the way along the length of the pavement, the nearest and the furthest points along its length cannot both be brought into focus together. The reason is obvious enough; since the nearest part of the pavement is closest to the camera its image is focussed farther from the lens and, similarly, the farthest point is focussed closer to the lens, so the plane of the image does not coincide with the film plane. Overall sharpness could be restored either by tilting the film panel back until it does coincide with the plane of the image, or by tilting the lens panel forward (i.e. so that it is closer to being parallel with the pavement) until the plane of the image coincides, more or less, with the film plane, or both. The disadvantage of the first alternative is that by so doing the steepness of the perspective effect, the foreshortening, is increased; that of the second, that by tilting the lens axis, the image will be moved across the screen, which may mean realigning the camera angle. The optimum position can be found in accordance with the so-called 'Scheimpflug principle' (Plate 33). This holds that maximum resolution of the image is found when extensions of the object plane, lens plane and film plane meet. More simply, if the camera is set up looking along an inclined surface and the lens panel tilted or swung until an imaginary line extended from it would meet the crossing point of the equally imaginary lines from the object plane and the film plane, maximum resolution will be achieved.

Some of the more advanced, and more expensive, monorail cameras are fitted with scaled quadrants which enable this inclination to be found by a single adjustment. With simpler models, it is quite easily found by eye; stand to the side of the camera and swing or tilt the lens panel until it seems to be in line with the imaginary junction described above.

All of these movements could, of course, be used for the opposite purpose; instead of rendering verticals parallel they could be made to appear even more convergent, or the plane of sharp focus could be decreased rather than increased, and so on. This is done, though only very occasionally, in commercial photography. By swinging the back panel so that it is less parallel with the principal plane of an object, a building can be made to look longer or taller, or a small car made to look larger – although much the same effect can be obtained by using a wide-angle lens and moving as close as possible to one corner of the car. It is difficult to think of any occasion when such distortion would be of use in archaeology. Very rarely it might perhaps be of value to reduce the plane of sharp focus on an inclined plane – to swing the lens panel so that the plane of focus and the object plane intersect at an acute angle and most of the foreground and background are deliberately thrown out of focus, thus emphasising one particular detail.

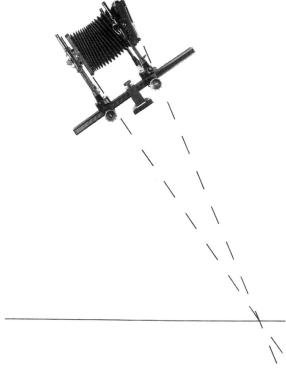

Plate 33   The Scheimpflug principle. The lens and the film panel are so arranged that extension of their planes would intersect with the plane of the object.

Quite apart from their use in changing the shape of the image, the rising and cross lens and film panels can be employed simply to move the image about on the screen without changing the position of the camera. At times this can be a minor convenience, for instance in centring the image of a drawing to give an even margin all round it. At times it can be very useful; for instance if the camera is pointed vertically down into a trench, then the effect of raising the lens, quite apart from maintaining the shape of structures, would be to get more of the trench bottom and less of the near trench wall. The fact that the camera does not have to be extended so far out can make the difference between stability and disaster.

Within limits, it is possible to achieve correction of converging verticals or horizontals by manipulation of the geometry of the enlarger rather than of the camera. If the head of the enlarger is swung, or the paper-holder tilted, the effect will be to make the image at one end of the negative smaller than that at the other (if the enlarger head is tilted, the end of the negative closer to the baseboard will be larger; if the baseboard is tilted, the opposite will apply). Some enlargers also make provision for tilting the lens panel; if this is done according to the Scheimpflug principle – at such an angle as to meet the intersection of the angle between the baseboard and the negative – optimum focus will be achieved. There are three disadvantages in correcting on the enlarger. One is that the overall shape of the negative will also be changed, two of its sides being no longer parallel, and unless there is plenty of background around the structure or object, it may not be possible to trim the resultant print to a rectangle. The second is that, depending on the focal length and the bellows extension of the enlarger compared with those of the taking camera, the image may be lengthened or shortened relative to its width. And thirdly, and especially when using a tilted paper-holder, one end of the print is at a lesser degree of enlargement than the other and therefore needs less exposure. This can be dealt with easily enough if tones and densities already vary in the print, but controlling it is no easy task should the background and the structure be even in tone from one end to the other.

Smaller camera formats lend themselves less readily to camera movements, partly because the compact design, especially of 35 mm cameras, leaves little or no room for movement, and partly because the shallower depth of focus given by lenses of short focal length means that swing and tilt movements are hardly possible. Lateral lens movements are, however, still possible by using *shift (perspective control) lenses*. These are always wide-angle lenses, in order to give a sufficient circle of coverage, and although the possible correction is not as great as with a large-format camera with movements, they can be most useful both for correcting convergence in architectural photography and for moving the image in close range work. For instance, if a photograph is to be taken of a rug, and it is important to obtain a square-on view, either the rug must be hung on a wall, which may not be at all desirable if the fabric is delicate, or it has to be photographed from above, using some sort of gantry. By using a shift lens, however, it is perfectly possible to set up a camera on top of a stepladder beside the rug, and, with the camera horizontal, shift the image into the frame. Two points need to be observed. It is difficult to estimate with any accuracy whether a small camera is horizontal or not, and it is desirable to use a spirit level (small cube-like levels can be bought which fit into the flash shoe on top of the camera). The second point is that, understandably enough, lens manufacturers extend the shift to the very edge of the lenses' covering power, and at close quarters the illumination at the farthest extent of the shift may fall off slightly, even though the resolution is still adequate. For this reason it is better not to use the last notch of the lens shift unless absolutely necessary.

Camera movements in all their applications are discussed in Stroebel (1986).

Darkslides

For those unfamiliar with their use, sheet-film holders, usually called darkslides (Plate 34), can be awkward to manipulate. Most will take two films, one on either face (hence they are also known as double-darkslides, or DDS). In essence they resemble thin rectangular boxes in which the film is held in such a position that when the slide replaces the focussing screen in a monorail or technical camera, the film is exactly on the plane the focussing screen had occupied. The film is protected from light by a sliding plastic or metal sheet (confusingly known as a 'shutter') which is withdrawn immediately before the

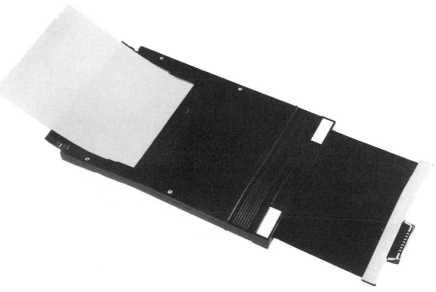

Plate 34   Double darkslide, showing the correct position for the filmnotch

exposure, but *after* the lens shutter is closed and tensioned and the aperture set. The shutter has a handling tag which is white or silver on one side and black on the other, and the usual practice is to set the shutter with the white side of the tag outwards when the film is loaded but unexposed, and to turn the shutter round to show black when the film has been exposed, thus avoiding possible confusion between exposed and unexposed films. It is also good practice not to withdraw the shutter completely, because if there is strong ambient light it can enter the slit into which the shutter fits and cause fogging.

A final precaution is always to check that the correct shutter is being withdrawn. A DDS, with a film on either face, has of course two shutters, and it is all too easy to withdraw the wrong one, which will not only leave the proper film unexposed, but will also fog the second film.

The darkslide is loaded by withdrawing the shutter and hingeing down a flap that runs along the bottom of the slide. The sheet of film is inserted by sliding it from the bottom of the slide under guide-rails at both edges; the flap is then hinged up again and the shutter closed. It is unloaded by the reverse procedure. There are two points on which care has to be taken; one is to ensure that the film is under both rails and fully pushed home (if it is not, there is a good chance of its jamming when the shutter is withdrawn before exposure); the other is to make sure that the film is the right way round, i.e. with the emulsion side outwards. All sheet films, except lith films, have a notch cut in one corner of one of the shorter sides. When the film is held so that its longer dimension is towards the user, and with the notch in the top right-hand or the lower left-hand corner, the emulsion face of the film will be uppermost, and it is in this position that the film has to be inserted in the slide.

Shutters

There are two types of camera shutter in common use: focal-plane shutters, built into nearly all 35 mm cameras and medium-format reflex cameras; and lens shutters (known by several names – between-lens shutters, bladed shutters, diaphragm shutters, and often Compur-type shutters, although this last is a trade name).

Focal-plane shutters consist of two blinds which move along or across the film plane, immediately in front of the film, either simultaneously but with a space between them, at fast speeds, or one following the other after an interval, at slow speeds. The length of the exposure is set by means of a speed ring, a control on top of the camera body. On automatic and semi-automatic cameras, the speed is electronically controlled, and if the camera battery is flat, they revert to a single manual speed, usually 1/75 or 1/100 sec (although some electronically controlled cameras will not work at all with a flat battery). Focal-plane shutters in modern cameras rarely develop faults, but they are very vulnerable to dust (as are all shutters, in fact), and if the camera is subjected to dry heat for a long time, they can develop pin-holes in the fabric of the blinds.

Compur-type shutters (Plate 35) are rather more complicated to operate since, on sheet-film cameras, both shutter and aperture have to be opened for focussing and the aperture set and the shutter closed and tensioned before exposure. They are built around the lens in a thick rim which also holds the aperture mechanism. The shutter itself consists of a number of overlapping metal blades – usually five – which pivot together to close the shutter and open apart when the shutter is fired. The basic controls are simple enough; the aperture is set by moving a small pointer against an f-number scale set around a quadrant of the rim, and the shutter speed by moving a milled ring, which forms part of the rim itself, and which is marked in fractions of a second – usually running from 1 sec to 1/400 sec – against a fixed point. All such shutters also include a position marked 'B', at which setting the shutter stays open for as long as the shutter release is depressed. Some also have a further position marked 'T'. When the ring is set to this position the shutter opens on the first depression of the release and closes on the second. The control which sometimes causes problems is that which holds the shutter open for focussing, simply because there are several different types of control in current use.

The simplest way of holding the shutter open is to set the ring to 'T' and press the release or, for shutters without a 'T' setting, to set it to 'B' and to use a cable release with a locking screw on it to hold the release down. More

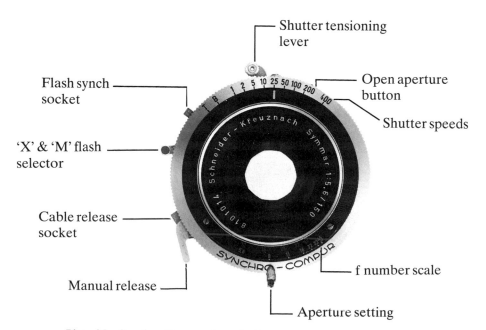

Plate 35   Synchro-Compur lens shutter.

modern shutters, however, incorporate another button which will open the shutter for focussing. Some will work only when the shutter is tensioned, and some whether it is tensioned or not. All shutters also have a release button or lever, tapped to take a cable release, and a short arm which is cocked back to tension the shutter before release. Most have, in addition, a co-axial socket for flash synchronisation, and yet another short lever which can be moved between positions marked 'X' and 'M' for electronic or bulb flash.

With all these controls in such a small compass it is as well to study an unknown shutter carefully before using it to make sure which does what. Unless the shutter is quite familiar, it is also as well not to try to set it just by reaching round the camera, but to check carefully that each control is properly set.

Light meters

Most SLR cameras, whether 35 mm or a larger format, incorporate a light meter which measures the light falling at the film plane (a through-the-lens or TTL meter). The correct exposure is set by turning either the aperture ring or the exposure dial until a needle is centred or an LED light changes from red to green. Many cameras have in addition automatic settings by which either the aperture is decided upon and the camera sets the appropriate shutter speed (aperture priority), or it sets the aperture to match the shutter speed (shutter priority), or both (fully automatic). The so-called multimode cameras offer all these alternatives, plus a manual mode, where the photographer decides on both aperture and shutter speed. Whatever the system, the film speed has first to be set on the camera, unless the camera has DX coding, a device that reads and sets the film speed from a bar code on the cassette. It is in any case as well to check the speed set from time to time: for some reason one of the commonest faults in using cameras with built-in meters is setting the wrong ISO speed.

Most such metering systems are 'centre-weighted', i.e. the reading from the centre of the screen counts for more than does that at the periphery, and that at the bottom of the screen counts for more than that at the top; this is to compensate for the fact that the top of most photographs is occupied by sky. A growing number of cameras use multi-cell systems which read and integrate the light reflected from different parts of the scene, or, by means of a switching device, take readings from only one small area, thus acting as spot-meters.

In most circumstances TTL meters work very well. The exceptions are when there is a great deal of light in the background, when an object in the foreground is likely to be under-exposed; or, vice versa, when the background is very dark and a foreground object is liable to be over-exposed (methods of assessing the exposure in these circumstances are discussed in more detail in Chapter 9). Some cameras incorporate a device – a Backlight Compensation Control (BLC) – designed to overcome this source of error.

The built-in meters on older cameras are usually controlled by a Cadmium di-Sulphide cell (CdS), while newer models rely on a Gallium Photo Diode (GPD) or a Silicon Photo Diode (SPD) cell. All are equally accurate, but the older CdS cells take longer to react to light, a disadvantage with automatic controls but rarely of any importance in archaeological or conservation photography.

For large-format cameras, or for medium-format non-SLR cameras, exposures are usually determined with a separate hand-held meter. There are also occasions when a hand-held meter is more convenient or more accurate in use, even though the camera is fitted with a TTL meter. Most hand-held meters use a CdS or SPD cell, although there are still plenty of the older type of Selenium cell meters in use. The Selenium meters are quite accurate in medium and high lighting levels, but rather insensitive in low light. There are two categories of hand-held meters; light meters with an angle of acceptance similar to that of a standard lens, and spot-meters with an angle of acceptance of only 2 or 3°. Most of the former can be used to measure either the light reflected from a scene or object, or, with the addition of a baffle, the light incident upon it.

Spot meters incorporate an optical system whereby the scene is viewed through a viewfinder within the field of which is a small circle, and it is only the tone within this circle that is measured when a trigger or button is pressed.

All meters, except TTL meters operating automatic or semi-automatic shutter circuits, present not one shutter speed/aperture combination, but a series of alternatives, all of which would yield a suitable dosage of light. Which combination is chosen depends on such factors as shutter speed, if the camera is hand-held or if the object is moving; or, more commonly in archaeology and conservation, on the selection of an aperture giving a sufficient depth of field.

The use of light meters is discussed more fully in Chapter 9. To sum up very briefly:

> The correct film speed must always be set on the meter.
>
> For a scene, or a group of people, or any structure or object with an average contrast range, a reading from the camera position with either a TTL or a hand-held meter should be sufficient; if a lot of sky is included, the meter should be tilted down slightly to favour the foreground.
>
> If the contrast range is very great, it is more effective either to take two readings, one from the lightest and one from the darkest part of the scene and to average the results (such readings are more easily taken with a spot-meter), or to take both an incident and a reflected light reading and average the results.
>
> If the object or the part of the scene of interest is very much darker

or lighter than the background, the reading should be taken on this part only, even if it means, with a TTL meter, moving the whole camera forward, taking the reading, and then moving it back; or on a grey card; or by using the incident light baffle only.

If the object of interest is distant or unapproachable, a reading can be taken on some nearby object of similar tone and in the same light, or on a grey card in similar light.

Light filters

There are many different types and colours of filter, and manufacturers tend to use their own codes of letters or numbers to describe their products, so it is not always easy to compare one make of filter with another. However, all filters fall into a few general classes, although the same filter may serve several different purposes. The most comprehensive system of filter types is the Wratten range used by Kodak, who also make the greatest number of filters, and this system will be quoted here.

Nearly all lens filters absorb light as well as changing its colour or quality. It is usually necessary to compensate for this loss by lengthening the exposure or by increasing the size of the aperture. With cameras that incorporate a through-the-lens meter, and with the lighter yellow, yellow-green and blue filters, this can be done by simply taking a light reading with the filter on the lens. When darker filters are being used, particularly dark red and dark green, this method is no longer accurate because the colour sensitivity of the film may not be the same as that of the exposure meter. In this case, or when a separate meter is being used, the meter exposure must be multiplied by a factor, known as the 'filter factor', specific to that filter. This factor is usually given on a leaflet supplied with that filter; for example, a pale yellow filter may have a factor of $\times 1.5$ or $\times 2$, while a deep red may be as high as $\times 25$. If a factor for a particular filter is not known, it can be found easily enough. A negative is made without a filter of an object or scene, preferably one containing several colours and a sizeable area of white or neutral grey. With the filter in position, a series of further negatives is then made, with progressively greater exposures. For light filters it would be advisable to increase the exposure in steps of half-stops, for dense filters in whole stops. The negatives are processed and compared, and the step nearest in density to the filter-less example will indicate the factor (1 stop is $\times 2$, two stops $\times 4$, and so on).

Filters for black and white photography

Distant views are often veiled because of the scattering of light by water vapour in the atmosphere. The shorter wavelengths, ultraviolet and blue, are those chiefly affected, and since black and white film is particularly sensitive to this part of the spectrum, the effect is often worse on a photograph than it is in reality. A *haze filter* excludes the UV (Wratten 2A or 2B) and will give a degree of haze penetration, while any filter that blocks the shorter wavelengths, yellow, orange and red, will have a similar or stronger effect. A few very expensive lenses, such as those made by Leica, incorporate UV-excluding glass, and the use of a haze filter is unnecessary. As a result of the high sensitivity of panchromatic emulsions to UV and blue, blue skies may be rendered as white on the print, and greens, to which such emulsions are not so sensitive, rather dark. A *correction filter* such as a light yellow (Wratten 6 or 8) or light yellow-green (Wratten 11) will darken blues and lighten greens, usually an advantage in photographs with sky, trees and grass. Some panchromatic films also have increased sensitivity in the red – deliberately heightened in order to increase their speed in tungsten light. If a correct rendering of red tones is essential, as it might be for instance when photographing an oil painting, this tendency may be corrected by using a light blue filter (Wratten 38).

Black and white emulsions record colours as shades of grey. It quite often happens that different colours will record as similar grey tones, and thus the contrast between different parts of the scene or object will be lost. *Contrast filters* accentuate the difference in the rendering of colours as tones, the general rule being that a filter lightens its own colour and darkens colours far away from it in the spectrum.

Filter	Wratten No.	Darkens	Lightens
Blue	38A	Red, yellow	Blue
Green	54	Red, orange	Green
Deep yellow	15	Blue	Yellow, orange
Red	25	Blue, green	Red, orange

It is sometimes useful to lose a colour altogether against its background; for instance if a yellow-stained print is to be re-photographed, by using a yellow filter all trace of the stain may be lost. When photographing a site or an artifact, however, it is rarely possible, or desirable, to suppress a colour altogether. All that is necessary is to accentuate an existing difference. For instance, the difference between the green of corroded bronze and the red-brown of corroded iron on the same tool may be accentuated by using either a green filter, which would lighten the green and darken the red-brown, or a red, which would have the opposite effect. It is important to remember that such a modification involves, necessarily, the distortion of tonal values, and such distortion should always be kept to a minimum.

Filters for colour photography
Obviously neither correction nor contrast filters can be used with colour film as they can with black and white. A red filter, for instance, would simply render the whole picture red. Some manufacturers, e.g. Cokin, do supply a

whole range of more or less strongly coloured filters, called 'Creative' filters (also known as 'effect' or 'pop' filters) by the use of which colours are deliberately distorted for aesthetic effect. In the same class are graduated filters, which grade from one colour to another, multiple image filters, 'starburst' filters, split image and soft focus filters, and similar gadgets. Their value is minimal so far as archaeological recording is concerned.

The scattering of light which may veil distant views can be as apparent in colour as in black and white photography; moreover, the scattered blue light can give an overall blueish cast, especially in the shadows. This effect may be overcome by using a 'Skylight' filter – a very pale pink or salmon-coloured filter which absorbs the UV and corrects the blue cast (Wratten 1A).

A number of filters are used with colour film in order to change the quality of the light to match that for which the film sensitivity is balanced. There is a series of *conversion filters* made specifically for matching light to film; details of these filters, and of the necessary adjustments in exposure times, are given in Table 1 in Chapter 5.

If a colour photograph is taken under mixed lighting, for instance a room lit at one end by daylight and at the other by tungsten bulbs, a colour cast is inevitable no matter what filter is used. This can be overcome either by replacing one of the forms of lighting, for instance by switching off the tungsten lights and illuminating the area by electronic flash, which is balanced for Daylight film; or, by covering the lights with filters, changing their spectral quality to that of daylight. Glass or gelatine filters of a large enough size would be expensive and of a higher optical standard than necessary, so a number of manufacturers supply sheets of acetate of the appropriate colour characteristics. In general, a better colour balance is obtained, and less light is lost, if a Tungsten film is used in daylight with the proper filter than if a filtered Daylight film is used under tungsten lighting.

In addition there are filters designed to compensate for the too-red effect of early morning and evening sunlight on Daylight film (Wratten 81A). Filters (FL-D) for use with Daylight film under fluorescent lights are also made by several manufacturers.

Kodak make a series of primary and complementary *colour correction filters* in graded steps for the fine adjustment of colour balance. These can be used over the light source or over the lens. They are designated by the initials 'CC' followed by a number indicating their density, and the initial letter of their colour; for instance, CC50Y is the densest of the yellow series. They are particularly useful for such operations as copying slides.

It should be emphasised that the balancing of colour film and light sources is a complicated business if exact results are required, and it is usually necessary to make series of tests. The above is only a rough outline; more information can be found in Kodak (1970).

Miscellaneous filters

Neutral density filters are neutral-grey filters, supplied in a graded series. They reduce the light coming through the lens without affecting its colour, and may therefore be used with either black and white or colour film. Their chief use is to control the exposure when it is necessary to combine a large aperture with a relatively long exposure time, in order to minimise the depth of field. They are little used in archaeology.

Normally the wave-front of light vibrates in all possible planes at right angles to the direction of the light ray. However, when light is reflected from the surface of many non-metallic materials it becomes polarized, i.e. it vibrates in one plane only. Such surfaces are glass, plastic, water, glaze, enamel, polished wood and so on. *Polarizing filters* (which are misnamed – they do not themselves polarize light) will in part suppress reflections from such surfaces (Plates 36 and 37). They are grid-like plates of parallel crystals which pass polarized light lying in the same plane as themselves, and block polarized light at any other angle. Since they necessarily block out a portion of the total light, they have a fairly high filter factor, $\times 2.5 - \times 4$. With a single-lens reflex camera, or with a camera with a focussing screen, the correct angle for the filter can be found by placing the filter on the lens and turning it while watching the image in the eye-piece or screen until the reflection is extinguished. With other types of camera it is necessary to look through the filter itself from the camera position, turn it until the reflection disappears and then mount the filter on the lens at exactly that angle. There are, however, a number of factors which limit the value of these filters. Firstly, they will only completely eliminate reflections at a fairly acute angle to the surface – less than about 40° – so they are ineffective for eliminating, for example, the reflection from a camera-mounted flash-gun in the glass of a showcase viewed square-on. Secondly, such a showcase may well be reflecting several lights from several different directions and very often as the filter is turned to extinguish one reflection, another emerges. And thirdly, they are very much more effective with a long focal-length lens, accepting light only from a narrow angle, than with a wide-angle lens, the angle of acceptance of which is likely to be wider than the filter can cover. They are also ineffective in suppressing reflections from metallic surfaces, since this light does not become polarized. To eliminate these reflections it is necessary to use polarizing sheets over the light sources as well as over the lens.

Polarizing filters may be used for either black and white or colour. In colour photography they have an additional function. Some of the light from a clear blue sky is polarized, and as was mentioned earlier, it is light from this end of the spectrum that is most likely to be scattered and to degrade the clarity of shadows and distant views. A polarizing filter will both darken the blue of the sky and give greater clarity and sharpness to a distant scene.

Black and white emulsions coated to record the infra-red part of the

Plate 36

Plate 37

Polarizing filter. Plate 36 shows glare reflected from a polished wooden box-lid; in Plate 37 the glare has been eliminated by means of a polarizing filter on the camera lens.

spectrum are also sensitive to the visible-light spectrum. In order to confine the image to the infra-red, it is necessary to filter out the shorter wavelengths. This can be done completely by using an *infra-red filter* which is visually opaque (Wratten 88) or partially by using a deep-red filter (Wratten 25). Infra-red film has an ISO number calculated on the assumption that one or other of these filters will be used. Infra-red may also be recorded on special colour films (sometimes known as '*False-colour*') coated to record green, red and infra-red instead of the usual blue, green and red; a strong yellow filter (Wratten 12) is normally used. Again, the ISO number is calculated on this assumption.

Nearly all emulsions record the UV, but if the UV image alone is required, it is necessary to use a visually-opaque *ultra-violet transmitting filter* (Wratten 18A) which will exclude all visible light. If, on the other hand, it is intended to record fluorescence excited in the UV and emitted in the visible spectrum, it is necessary to use a light source radiating only UV (usually a mercury discharge lamp or fluorescent tube with a cobalt glass envelope, also known as a 'Wood's glass filter'), with all other light eliminated and an *ultra-violet barrier filter* over the lens which will *exclude* the UV (Wratten 2A, 2B or 2E). Obviously it is important to distinguish between UV-transmitting filters and UV barrier filters; unfortunately both are often referred to simply as 'UV filters'.

Infra-red and ultra-violet filters are discussed more fully in Chapter 11.

One final type of filter is worth mentioning, the so-called '*Pan-vision' filter* (Wratten 90). These are dark grey-amber filters which, when looked through, give roughly the tone relationships of different colours when photographed on panchromatic black and white film in daylight. They are not intended for use over the camera lens, but for assessing the appearance of a coloured object or scene to be photographed in black and white.

Most filters can be bought either as glass or as gelatine. Glass filters, which are the more expensive, are normally supplied to fit individual lenses, or are used with some sort of adaptor which will fit several. Glass filters should be treated as lenses – kept dust- and scratch-free and cleaned only with great care. Gelatine filters are supplied in sizes of 50 to 150 mm square (although some are available in larger sizes) which are cut to fit lens-holders or adaptors. They also should be handled with care as scratches or fingerprints may affect the image.

In dusty conditions it is advisable to leave a glass UV barrier or haze filter on the lens permanently. This will protect the lens itself without adversely affecting any exposure.

For use on an excavation, a kit consisting of a haze filter, yellow, red and green contrast filters (Wratten 15, 25 and 54), a yellow-green correction filter (Wratten 11) for black and white photography, together with a skylight filter (Wratten 1A) and an evening-light filter (Wratten 82A) for colour, should deal with most problems. A Tungsten-to-Daylight filter (Wratten 85B) or Daylight-to-Tungsten (Wratten 80A) might also be needed, and a polarizing filter might occasionally be of value.

Scales and information boards

Whatever the subject, all archaeological photographs should include a scale. This is not quite an unbreakable rule – very occasionally a scale might be obtrusive or redundant – but it holds good for the vast majority of cases. With most site photographs, and with photographs of large objects, the purpose is not so much to provide an exact measure of size (no one is ever likely to use a pair of calipers to work out the dimensions of a wall or a statue from the scale of a photograph – these would be far more accurate taken from a plan or drawing), but to give the eye a comparison, something of known size, so that the scale and proportions of the image can be judged. It is for this reason that very often the best scale, particularly in photographing architecture, is a human figure. Given this, everything else falls into place. Obviously the figure or figures must not be so obtrusive, nor for that matter so attractive, that they distract the eye from the archaeology, and they have to be placed with some care. Too stiff and too conscious of the camera and they look awkward and unreal; too relaxed, and doubt is cast on the serious-mindedness of the dig. Again obviously, they must not be so placed as to mask any important features. It is sometimes held that any figures in a site photograph must appear to be working, but this can be difficult to arrange, and nothing looks more ludicrous than a photograph including some member of the team holding a pick over an untouched surface and clearly bored with the whole charade. A reasonable compromise is to have the figure holding a ranging pole (upright!).

Human figures apart, the standard scale for site photographs is a two-metre ranging pole, red and white, marked in 50-centimetre sections. If resources permit, it is as well to keep a couple of poles exclusively for photography, repainted every season and washed from time to time. For smaller areas, 1 m, 50 cm and 25 cm scales are essential, red and white or black and white, and with the length of one white section painted on. It is irritating to see a photograph of some feature of indeterminate size, such as an oven, with a scale in the picture of equally indeterminate length – a black and white stick which could be a metre long divided into 10 cm divisions, or could equally be 10 cm long divided into centimetres.

Scales should always be placed so as to appear upright or horizontal in the frame; for some reason a leaning scale looks uncommonly careless, though it may occasionally be more informative for a horizontal scale to run obliquely to emphasise the angle of a wall. If the picture has any depth in it, e.g. looking along a trench or along the length of a building, there should always be scales, whether human figures or 2 m poles, near both the front and the rear of the area. This is particularly important if a wide-angle or a long lens is in use, since the eye does not necessarily detect steepened or flattened perspective, and the relative sizes of the two scales provide a visual clue. If it is at all possible, the use of trowels, brushes or other bits of equipment as scales should be avoided; they are usually rather obtrusive, and not very effective. Trowel blades can vary from about 15 to 7 cm in length, or even less with a veteran trowel, and will therefore give very little indication of size. Geologists often use their hammers as scales, but the standard wedge-ended geological hammer can be anywhere between 20 and 50 cm long. Some of the more conscientious mark the handle in centimetres, which provides a better, though grubby, scale.

On some digs and surveys it is standard practice to include an information board in the photographs, marked with the location, square, level and so on, or even to put large labels on the different features, and to put in north points or compass circles. This is quite often done with photographs of graves, where one grave looks very like another and orientation is of particular interest. If this is the policy of the dig, well and good, and certainly such photographs provide a useful check on other records; but inevitably they appear cluttered, and the scales, north points and markers may look more obvious than the feature itself. A page full of such photographs in a final report is not at all attractive. It is always as well to take two photographs in such circumstances, one with and one without the boards, etc. Information boards can either be of metal, with magnetic letters, such as those used for film titles, or, a good deal cheaper, café menu boards with plastic letters in slots. About 20×30 cm should be large enough for most purposes. For quick, standardised photographs of such things as soil sections, it may be worth marking the edge of the board in centimetres, dispensing with separate scales, and making a small north point to fit on the board. If the board is used upright or sloping, the usual map convention is used; if the photograph is taken facing north, the N point points to the top of the frame, if facing south, to the bottom.

On many digs it is not considered necessary to put a scale into photographs of skeletons, unless the skeleton is of a child, dwarf or giant, at least not with an extended burial. Anthropometric measurements are much too fine to be aided by such a scale, and any scale is sure to obscure an edge of the grave.

It has been suggested (Houlder (1980)) that all structures and objects on site should be photographed surrounded by a 'box-scale' – a skeleton cube of scales – so that if necessary a three-dimensional perspective grid can be projected over the photograph and a contour plan be drawn by photogrammetry. While in theory this may be a desirable provision, the time and labour necessary to construct such a scale and to erect and orientate it for every photograph would be considerable.

For the photography of objects and small details, scales of 20, 15, 10, 5, 3 and 1 cm are useful, and 1 cm and 0.5 cm scales divided into millimetres for close-up work. This may seem an unnecessarily large number of different lengths, but it is of value to match the size of the scale to some extent to the size of the object. Certainly a 1 cm scale next to a 20 cm high pot is of little value, or even worse a 10 cm scale next to a 2 cm coin.

The longer scales, 1 m down to 25 cm, are best made of lengths of hard-wood, thick enough not to warp or bend and wide enough to be visible. A rough guide would be 4×2 cm for a 1 m scale, and 2.5×0.5 cm for a 25 cm scale. One side and one edge should be painted with black and white divisions, and the other edge in red and yellow. The latter is preferable, though not vital, for colour photography, where black and white divisions are apt to look rather glaring. Matt or eggshell paint should be used, because gloss paint is too reflective. Some photographers prefer to use a scale of triangular section, but this of course rules out the possibility of alternative colour schemes.

The smaller sizes, from 20 cm down to 3 cm, can be made simply enough by drawing them accurately on tracing linen, contact-printing this drawing on to lith film to give a negative, and contact-printing the scales from this negative. It is worth drawing several sizes on one sheet to make printing more economical. The prints are dry-mounted on board and trimmed. If an unwanted bromide print is also dry-mounted on to the back of the board the scales will be less likely to warp. Scales for close-up work have lines too fine to be drawn at same-size at all easily, and it is better to draw them enlarged three or four times and photograph the drawing. If a large-format camera is available, it is easier and more accurate to photograph them to the correct size on lith film (which is size-stable) and to contact-print them rather than try to focus them to the correct size on an enlarger. Once the negatives have been made, any number of scales can be printed and they can be regarded as expendable; certainly they should be discarded at once when they become battered or dirty. Few things look worse than a smudgy scale in a close-up photograph.

Small scales can also be printed, although with rather thick lines, on a graphics computer or, if the facilities are available, engraved on plastic or matt metal.

4

LIGHTING BY FLASH

This chapter deals with the equipment for flash lighting and with its general use. Equipment and methods are more or less similar in every situation, but some particular applications are discussed under the relevant headings elsewhere. A comprehensive account of flash equipment can be found in Langford (1989) and of its use in the field in Blaker (1976).

Types of equipment

Bulb or *expendable flash* is nowadays little used largely because of the high cost for each exposure and the inconvenience of carrying a supply of bulbs. The exception is when it is necessary to light a large interior from several points simultaneously, when the relative simplicity of arranging a long firing-circuit, and the availability of high-output bulbs, become invaluable.

The construction of the bulbs themselves is simple enough. The bulb contains a fine foil of magnesium/aluminium (or, for small bulbs, zirconium) in an oxygen-enriched atmosphere. A small wire filament in the centre of the bulb ignites the foil when a current of 3 V or more is passed through it. Bulbs are available in several sizes, giving a wide range of light output,[1] from the small 'Magicube' bulbs fitted to snapshot cameras, with a peak light output of less than 500,000 1m to the largest 'S-type' bulbs, with an output in excess of 5,000,000 1m. Bulbs also differ (a) in the time they take to reach their peak output (AG1 type, 15–18 milliseconds (ms); M type 20 ms, S type 30 ms); (b) in the duration of the flash, small bulbs have a total duration of from 30 to 40 ms and large ones from 50 to 60 ms, although with a synchronised shutter not all of this light is used, while focal-plane bulbs, FP, which are designed to give a long and even output of light to match the travel of focal-plane shutters, have a duration of 40–50 ms; (c) in the colour of the light (clear bulbs have a colour temperature of about 3,800°K, blue-coated bulbs about 5,500°K); and (d) in the type and size of cap (bayonet, screw, capless, etc.).

Firing is normally from a dry battery via a capacitor circuit, although for a

---

[1] The different terms used to measure the energy, output and effect of light sources, including flash, are manifold and confusing. The output of flash bulbs is usually expressed as lumens (units of light measured at a surface, [1m]) or lumen seconds (lumens multiplied by duration in seconds, [1m/s]); and of electronic flash as joules or watt-seconds (units of energy, 1 J = 1 W/s). Both expressions can be deceiving, however, since the effect of the flash depends also on the design of the reflector and on the camera shutter. A more realistic measurement, and the one normally given in the specification of a flash unit, is a standard *guide number*. As explained later, this is a multiple of distance and f-number, and for purposes of comparison it is specified for a film of 100 ISO.

54

one-off arrangement it is possible to fire a number of bulbs simultaneously from a car battery.

Electronic flash units are rather more expensive than is the equipment needed for bulb flash, but very much cheaper per flash – no more than the cost of the electricity. The tube itself is of toughened glass, filled with a rare gas, usually xenon, and with a tungsten electrode at each end. High-voltage current is built up in a capacitor and, when triggered off, causes a brief, intense, fluorescent discharge in the tube. There are a great many kinds of unit on the market, and designs are constantly changing, so any list of the various types would be immediately outdated. There are, however, a number of basic features which, in one form or another, have to be considered.

Within the range at present available, the main division is between portable units, which are often hand-held and can be carried as camera accessories (many 35 mm cameras now incorporate a small flash unit in the camera body); and studio units, which replace tungsten lighting stands. The smallest of the portable units weigh no more than 100 g and, with a fast film and a standard lens, throw adequate light for 3 or 4 m. The largest, the so-called hammer-head units, weigh up to 1,000 g, and can illuminate up to a distance of 10 m or more. All have a power source, most commonly two, four or six 1.5 v batteries (AA), although a few units can be used with a separate wet- or dry-cell power pack. Rechargeable 1.5 v batteries can be used, but although these are cheaper in the long run than replaceable (expendable) batteries, they do not carry the same charge and do not give the same number of flashes per battery. Replaceable batteries also have the advantage of being obtainable virtually everywhere in the world, since they are of course the same type as those used in transistor radios. Many units can also be connected to a mains electricity supply via a transformer.

All units have an on/off switch, and if the unit can be connected to mains power, a three-position switch: AC (or External Power)/Off/DC (or Internal Power). When the power is switched on, there is a delay of several seconds (the length depending on the characteristics of the unit) before the capacitor is charged. Most have an audible warning to indicate that the capacitor is charging, and a neon signal to show when it is fully charged. This is of importance, since it is possible to trigger off the flash before the capacitor is fully charged.

The flash can be triggered either manually or, by means of a cable or a hot-shoe connection, by the camera shutter. Shutters of the between-lens type are normally fitted with a single co-axial socket and a lever that can be set for 'X' (for electronic flash), or 'M' (for medium-peaking flash bulbs). With either type of flash, any speed setting can be used, although it is advisable not to rely on the fastest speeds being synchronised correctly on an old shutter. With focal-plane shutters, however, flash can be synchronised only with the slower speeds, since the flash has to fire when the shutter is fully opened.

Most cameras with focal-plane shutters, including most 35 mm cameras, have a setting marked with an 'X' on the speed-ring, which is the fastest speed at which electronic flash can be synchronised. Usually this is 1/60 or 1/75 of a second, although some cameras with vertically operating blinds can be used at faster speeds. There are normally two sockets, one marked 'X' for electronic flash and the other marked 'FP' for focal-plane flash bulbs.

Studio flash takes the form of large flash units designed as stand lights (Plate 38). They are powered directly from the mains supply, and most incorporate 'Modelling lights' of 200 w or more, positioned in the centre of ring-shaped tubes. The position and balance of the lighting can be arranged by means of these lights, thereby overcoming the greatest single disadvantage of flash: the fact that the effects of fine adjustment of the angles or distances

Plate 38   Lighting units. These are, from left to right, a boom-light for tungsten bulbs, an 800 w tungsten-halogen flood, a tungsten flood on a side arm, and a 1 m square 'soft-box' diffuser for studio flash.

of the lights cannot be assessed except by trial and error, or by Polaroid test exposures. Studio flash systems also include a variety of reflectors, baffles and spot attachments which allow of different kinds of lighting. Several flash-heads can be linked to fire at the same time, either by a connecting cable or, better, by means of 'slave units' (this applies both to studio flash and to smaller units). These are relatively insensitive photoelectric cells which will not respond to ordinary levels of lighting but which trigger off the flash-head to which they are attached only when another flash fires. In use, one flash-head is linked to the camera shutter, and when this is fired the others operate virtually instantaneously.

Flash exposure
With normal photography by continuous light, the total exposure – the 'dosage' of light received by the film – is a function of the length of exposure, controlled by the shutter, and intensity, controlled by the aperture; and, within limits, these two controls are directly reciprocal, i.e. a long exposure with a small aperture will produce the same result as a short exposure with a large aperture. When flash is used, however, one of these factors, the length of time for which the shutter is open, is no longer relevant, since the length of exposure depends now on the duration of the flash itself. A small electronic flash unit might have a duration of 1/300 of a second and a large unit one of 1/1000 or shorter. But as well as differing in length of flash, different sizes of unit have widely disparate light outputs, so some measurement is necessary to relate light output to aperture, and which will take account of film speed. The basic unit for this purpose is the guide number (GN), which is specific for each flash unit and also for flash bulbs. The number is a multiple of the aperture (expressed as the f-number) and the distance of the flash from the object, specified in feet or in metres. It is usually given for a film speed of 100 ISO. A small unit might have a GN (based on metres) at 100 ISO of between 15 and 20, a large unit of 40 to 50, and a studio unit of 50 to 200. Using a flash unit of, for instance, GN 50 (metres at 100 ISO) at a distance of 5 m, the aperture should be set at:

$$\frac{50}{5} = f10$$

Alternatively, if for reasons of depth of field an aperture of f16 is necessary, the flash unit should be set at a distance of:

$$\frac{50}{16} = 3.1 \text{ m}$$

It is important to note that 'distance' refers to the distance of the flash unit from the object; within limits, the distance of the camera is immaterial. A guide number can be adapted for film speeds other than 100 ISO by multiplying it by 1.4^2 for each doubling of the speed, and dividing it by 1.4 for each halving; so, for instance, a GN of 50 would become 70 for 200 ISO, or 36 for 50 ISO.

Even the simplest electronic flash units now incorporate some form of table or dial which shows the distances or f-numbers for various film speeds; for straightforward photography using one flash unit as the sole source of light, it is therefore rarely necessary to make any sort of calculation. In situations involving multiple flash, however, and where the flash is not the main light source, as is explained later, very often the simplest way to arrive at the correct exposure is to use the guide number. It is important, however, to realise that there is no sort of measurement involved. The calculation will simply give an exposure which the manufacturers think to be adequate under normal conditions, and the assumption is based on a domestic interior. If, for instance, a photograph were taken outdoors, at night, with no reflecting surfaces, then the exposure would probably have to be increased by one or two f-numbers; if it were of a light-coloured object in a small room with white walls, it might need one stop less.

Most of the larger and more expensive portable flash units now incorporate an automatic control, a self-regulating device which adjusts the length of the flash according to an automatic reading taken with a light sensor built into the flash unit. This light sensor measures the light reflected from the subject during the flash, and cuts off the flash accordingly. Most such units have to be set for distance or f-number, and all have to be adjusted for different film speeds. On some models the light sensor can be removed from the flash unit and fixed to the camera, so that wherever the flash is located, it is the light being reflected back to the camera that is measured. The most sophisticated forms at the moment are the TTL dedicated units. These are designed for specific models of camera, and use the camera circuitry to achieve the correct exposure. TTL units have the same advantage of measuring the total light reflected back to the meter of the camera, including the ambient light, and of adjusting the length of flash, and in addition they adjust the shutter speed accordingly.

Exposure using studio flash is most readily determined by means of a *flash meter*, a light meter that measures the total dosage of light rather than, as ordinary meters do, the level of light. In use, the camera cable is linked to the meter, and a trigger on the meter fires the flash. Readings can be taken either of the light reflected from the object, or of the light incident upon it, the film speed having been set on the meter dial. The reading is given in f-numbers, and the same care has to be taken, as with an ordinary meter, to ensure that the reading is taken from the object and not from the background.

---

[2] i.e. $\sqrt{2}$, following the inverse square law of light: when a surface is illuminated by a point source of light, the intensity of illumination at the surface is inversely proportional to the square of its distance from the light source.

The use of flash

An unmodified, direct flash, whether bulb or electronic, gives a single, intense source of light. Used along, or nearly along, the lens axis, as it is if the flash-head is on the camera shoe, the effect is to flatten shape and detail in the object and, since light from a point source falls off very steeply, to illuminate surfaces close to the camera while leaving those more distant in darkness. So, although this is the most convenient position for the flash, if it is the main light-source it gives better results to position the flash off the camera and away from the lens axis. With studio flash, where the units are free-standing, they can be positioned in the same way as any other type of lights; with smaller units, however, it may be a matter of holding the flash away from the camera as far as the length of the connecting cable allows. Some small flash units can only be connected to the camera shoe, and have no facility for use off the camera; these should be avoided as too inflexible.

With the flash away from the camera, if only by 10 or 15°, a good deal more of the shape and detail of the object can be recorded, but inevitably there will be shadowed areas on its unlit side with little or no detail. It is important therefore to be able to introduce light into these areas. The simplest way of doing this is to use a reflector – either white paper or, better, a sheet of aluminium foil – to direct reflected light from the flash into the shadows. This can be quite effective with objects of low relief, but objects that are strongly three-dimensional, like pots or portrait busts, whether in the studio or *in situ* in the ground, will still show a considerable gradient of contrast from one side to the other. It is perfectly possible to use two or more small flash-heads, in the same way as studio flash is used, linked by connecting leads or by slave-triggers (a great advantage of the latter is that units made by different manufacturers, incompatible in other ways, can be used together). A difficulty can arise if the different heads are set to 'automatic', controlled by their photoelectric cells. If, for instance, the main light is to the left of a three-dimensional object, with a subsidiary fill-in light to the right, a desirable ratio of light between the two might be 2:1 or 3:1. But moving the second head away from the object will not achieve this ratio, since its meter will automatically ensure that something like a 1:1 ratio is maintained. The easiest way to restore the balance is to set for a different, faster, film speed on the right hand head. If the main light is set for 100 ISO, for example, and the fill-in for 200 ISO, the ratio will remain at approximately 2:1.

Alternatively, the same flash head can be used several times, much as a single tungsten light can be used as a moving light. It is possible, just, to use the synchronisation mechanism, re-cocking and releasing the shutter for each flash (with a focal-plane shutter, the rewind button must be held down while re-tensioning the shutter, otherwise the film will be advanced). In doing this, however, there is a fair possibility that the camera will be moved slightly, giving a double image. It is safer to hold the shutter open throughout, using the flash on the 'manual' button and to have an assistant hold their hand, or preferably a card, in front of the lens between flashes.

This sort of multiple flash technique can also be used for photographing interiors and large areas generally, either when a single flash would be insufficient or (a more common situation) when a single flash or a series of flashes from the camera position would give too great a fall-off of light from the front to the back of the picture. For instance, to photograph the length of a barn or a church or a pillared hall, the camera can be set up at one end, looking down the building, and flashes fired off from behind each pillar in turn (Plate 39). If each flash illuminates a separate area, or if the lit areas overlap slightly, only one exposure calculation need be made. Working from the guide number, adjusted for the film speed, an f-number is calculated, and this will hold good no matter how many flashes are used, provided that they are not lighting the same area. Occasionally it may be necessary to use more than one flash to light an area, if the unit is not powerful enough to allow of a sufficiently small aperture. The guide number is then multiplied, not by the number of flashes, but by the square root of the number. Thus, for example, if two flashes were used, a guide number of 30 would become $30 \times \sqrt{2} = 30 \times 1.4 = 42$; for three flashes $30 \times \sqrt{3} = 30 \times 1.7 = 51$; for four flashes, $30 \times \sqrt{4} = 30 \times 2 = 60$, and so on.

There are two stipulations in using this technique, however. One is that there should be virtually no ambient light. In the course of photographing an interior by this method, for instance, the lens might be open for a total of 5

Plate 39   Interior of a barn lit by daylight and two subsidiary flash-heads.

minutes or more. Even the smallest and dimmest window or other light source would in that time be recorded as a burnt-out blur. The other requirement is that the flash – and the person holding it – should be out of sight of the lens each time, for obvious reasons. A figure, either the flash operator or someone else, is sometimes included in one of the flash exposures to act as a scale, but the practice of putting the same figure into a photograph three or four times in different places should be deprecated; it has a certain shock value, but it is undoubtedly distracting to anyone looking at the photograph or viewing the slide for the first time.

In addition to these various ways of using more than one flash, it is often valuable to diffuse or spread the light, both to give a softer and less directional illumination and to reduce slightly the steepness of fall-off that results from the point-source nature of flash-heads. One of the simplest ways, if circumstances permit, is to 'bounce' the light off an adjacent ceiling or wall so as to give a broad and more or less even beam. With automatic or TTL-metered flash, no adjustment need be made, beyond the obvious necessity of having the sensor facing towards the object and not towards the wall or ceiling (most automatic flash units incorporate a device whereby the head itself revolves or tilts while the meter faces forwards). With non-automatic and bulb flash, allowance has to be made in the guide number calculation for the increased distance from flash to object, which becomes the sum of the distance from flash to reflecting surface and that from reflecting surface to object. Allowance must also be made – and this can be no more than an estimate – for the absorption of light by the wall or ceiling. Even a clean white ceiling will absorb light equivalent to at least one f-number, and – an additional hazard – a coloured surface will reflect coloured light, affecting the rendering of both positive and negative colour film. Some small units can be fitted with a reflector, a useful if rather unwieldy contraption consisting of a frame holding a white card, mounted on the flash unit, which is set vertically and angled to reflect the light forward. More effective are white or silvered umbrellas, arranged with their concave side towards the object, and with the flash-head directed into them. These give a broad, fairly soft, but still directional beam of light similar to that of a tungsten floodlight. They are routinely used with studio flash, but they can also be arranged for use with smaller units; they can even be hand-held with a little ingenuity.

It must be emphasised, however, that exposure determination, especially using guide numbers, becomes rather unreliable using any of the above methods, and it is always worthwhile to make several exposures at different apertures.

So far this chapter has been concerned mainly with flash lighting as the main source of illumination. It can also be used effectively as a supplement to other lighting, to introduce light into shadowed areas or to highlight parts of an object or scene (Plates 40 and 41). Consider, for instance, the requirements

Plate 40

Plate 41

Supplementary flash. Plate 40 shows the interior of a mill lit only by existing light. In Plate 41, the ambient light is supplemented (and slightly overwhelmed) by a single flash on the camera.

of a photograph of a doorway from a viewpoint inside a building, but showing also the vista through the opening. An exposure long enough to give detail in the interior surface of the doorway might render the exterior as a formless white blur, especially if it were sunlit; while an exposure short enough to suit the exterior might record the doorway itself as no more than a silhouette. By using flash, both could probably be rendered acceptably. With this and similar situations where the flash is a subsidiary light source, it should be as close as possible to the lens axis, otherwise there is a strong chance of recording two conflicting sets of shadows, one from the sun and the other from the flash. In these cases automatic, and still more TTL flash controls, become ineffective, since they will take account of the exterior light. It is safer to rely on using the guide number, and for this the calculation is simple enough. An exposure reading is taken of the exterior (if a focal-plane shutter is being used, the length of exposure must be no shorter than that specified for flash). The f-number decided on is divided into the guide number, and the flash positioned at the resultant distance from the doorway. If the calculation is absolutely accurate, this would result in both exterior and interior being identically lit, which might well be confusing; it might be as well therefore to move the flash back a little from its indicated position to achieve a better balance. Again, it would be worth making several exposures, this time adjusting the position of the flash rather than the f-number.

More rarely, it may be desirable to aim for the opposite result, with the doorway lit and the exterior, sunlit or not, rendered completely dark. This can also be achieved by flash, although it may not be possible with a focal-plane shutter, with its limitations on the length of exposure. The aim is to work with a short exposure time, or a small aperture, or both, so that the exterior is very much under-exposed, while the flash is brought close enough to the doorway to illuminate it adequately. This minimum distance is first decided upon (remembering that the flash head or heads must cover the whole doorway and must not be in the frame) and divided into the guide number to give the f-number. It may be necessary to use quite a powerful unit, or several units, to give enough light. It should be said that this effect – of a lit object against a dark background – is more usually achieved by accident than by design when using flash out of doors or in a large space, and it is often necessary to extend the exposure beyond the flash minimum to enable ambient light to be recorded outside the area lit by the flash.

Two other uses of flash in field photography are worth mentioning. Firstly, flash can be used to add highlight detail to a dull and low-contrast surface or structure. Here the steep fall-off of undiffused flash is of advantage, picking out the detail in the area nearest the camera. TTL-metered and automatic flash are usually adequate, although tending to over-exposure. Guide-number calculations are liable to be deceiving, however, since they make no allowance for ambient light. Very roughly, if an ordinary meter reading is taken (again, at a speed compatible with flash, if a focal-plane shutter is used) and this exposure halved; and if a guide number exposure is also worked out, adjusting the flash distance to give the same aperture, and this also is halved; then the two together should add up to a reasonably correct total. The easiest way to work out such a calculation is to double the film speed in both cases.

Secondly, flash can be used to bring light into the shadows of an object or structure that is lit frontally or from the side by the sun. For this purpose the flash should be used from close to the lens axis, otherwise double shadows will be inevitable. TTL flash metering may be ineffective for this situation, since it measures total light, and if the greater part of the frame is strongly sunlit, it may quench the flash before any appreciable light is flashed into the shadows. To a lesser extent, automatic flash may suffer the same deficiency – less because few are sensitive enough to be much influenced by ambient light. Probably the simplest method of calculation is to arrive at a flash distance by means of the guide number, using the aperture, at twice the film speed, resulting in a flash exposure for the shadows at a ratio of about 1:2 compared with the exposure for the ambient light. Any more than this and the flash is likely to affect the sunlit areas also. The method, again, is only approximate, since it takes no account of the reflective quality of the lit surface, so again it is advisable to make several different exposures, varying the ratio between sun and flash.

Mutatis mutandis, flash can be used to fill in shadows in artificial light, bearing in mind that electronic flash is colour-matched for daylight-type film, and filters will be needed to make it match with tungsten-type film.

5

PHOTOGRAPHIC MATERIALS, PROCESSING AND PRINTING

For conservation and post-excavation work generally, processing equipment and a reasonably convenient darkroom are necessary facilities. Museums and similar institutions will normally have the back-up of a photographic department, and perhaps even the luxury of a technical staff, although for some a temporary darkroom and the simplest equipment will have to suffice. Similarly, some digs may be within reach of a base with a fully-equipped darkroom while others may have to manage with the minimal facilities that can be contrived on site. But while the photographic requirements of a museum or conservation department will probably be assessed in terms of space, personnel and budget, the decision whether or not to process film on an excavation site involves other considerations. As well as the requirements of extra equipment, materials and space, and the occasional diversion of personnel from tasks that may appear more urgent, there is the fundamental question of the quality of the record.

In the field, it is a principle that no structure or artifact should be destroyed or removed until it has been fully recorded; this means, so far as the photographic record is concerned, until at least the film is developed and checked as being technically satisfactory and as showing whatever is necessary. This principle is disregarded often enough for colour film, otherwise delays might be intolerable, but it should not be lightly abandoned so far as black and white negatives are concerned, since these are often the primary, and sometimes the only, record of a structure. But while field processing guarantees that the structure is recorded, and is seen to be recorded, so that excavation can be continued with a clear conscience, conditions may not be conducive to clean, reliable and consistent processing. The value of an immediate record is greatly reduced if that record is of doubtful quality.

One is not, of course, faced only with the alternatives of processing and printing everything on site, or of keeping all the exposed film, both colour and black and white, until the end of the season and then processing *en bloc*. Many digs employ a local commercial laboratory for processing, others arrange for their photographer to spend one day a week or so in a nearby commercial or institutional darkroom, while others again send batches of film, by a safe hand, back to their base organisation every few days. Whichever of these methods is employed, it is important first of all to ensure that the quality of processing will be adequate (this applies particularly with

65

local commercial arrangements – a village photographer normally engaged in wedding and passport photography may have neither the equipment nor the experience to deal with anything else). It may at least be advisable to specify the developer to be used, or even to supply it. Secondly, it is vital to devise some system whereby the excavation director or photographer can be told immediately if something is going badly and consistently wrong; if all the frames on a film are overexposed, for instance, it may mean a fault in the meter, or if there is a constant colour cast on colour film, it would suggest the need for a correction filter. If the decision is made to process films on site, two factors are of paramount importance: one is the need for clean working conditions, and the other is the necessity for adopting, and sticking to, completely standardised methods.

Darkrooms
If all that is needed is to develop black and white film, it is quite possible to manage without a darkroom at all, by loading developing tanks in a *changing-bag* – a light-proof fabric bag with a zipped or flapped entrance and elasticated armholes for access. Films and developing tanks are put in through the flap, with is then closed, and cassettes or dark-slides opened and the tanks loaded by manipulation through the armholes, which should also be light-proof. However, although a changing-bag will serve for such occasional loading, it is not at all pleasant or convenient to use, and in hot or humid weather it is all too easy to get fingermarks on to a film. One stage better is to construct a *changing-box*, a light-tight cubical box with sides of 30 to 50 cm and a close-fitting, drop-on lid and elasticated sleeves attached to armholes in the sides. Such a box does at least avoid the chief annoyance of changing-bags – the fact, that, inevitably, tanks, cassettes or slides, film and scissors end up in a jumble at the bottom of the bag.

Darkroom tents are available commercially; these are constructed like frame tents, with walls, roof and floor of black plastic sheeting, and with room enough for a bench, an enlarger and one operator. Erected indoors, they are usable if rather claustrophobic; but used outdoors and in direct sun they quickly become like ovens, to the detriment of both materials and photographer.

If circumstances permit, it is usually more efficient, and certainly makes for better working conditions, if a room or part of a room can be converted to a *temporary darkroom*. Black plastic sheeting can be taped over walls and ceiling, both as light-proofing and, equally important, as dust-proofing. The greatest problem usually is to provide adequate ventilation while keeping out light. Given a window space, an arrangement of overlapping sheets of plywood or hardboard, with all surfaces painted black to minimise the reflection of light, will give a certain amount of air circulation, but this will not be very effective unless another, similarly baffled, ventilator can be rigged up elsewhere in the room, preferably near to the floor, to allow of a through-current of air. Where space allows, a baffled entranceway, so arranged that access is by way of two right-angled turns, is effectively light-proof and allows air to move through the darkroom. Quite a small electric fan, if mains power is available, makes a surprising difference in a small room. It will rarely happen that a darkroom is so hot and airless that a photographer cannot work in it, or that materials will be irretrievably damaged; but a stuffy and uncomfortable working environment is highly conducive to hasty and slip-shod work. Understandably, one's aim becomes to finish and leave as soon as possible, and care and concentration suffer. Very often it is possible, and preferable, to work at night when a window can be left open and temperatures are likely to be lower. This applies in summer even in a temperate climate; in hotter climes, it is often the only resort. It may also be necessary to net doorways and ventilators against insects.

The floors of temporary darkrooms often present problems. Concrete, brick, untreated boards and compacted floors can become very dusty, while tiles and linoleum can be slippery to the point of being dangerous when wet. The best solution may be to use duck-boards, which will at least leave a dust-producing surface undisturbed, or on a hard and slippery surface to use plastic matting which can be removed and easily dried out. It is also possible to spray friable surfaces with petrifying fluid or concrete surfacing compound, which will harden and seal the surface, at least temporarily.

A darkroom which is to be used only for loading and processing film is furnished easily enough. It is always preferable to have two benches, one for dry operations – loading spirals, opening slides and the like – and the other for wet use – developing tanks and dishes. Both should be at a convenient height for working (90 cm for standing, 70 cm for sitting), and the wet bench should have a waterproof, easily wiped surface; for temporary use, plastic sheeting is adequate. A slight added convenience is to have a raised lip, perhaps 0.5 cm high, around the edge of the dry bench, so that cassettes or spirals rolling across the surface will not end up on the floor.

If the darkroom is to be used for more than this, its layout, and indeed its usefulness, will depend very much on whether or not running water and mains electricity are available. Processing and printing can be carried out without a mains water supply, although in the case of printing not very conveniently, so long as there is some supply of water nearby; but printing, beyond contact printing which can be done using a torch, needs a mains supply of electricity or a generator.

Mains electricity must, obviously, be treated with caution in a darkroom. Cable should never be allowed to trail around the room; all appliances should be earthed, even if they are connected to the lighting rather than to the power supply; and any switch within the reach of wet hands should be of the cord-pull type.

The design and construction of *permanent darkrooms* lies beyond the scope of this book, and professional advice should be sought; the subject is treated at length in Langford (1974). Very briefly, close attention should be paid to the direction and magnitude of the flow of work, and to ensuring reasonably comfortable working conditions. The environment of even a well-designed, well-ventilated and adequately safe-lit darkroom can become oppressive after some hours, and quite minor inconveniences – a bench too high or too low, or a switch that has to be reached for – can become major irritations and consequently distractions.

Darkroom equipment

As is the case with cameras, it is rarely possible to justify the cost of the types of processing equipment ideally suitable for an excavation. Much more commonly it is necessary to manage with borrowed equipment or with the cheapest available. Certain items, however, are vital and it is these that are discussed below.

Developing

There are two main types of 35 mm and roll-film developing tanks available, with minor variations within each type: plastic-reel tanks and steel-reel tanks. Plastic-reel tanks are simple to load, fairly cheap and widely available. Their disadvantages are their relative fragility, the tendency for the reels to clog in time from a build-up of gelatine and silver debris, and their difficulty in use in hot or, worse, very humid weather, when the acetate base and gelatine soften and becomes tacky. Steel-reel tanks are much tougher – in fact almost indestructible. The reels are virtually self-cleaning, and heat and dampness make little difference. They are relatively expensive, and (perhaps their major drawback) loading the reels takes a degree of skill and practice. Both types of tank can be used for 35 mm or for 120 film (plastic reels are expandable, but separate sizes of reel are necessary for steel tanks); and both are supplied in different heights to accommodate different numbers of films, one to five 35 mm films in plastic, one to ten in steel. For most digs, one double and one triple tank of either type would probably suffice; a double 35 mm tank will take one 120 film and a triple tank will take two. Plastic reels must be completely dried before they can be used, so three or four spare reels will be of advantage.

There are a number of daylight-loading tanks available which need no changing bag or darkroom. With these, a 35 mm film, still in its cassette, is set in a container, the film-lead attached to a clip on the reel, and after both are covered with a light-tight lid, the film is wound on to the reel. The advantages are obvious, but in practice such tanks are fiddly to use, they will take only one film, and they are difficult to agitate and to clean.

What type of tank is preferred for processing sheet film depends very much on the throughput of films. For occasional use, perhaps one or two films a day, small tanks with light-tight lids and funnels are adequate, although rather wasteful of chemicals. One litre of undiluted sheet-film developer should, in theory, be enough to develop about twenty five 5 × 4 in films. Tipped in and out of a small tank a number of times, however, it will become oxidised and unusable very much sooner. There are a number of small tanks available; most hold less than 1 litre of developer, and most are designed to take six 5 × 4 in films. It is wise, however, to develop no more than four at once, otherwise there is too great a chance of the films touching during processing. If a much greater number of films is to be processed, and if a darkroom is available, it is worth considering using a line of deep tanks, either 6 litre or 14 litre. For black and white negatives, three tanks are necessary – developer, stop and fix – as well as a washing tank. All need lids, and the developer tank should also have a floating lid to minimise oxidation. Apart from the advantages of speed and convenience, the relatively large volume-to-surface ratio of developer means it will oxidise more slowly, especially if the floating lid is kept on when the tank is not in use; nor will it be so affected by changes in air temperature. Ten or twelve film hangers will also be needed, as large or larger than the largest size of sheet film in use.

The minor items needed for a site developing room should include: a thermometer, the dial type with a bi-metal probe being a good deal more robust and easier to read than the glass-tube variety; plastic measures and funnels, and a clean plastic bucket marked with litre divisions; and a timing clock with a dial, at least 10 cm across (clocks smaller than this are difficult to read or to set accurately).

Of considerable importance is the question of film drying. While films, whether sheet, roll or 35 mm, are drying, they are particularly susceptible to damage. The gelatine is soft and swollen, and any dust blown against it, especially hard-edged particles of silica, may become embedded immovably. Such films are also easily scratched and, if disturbed in any way before drying is complete, may suffer from drying marks, tear-shaped dense areas where water, running back across a dried part of the film, has expanded the gelatine. In the face of these dangers, it is worth going to a lot of trouble to ensure that films are dried in a dust-free atmosphere and that they remain untouched and undisturbed until all the moisture has evaporated. The best equipment is a professional drying cabinet with an updraught of warmed, filtered air. Those that will take a full length of 35 mm film are preferable; in shorter cabinets, 35 mm films have to be looped, and there is a strong possibility that the frame at the bottom of the loop will be marked. Such cabinets are, however, expensive and are hardly justifiable for a dig darkroom. A reasonable substitute can be arranged, using a cupboard or screened-off corner of a room, or even a pair of crossed wire coat-hangers draped with a sheet of polythene. Heat is not necessary except in the most humid environments – and even there it should be very gentle – but it is essential to make sure that a suddenly opened door, for instance, will not cause the films to sway and touch one another or a wall, or that somebody walking across the floor will not raise a cloud of dust. Top clips are necessary to hold the film in the cabinet or on a line, and bottom clips on each film to weigh them down and prevent their touching. Stainless steel film clips are best, but failing these, ordinary plastic (not wooden) clothes pegs will serve.

Contact printing

Even if darkroom facilities are minimal, it is usually worth making contact prints from black and white negatives for filing purposes, for catalogues, and to check the quality of the record; it is easy enough to tell whether an object has been correctly photographed by looking at the negative, but not at all easy with a negative of a structure or section. If mains electricity is not available, contact prints can be made using two torches, one with red contact tape over the lens acting as a safelight, and the other as the exposing light.

Contact frames designed for 35 mm, 120 or sheet film are easy to use and give a white border along the film edges when printed, which is useful for numbering. At least three A4-size dishes are needed (developer, fixer and washing). Stainless steel dishes are a good deal more expensive than plastic, but they are unbreakable and do not become stained as plastic does.

Enlarging

For a darkroom used for enlarging, an electricity supply is necessary, and piped water is of great advantage. As far as equipment is concerned, the line between a temporary dig darkroom and something more permanent becomes blurred; much the same kinds of equipment would be used in both, and choice becomes a matter of availability, budget and personal preference. However, it is worth briefly considering the pieces of essential equipment, if only because equipment used on digs, or by departments or organisations without professional photographic staff, needs to be simple in operation, robust and easily dismountable, desiderata that are not necessarily mentioned in manufacturers' specifications.

The first question to be decided is the size of the enlarger. An enlarger big enough to take 6 × 6 or even 6 × 9 cm film is not very much larger than one that deals only with 35 mm. It is desirable though not essential to have two lenses, a 40 or 50 mm for 35 mm film and a 90 or 100 mm for 6 × 9 cm; and two or three film-holders. Glassless film-holders are much to be preferred – those with glass are too likely to pick up dust – and adjustable borders are an advantage. Square-section columns are generally more rigid than round, and all parts, particularly the column, should be black rather than bright metal. There are several makes available on which the enlarger head can be replaced by a camera arm and the enlarger used as a vertical camera stand; this is a most useful facility on a dig.

Enlargers designed for negatives bigger than 6 × 9 cm come into a different, and rather more expensive, category. Although essentially they are no more than scaled-up versions of 35 mm enlargers, they cost quite a lot more, presumably because they are manufactured for a specialist rather than a mass market. However, large-format black and white enlargers are quite common on the secondhand market, since most large laboratories and studios now use colour enlargers for all their work. But like secondhand professional cameras, secondhand professional enlargers should be approached with caution; check the stability of the column, the squareness of the negative and lens stages (which may or may not be adjustable), and the amount of play on the column drive and the focussing wheel. Burnt-out wiring and lamp-holders are easily replaced, but replacing worn or missing parts, or cracked or torn bellows, may be very expensive indeed. Long-focus enlarging lenses are similarly expensive (150 mm is the standard for 5×4 in), although again there are plenty of good secondhand lenses available which, so long as they are unscratched and the coatings untarnished, are quite adequate. It is worth bearing in mind that a good enlarging lens is also a good lens for copying and for macro photography.

There are few, if any, digs on which a large-format enlarger would really be justified, unless perhaps where long-term architectural work is in progress. Nevertheless, for base-camps and laboratories such an enlarger is essential if large-format photography is to be done at all, and some at least can carry adaptors enabling negatives down to 35 mm to be printed.

Small enlargers can be rewired to take low-voltage bulbs powered by generator or batteries, but since such bulbs are smaller and closer to a point source than are standard enlarger bulbs, it may well be necessary to re-focus the illumination whenever the enlarger head is moved up or down the column. To enable this to be done, the bulb-holder must be of the type fixed on the end of a tube that is adjustable, up and down, within the enlarger head. The procedure is simple: a negative is brought to size and focussed, and it is then removed and the tube adjusted up or down until the rectangle of light on the board is evenly lit.

It is useful, though not essential, to have a timing clock wired into the enlarger circuit rather than to time exposures by counting or by watching a clock face; but such wired-in timers are made only for use with mains electricity.

Solidly built paper-holders are not only longer lasting than light-weight models, but they are far less likely to move if jarred between exposures.

Two small safelights, one beside the enlarger and one over the developing dish, are more efficient than one larger general one. The appropriate filters are:

	Ilford	Kodak
Bromide paper	5	OC
Lith material	LR	1A

Safelights should be tested on setting up, and at the beginning of each season; safelight filters can develop hairline cracks, hardly perceptible to the eye, but enough to fog paper slightly. The quickest way to test these is to place a hard-edged object – a coin or a pair of scissors – on a sheet of the material in use, leave it under the safelight for perhaps twice as long as it would normally be exposed, and develop the result. If even the slightest trace of the object's outline can be seen, the filter is faulty, the lamp too strong, or the safelight too near.

Minor items of equipment such as plastic forceps, dodging cards and focus magnifiers should always be packed with the enlarger, not because they are particularly difficult to come by or even essential, but because they are very lose-able, and to replace them in the field may take disproportionate time and effort.

Equipment for colour photography
So far, these notes have been concerned mostly with the processing and printing of black and white materials. Processing negative and positive colour film requires little more skill, but it does call for closer control of temperatures during processing, and for a very precise and standard way of working, if results are to be predictable and repeatable. For this reason, where there is an alternative, it is better not to process colour film on site or in any but stable conditions.

The essential equipment is much the same as for black and white. Small spiral tanks, both plastic and metal, are quite suitable for processing colour film in small quantities. When the ambient air temperature, and the temperature of the water, is lower than the processing temperature (20°C for black and white, 38°C for the E6 colour process), it is well worth contriving a tempering unit – a bath or sink, filled with water at about 0.5°C above the processing temperature, in which the processing tank and the various bottles of solutions can stand. For a larger flow of work, rotary processors, in which a spiral tank revolves with regular agitation in a temperature-controlled water-bath, are worth investing in, and when the costs of processing are compared with the charges of commercial laboratories, they soon repay their initial cost.

Colour printing entails similar restraints, and is more or less ruled out for on-site work. Although, given reasonably good working conditions, an ordinary black and white enlarger can be used for colour printing by means of complementary filters, an enlarger with a colour head is easier and more flexible in use. The cost of enlargers with built-in filtration, however, is considerable, they can be used only with a mains electricity supply, and a voltage stabiliser and a wired-in timing clock are highly desirable.

Film
Black and white film is the basic raw material of archaeological and conservation photography; relatively cheap, easy to process, stable, and yielding

sufficient detail for most purposes. For field use, a medium-speed, panchromatic emulsion, about 100–125 ISO, will meet most needs. These films, such as Kodak T-Max 100 or Plus X, Ilford FP4 Plus and Agfapan APX100, have the advantage of sufficient speed for site and survey photography and a grain structure fine enough for the recording of finds and most small objects. It is thus unnecessary to carry more than one type of black and white film for use in the field.

For close-up and laboratory work, a slower, finer-grained film is to be preferred: Kodak Technical Pan, Ilford Pan F Plus or Agfapan APX 25. Recently, however, manufacturers have been developing the use of finer silver halide particles, in particular the 'tabular-grain' technology, which should give as good resolution as the present 30–50 ISO films do, with two or three times the film speed and with conventional processing. Most of these black and white films are available in 35 mm, roll-film and sheet film formats, and some at least of the 35 mm films can be bought both in cassettes and in lengths of 5, 17 or 30 m. Both black and white and colour film costs roughly twice as much bought in cassettes as it does in bulk, and at present-day prices, for any project that involved more than about twenty 35 mm films, it would be advantageous to buy film in bulk, with a loader (a device whereby bulk film can be loaded into cassettes in ordinary room-lighting) and empty cassettes.

Colour positive film, i.e. transparency film, is used in archaeology and conservation almost entirely for slides, and only very occasionally for publication. In any case, publishers prefer formats larger than 35 mm – the standard size for slides – although most will accept 35 mm if nothing else is available.

There are many positive films on the market (and the number is growing) all of which will produce satisfactory results in general use. But, unlike colour negative film, where minor errors of exposure and departures from a correct colour balance can be compensated for during the printing stage, positive film has to be correctly exposed and the colour balance of the film has to match the lighting fairly closely to achieve good results. Because of the need for accuracy with slide film, it is always worthwhile to bracket exposures, preferably in steps of half-stops, if there is the least doubt of the lighting conditions.

The proportions of the colours of the spectrum in light from various sources are very different. Tungsten bulbs, for instance, emit more red and yellow than does sunlight, and the light reflected from a clear blue sky contains little, if any, yellow (which accounts for the blue shadows in a scene under a blue sky).

The term *colour temperature* is used as an objective measurement of these differences. It is based on the temperature to which a standard metal block has to be heated to reach a colour comparable with the light source under test, and it is always expressed in degrees Kelvin (K = °C + 273). Thus a

Table 1. *Colour conversion filters and exposure adjustments*

Light source	Colour temperature	Filter (Wratten) and filter factor	
		Tungsten film	Daylight film
Noon sunlight Blue flash-bulbs Electronic flash	5500K and above	85B + ⅔ stop	Not needed
Photoflood bulbs Clear flash-bulbs	3400K	81A + ⅓ stop	80B + 1⅔ stops
Photographic lamps	3200K	Not needed	80A + 2 stops
Domestic lamps	2800K	82C + ½ stop	Not recommended

domestic bulb, which emits a high proportion of yellow and red, has a low colour temperature, 2000–3000 K, while noon sunlight, with a higher proportion of blue, has a colour temperature of over 5000 K. Negative and positive colour films are balanced to give a correct colour response at specified colour temperatures: tungsten-type film at 3200 K and daylight-type film at 5500 K. Within limits, each type can be used with light sources of other colour temperatures by the use of colour conversion filters; blue to enable Daylight film to be used under tungsten light, and amber to enable Tungsten film to be used in daylight. The commonest light sources, colour temperatures, filters and filter factors are shown in Table 1 for the two types of film. For precise colour match, however, it may be necessary to supplement these filters with additional colour correcting filters.

Most colour positive films are balanced for use in daylight, in fact for 'Mean Noon Sunlight', with a nominal colour temperature of 5500 K. There are a few balanced for use with tungsten lamps, for example Ektachrome 64T and Ektachrome 160T balanced for a colour temperature of 3200 K. Quite reasonable results can be obtained by using tungsten-type film in daylight, with the appropriate filter (see Chapter 3) but unfortunately the converse is not generally true. Using daylight-type film, filters, under tungsten light, are rarely satisfactory; this, however, would be the preferred system on a dig, where the most likely requirement is for a film to be used mostly in daylit scenes with only occasional frames of artifacts under tungsten light. In these circumstances it would be preferable to light artifacts by electronic flash, which matches daylight film, rather than by tungsten lights.

The various brands of positive film differ slightly in their responses to colours, although in most cases the differences are small enough to be unnoticeable unless directly compared, and are not important unless absolute colour fidelity is required. For use in the field, and especially where conditions of storage are not ideal, there is much to recommend Kodak's Kodachrome film. This has long been available as 35 mm cassettes at 25 and 64 ISO, and recently a 200 ISO type has been introduced as well as a 120 format. The price, which includes processing for film bought in Europe but not for film bought in America, is rather high, but the warm tones of the resultant slides seem to suit site photographs and, above all, the colour balance and other characteristics are not greatly disturbed by poor conditions of storage, and it is said to be more archivally stable than any comparable film. With many positive films, overheating or use of ageing stock will result in an overall greenish cast, which will probably be unacceptable. In similar conditions, Kodachrome takes on a slightly golden appearance, which is not too misleading in site or object photographs, although it may make the staff look too healthy.

When slide films are sent for processing, whether to the manufacturer or to a commercial laboratory, it is as well to specify that they should not be mounted, but should be returned uncut, otherwise it may be difficult to match the slides to the photographic register.

Colour negative film is increasingly being used as the sole recording medium on surveys and excavations. This is not necessarily a desirable development (see Chapter 8) but its growing popularity is in part due to convenience and in part to the increasing difficulty in some parts of the world of finding commercial processors capable of or willing to process black and white film. An essential requirement, if such film is to be used, is good quality printing of the negatives and since it is rarely worthwhile to undertake colour printing on a small scale, this means using commercial laboratories. There is a clear distinction, both in price and in quality, between laboratories catering for the amateur mass market and those providing a service to professional photographers, and it is only the latter that can be relied upon for accurate and consistent results.

There are a great, and growing, number of colour negative films on the market, all claiming some advantage of speed, gradation or colour rendition, but for general use most films of speeds between 100 and 200 ISO will provide good resolution at reasonably short exposures. As with black and white films, a slower film with high resolution, like Kodak Ektar 25 or Agfacolor Ultra 50, is to be preferred for close-up work. Accuracy of exposure is not so vital as it is with colour positive film, since some compensation can be made at the printing stage. A correct matching of the film to the colour of light is still necessary, however, because although the balance can to some extent be restored during printing, a wide mismatch may result in a distorted rendering in the print. Most colour negative films are balanced for used in daylight but will yield reasonably good results to tungsten light with a colour conversion filter (Wratten 80B or something similar). There are negative films made especially for short exposures (1/10 sec or less) with daylight or electronic flash, e.g. Kodak Vericolor Type S; and for long exposures (from 1/50 to 60 sec) with tungsten lighting, e.g. Kodak Vericolor Type L. When the colour match is critical, these are much to be preferred to the general-purpose films.

As is the case with specialist colour positive film, conditions of storage have to be more carefully controlled than they do for general-purpose film.

Processing chemicals
Black and white processing

There are many photographers who maintain that satisfactory standards of processing can be attained only by making up solutions, especially developer, from the raw chemicals and finding formulations that suit the work in hand. If time and skill permit, there is much to be said for this approach (a comprehensive account of formulae and methods is given in Jacobson and Jacobson (1978)), but most archaeologists and conservators have perforce to rely on manufactured developers. These have at least the virtues of consistency and simplicity in use, and there is a wide range of formulations to choose from. For general-purpose processing, whether on a dig or in a laboratory, by far the most satisfactory method is to find a film/developer combination that gives satisfactory results and to stick to it, using absolutely standardised methods. Given a medium-speed film such as Agfapan APX 100, Ilford FP4 Plus or Kodak Plus X, one of the general-purpose fine-grain developers like Agfa Rodinal, Ilford ID11 or Kodak D76 will give good results on nearly all occasions.

There are, of course, times when some other combination of film and developer will give more control over speed, contrast and resolution. Ilford, for instance, have departed from the usual match of one emulsion at a single recommended speed with one developer; they now offer an extended choice of speeds and of degrees of contrast from among three emulsions (PANF, FP4 and HP5) and three developers (Perceptol, ID 11 and Microphen). Since each of these three developers has a good shelf life, it might well be worth keeping them in a laboratory or a permanent darkroom, even if not on a dig. If lith film is being used, a lith developer – or at least a high-contrast developer such as D 19 – is necessary, and there are a few other emulsions, e.g. Kodak Technical Pan, which call for special developers.

Packed developers always enclose instructions for mixing and storage, which should be followed as carefully as possible. It is important that the developer powder be dissolved in water at a temperature of about 50°C (this temperature is not critical, but if it is very much higher insoluble compounds may be thrown down, while solution is almost impossible at very much lower temperatures). The water used should be reasonably clean and free from visible suspended particles; if there is any doubt the water should be filtered, but dissolved material seems to do little harm. Ideally the pH of the water should be neutral, but any hard or soft water that is drinkable should be usable, and indeed it is possible to use sea water as solvent if need be.

On a site, and particularly in hot weather, it is very much better to make and use developer in small quantities – a litre or so at a time – rather than make up five or ten litres some of which might oxidise before it can be used. However, packed developers cannot safely be subdivided, so it is necessary to buy the material, rather expensively, in small packs. In hot weather, rates of oxidation increase, and it is preferable to keep the developer in small, tightly stoppered, brown glass bottles, full to the top. It is also possible to buy aerosol cans filled with nitrogen with which bottles can be topped up as they are emptied. Some developers are supplied as concentrated liquids that are watered down to working strength; while these are convenient, particularly since they avoid the need first to heat the water to mixing temperature and then to cool the liquid to working temperature, they are relatively expensive, and, if stores are to be shipped, rather vulnerable. If there is a choice, as with some developers, between using undiluted stock solution a number of times, or diluted solution once only, the latter is to be preferred. Not only does this improve consistency of results, but it also reduces the extent of oxidation. For deep tanks, however, developer is used at a standard working dilution, and its strength and quantity kept up throughout its life by topping up either with fresh developer or, more effectively, with a replenisher formulated for the particular developer. With most developers, up to about 25% of their original volume can be replaced with replenisher.

Apart from the type of film and the type of developer, the factors affecting the density, evenness, contrast and, to some extent, resolution of the resultant negative are temperature, agitation and the duration of development.

The standard working *temperature* for most black and white developers is 20°C. Below this, reasonable results can be achieved down to about 13°C by extending the development time. For the films and developers previously named (Agfapan 100, FP4, Plus X, Rodinal, ID11, D 76), and assuming a development time of 10 minutes at 20°C, compensation can be achieved thus:

Temperature	13	14	15	16	17	18	19	20	°C
Development time	19	17	15	14	13	12	11	10	minutes

Although development below 13°C is possible, it calls for modification of the developer formulae, and in any case such temperatures are unlikely in archaeological work. Indeed, since warming liquids is a great deal easier than cooling them, it is usually possible to develop at the standard temperature even in cold conditions, and this should be done whenever possible, since extending the development time can affect the contrast of the film.

A more frequent situation is the need to develop at temperatures higher

than standard. Again, with the same films and developers, higher temperatures can be compensated for, within limits, as follows:

Temperature	20	21	22	23	24	25	26	27	°C
Development time	10	9	8	7.5	7	6.5	6	5.5	minutes

At temperatures higher than these, the fog level of the film increases rapidly,
the gelatine softens and becomes unstable, and the granularity increases. It is
possible to work at higher temperatures by using specially formulated developers, pre-hardening baths and anti-foggants, but it is much better to avoid
the necessity if at all possible. Even in desert or tropical climates it is usually
possible to bring temperatures down by storing solutions in refrigerators or in
running water, or by working at night or in the early morning. Low- and
high-temperature processing is discussed at greater length in Jacobson and
Jacobson (1978), in John (1965) and in the Kodak Data Booklet GNS:
Photography in the Tropics.

The standard method of *agitation* for spiral tanks is to invert the tank a
couple of times every minute and, for deep tanks, to lift the film out
completely and replace it every two minutes. These procedures should be
adequate, but it is also important with spiral tanks to ensure that the film is
completely covered and soaked at the commencement of development. The
tank should be agitated continuously for the first 30 seconds or, better, it
should be filled before putting the film into it, and the film agitated in the dark
without taking it out of the developer; the light-tight lid should then be put on
and the process continued. It is also wise to tap the tank sharply on the bench
at the beginning, to dislodge possible air bubbles (remembering however that
plastic tanks are by no means unbreakable).

If an exact match of tones and contrasts between films is desirable, it is
advantageous to pre-soak the film in water at the same temperature as the
developer for five minutes or so before processing (a similar procedure is
recommended for most colour development processes). Because this soaking
softens the gelatine and allows the developer to penetrate the emulsion more
quickly, it reduces the subsequent developing times by about 10%.

Having standardised film, developer, temperature and agitation, the
remaining variable, *time*, can be adjusted to give some control over the
density and contrast of the film. The limits of this adjustment for any
combination of film and developer can be found only by experiment, but as a
rough guide, with the medium-speed films previously named, development
time could be cut by up to about one-third to reduce contrast, or it could be
doubled for maximum contrast. However, if either adjustment is made,
compensation has also to be made in the exposure, otherwise the negative will
be too thin, if underdeveloped, or too dense if overdeveloped. For minimum
contrast, exposure should be doubled, i.e. increase by one stop; for maximum
contrast it should be halved, i.e. decreased by one stop. These figures are only

an approximate guide, but it should be emphasised that the manufacturer's recommendation of film speeds and development times should also be treated as no more than a guide, to be modified in the light of experience. In particular, photographs of structures and sections in shadow can be of very low contrast and can be much improved by extended development, while scenes in direct sunlight or lit by flash will be of very high contrast, benefitting from reduced development.

It is always necessary to rinse a black and white film for a minute or two between development and fixing. It is better, however, to immerse the film in a *stop bath*, which will neutralise the developer, preventing its carry-over into the fixer, and thus avoid the possibility of dichroic fog. A 2–5% solution of glacial acetic acid, citric acid or potassium metabisulphite is adequate, although commercially produced stop baths also have a useful indicator which, by a colour change, shows when the bath should be discarded. If processing is to be done at high temperatures, a stop-hardening bath is preferable, since this prevents excessive swelling of the gelatine. A solution of 3% potassium chrome alum and 6% sodium sulphate (anhydrous) will serve. Immersion should be for about one minute.

For *fixing* the film, any acid fixer should be effective, but hardening acid fixer is not recommended. As with developers, concentrated liquid fixers are more convenient, but rather more expensive and more vulnerable in transit. It is important not to use the fixer to, or beyond, exhaustion; the simple fact that the film appears to be clear after fixing is not necessarily proof that it is completely fixed. With site photographs, all negatives should be regarded as being potentially of archival value, which means, above all, adequate fixing and washing. One litre of fixer (whether sodium or ammonium thiosulphate) will fix about one hundred 5 × 4 or twenty-five full length 35 mm negatives, but this is the outside limit and it is safer to work to a lower margin.

As was said earlier, adequate *washing* of black and white films is essential. If running water is available, 15 to 20 minutes' washing with the tank so arranged that the water, through a tube, is carried in at its base, is enough. If there is no running water, a spiral tank, or a dish for sheet film, can be filled, discarded, and refilled about ten times at five-minute intervals. If permanence is essential, or if water is scarce, the film can be immersed in a hypo eliminator solution after a brief wash, and then washed again for 5 or 10 minutes. This should remove all residual salts. (Hypo eliminator can be obtained from manufacturers e.g. Kodak Hypo-Eliminator HE-1.) If there is insufficient water for adequate washing, films can be rinsed briefly, dried, and then rewashed thoroughly up to about one year later. When necessary, film can be washed in sea water, so long as a final wash of five minutes or so is given in fresh water. If the washing water is hard, or of doubtful quality, it is advisable to give the film a final rinse in distilled water – or at least in filtered water – to which a few drops of wetting agent have been added.

As has already been emphasised in the section on darkrooms, it is essential that *drying* of film be done in a dust-free environment, and to ensure that the film is undisturbed until it is completely dry.

Colour processing

The processing of colour films, whether positive or negative, is not a highly skilled business, nor does it call for elaborate equipment, but as was said earlier, it does entail close control over times and temperatures. At the level of throughput likely in an archaeological or conservation unit, the simplest and most reliable method is to buy processing kits, which include all the chemicals and instructions, and then to stick slavishly to these instructions. Compared with black and white, the extent to which processing can be manipulated is in any case limited, and by following the manufacturers' rules, reasonable and consistent results should be obtained.

Materials for printing

Black and white paper

Bromide paper is obtainable in a wide range of sizes, weights, surfaces and contrast grades, on both fibre and resin-coated (RC) bases. RC paper has the advantages of speed and ease of handling, and needs less washing water; fibre-based paper is cheaper and more permanent, and time is rarely at such a premium that a few minutes saved is important – in fact, the longer developing period of fibre is an advantage, giving time for manipulation.

Most of the other variables can be dealt with quickly. Neither on a dig nor in a laboratory is there likely to be need for anything but white glossy paper. Occasionally exhibition prints may be called for, and a rough-textured paper is preferable to a glossy surface for these, but such paper can be bought in small amounts as needed. Single- or medium-weight paper is suitable for most purposes; the only exception is when making prints to be stuck in registers, when light-weight paper – also called document paper – is preferable because it is less bulky. On a dig, the largest, and probably the only, size of paper needed with be A4 or 10 × 8 in; this is large enough to contact-print 36 exposures of 35 mm film, and any smaller prints can be cut down from this. In a more permanent darkroom, a couple of smaller sizes, perhaps 5 × 7 in (12.7 × 17.8 cm) and 6½ × 8½ in (16.5 × 21 cm) could be useful.

Both RC and fibre-based bromide paper are obtainable in different contrast grades, and by using the appropriate grade of paper the contrast of the negative can be modified. For most brands of paper the range runs, and the boxes are marked, from 0 to 4, 0 being the softest and 4 the hardest. A negative of average contrast should give a full range of tones on Grade 2; but if the resultant print is hard, i.e. the blacks are dense and the whites rather blank and featureless, Grade 1 should give a fuller range of tones, while if the result is soft, i.e. the blacks are only dark grey and the whites light grey,

Grade 3 might give better results. Grade 4 (and Ilford Grade 5) is mostly used for line originals, or for subjects of extremely low contrast, such as details of rock engravings; while if a negative is so hard that only Grade 0 will give a reasonable print, there is probably something amiss with the lighting or the negative processing.

RC and fibre-based paper are also supplied with a variable-contrast emulsion, whereby a similar degree of control over the contrast of the print – perhaps not quite as much as can be managed with the different contrast grades – can be obtained by changing the colour of light of the enlarger, by means of filters.

There is much to be said for using only variable-contrast paper when the throughput is relatively small. Certainly on an overseas dig, or any place where the replenishment of materials might be difficult, the advantages of carrying only one grade of paper are obvious. Since the enlarger filters are vital with variable-contrast paper unless the enlarger in use incorporates a colour filtration head, it would be as well to carry a spare set – such small items are apt to get lost.

What type of paper is used in a more permanent darkroom is largely a question of personal choice. Most photographers have their own preferences between makes and types of paper, and cost differences are not great. Most would agree, however, that fibre-base paper, properly fixed and washed, is more permanent than RC paper, and should always be used for any sort of archive, and that publication prints should always be made on glossy, glazed paper.

Chemicals for black and white printing
There are a considerable number of paper developers available, suited to fibre or RC paper, in liquid or powder form. Choices are not so finely balanced as they are between film developers, however, and most will serve equally well, so long as they match the base-type of the paper. Again, considerations of time and temperature are not so critical as with film; although 20°C should be aimed at, a few degrees one way or the other will simply shorten or lengthen development time.

If the darkroom is warm, developer in the dish will oxidise quite quickly, especially if it is shallow and has therefore a low volume-to-surface ratio. But it is a false economy to use too little developer; it is better to keep the depth of liquid in the dish to at least one centimeter, and to use a dish no larger than the largest print.

Many workers prefer to use only a dish of water between the developer and the fix, since this allows of greater flexibility in processing – the print can be brought back to the developer for further partial development, etc. If the darkroom is warm, however, and if a considerable number of prints are being processed, it is better to use a *stop bath*, either instead of the water or after it,

in order to prevent staining and to prolong the life of the fix. A 3 or 4%
solution of acetic acid is all that is needed. An *acid-fixing bath* should always
be used, either ammonium or sodium thiosulphate (sodium thiosulphate –
hypo – is cheaper, but can have an unpleasant smell in an unventilated
darkroom), and prints should be moved about in the fixer, but not left in it for
much longer than the recommended period, otherwise, in ammonium thiosulphate fixers, they can start to bleach, and RC papers (which need a very short
fixing period – about 2 minutes) can split at the edges. For permanence, and
with a high throughput of prints, there is much to recommend a two-bath
fixing system – the prints being immersed first in fresh fixer, and then moved
on to an older bath. A convenient method is to make up a fresh bath for every
session, using the previous day's bath as the second fix, discarding this at the
end of the day. The fresh fix is then demoted to second fix for the next day,
and so on. At the manufacturers' recommended dilution, one litre at working
strength should fix adequately about 50 sheets of A4 paper, but this should be
regarded as a maximum.

RC papers need only a few minutes' wash, but fibre-based papers have to
be washed very thoroughly if future staining and fading is to be avoided; they
should have at least thirty minutes, and preferably longer, in a tank so
arranged that the papers are swirled about, or parted from each other, and so
that all surfaces have access to fresh water. If the site has no piped water this
may not be possible, and it becomes necessary either to rewash the prints later
or to use a hypo clearing agent. This insistence on permanence may seem
excessive for printing undertaken on digs or the like when, presumably,
archival or publishing prints can always be made later and in better circumstances; but on many digs prints are made to go into registers and catalogues
or on to conservation record cards, and these should certainly be as permanent as possible.

The *drying* of RC prints can be done satisfactorily even without a hot-air
drier, if they are laid on clean paper or hung on a line; the same applies to
fibre-base prints but they are apt to dry crinkled or curled. If need be, they
can be dried flat by interleaving the wet prints with sheets of clean blotting
paper (although the process may take a very long time) or by squeegeeing
them on to glass. It is better if possible to use a heated drier/glazer; the rotary
type are heavy and expensive, but flat-plate driers are relatively cheap.

Colour printing
Like colour developing, colour printing, whether from negatives or positives,
calls for very well-controlled darkroom conditions and exact working
methods. In addition, establishing correct filtration and exposure for any
particular film/paper combination may take some time and be quite costly in
materials. Unless a fairly steady run of work is contemplated and a well-
equipped darkroom is available, most archaeological or conservation organi-

sations would scarcely find the investment in equipment, materials and labour justifiable. Printing from colour negatives, in particular, is now so mechanised and so widely available commercially that it has become cheaper to send work out than to do it oneself.

Quantities of materials

Estimates of the quantities of photographic materials that may be needed for an excavation cannot be more than an approximation. As well as the size and complexity of the site and the expected length of the season, there are many other factors to take into account: whether there are likely to be large quantities of pottery, flints, grave goods or the like, whether it will be necessary to re-photograph artifacts after treatment or bones after excavation, and so on. If during the course of the dig specialists will be present studying such things as organic remains, building methods or the site's geomorphology, or if there are to be surveys of other sites in the area, yet more photographs will certainly be called for.

Most directors or funding bodies need an estimate of cost before the season starts, an estimate which should of course include a reasonable though not extravagant margin against wastage, accidents and the unexpected generally. Very often, naturally, the estimated requirement and the actual grant figure are widely different, and the desirable has to give way to the practicable. Generally speaking, however, the photographic budget cannot be greatly cut without seriously affecting the record of the site. Savings can and should be make by bulk buying and by buying from discount houses, but such savings are marginal. Again, a decision not to print on the site to save the cost of materials is simply postponing the expenditure until a future and perhaps less convenient time. It should be said that, at the moment at least, the chances of finding a manufacturer to sponsor a dig by supplying free photographic materials are slim indeed. Applicants are many, and unless the project is particularly glamorous or newsworthy, it is unlikely to appeal to their public-relations departments.

Consideration has also to be given to the logistics of supply. On many overseas excavations and surveys the entire stock of film, paper and chemicals for the season is shipped out and any surplus is brought back at the end. This arrangement is usually satisfactory, but enquiry should first be made about local costs – it may be that the dig is bringing in materials that are available, and perhaps cheaper, locally; and about whether the import of substantial quantities of photographic materials might attract customs or import duty.

Probably the simplest way to estimate quantities is to take the expected number of working days in the season and to try to calculate, however roughly, the likely number of photographs on a typical day. Thus, a two months' season might involve forty eight working days. Using only 35 mm cameras, a medium-size dig – neither a simple bank-and-ditch, nor yet an elaborate town site – might call for one 36-exposure length of black and white film and half a roll of colour film per day. Allowing a slight margin, this could total fifty cassettes of black and white and twenty five cassettes of colour for the two-month period. Using a spiral tank and developer, diluted 1:1 and used only once, this amount of black and white film would call for 7.25 litres of developer – or 8 litres allowing for spillage and evaporation. It should be possible, just, to fix fifty 36-exposure cassettes in one litre of fixing bath, but it would be safer to double this figure. About 50 ml of glacial acetic acid should be enough to provide a stop bath for all the films.

35 mm or roll films, then, are simple to estimate for; so many films per working day, and amounts of developer and fix in direct proportion. Estimating for sheet film is less easy. It would hardly be necessary, for instance, ever to photograph all small finds on 5 × 4 in film, nor could one justify bracketing exposures on sheet film with as free a hand as on 35 mm or 120 film (although it is certainly worthwhile to duplicate important shots in case of accidents). In particular, the requirements of a site with standing architecture cannot really be estimated on the simple basis of so many days' work, so many photographs. It might well call for ten or twenty sheet films per working day on occasion, but this number is unlikely to be maintained throughout the duration of the dig. If work were commencing on some fairly large-scale group of buildings such as a fort or an abbey, one of the first photographic tasks would probably be to record all the remains above ground, which would mean that in the first season, or in the first part of the season, there would be a need for many large-format photographs. But excavation or restoration work on such a site is, of its nature, slow, and the need for large-format photographs thereafter might be much less. In such cases estimates can be based only on a preliminary survey. Fortunately large-scale digs of this sort are usually planned well in advance, and there should be opportunity to make such a survey.

Negative envelopes of the correct size should be provided for all films.

The quantities of processing chemicals needed are also less easy to estimate for sheet films than for 35 mm or roll film. Unless all the sheet films are to be dish-processed – a tedious and unreliable method – it would be wasteful in the extreme to discard the developer after each film or batch of films had been developed. One litre of working-strength developer of the ID11, D76, Rodinol type will process some 3300 cm^2 of film emulsion, i.e. about twenty-five 5 × 4 in negatives. But this is the outer limit, and a safer estimate would be twenty 5 × 4 in negatives, or about thirty 6 × 9 cm negatives, per litre, evaporation and carry-over of the liquid being dealt with by use of a replenisher. Thus, one filling of a 14 litre deep tank would be enough to develop 280 5 × 4in films or 420 of 6 × 9 cm. One filling of a fixing tank of the same size would be more than enough to fix these numbers of films, and a 14 litre tank of stop bath would need 420 ml of glacial acetic acid. The equivalent quantities for the smaller size of deep tank of 6 litres would be 120 5 × 4 in films or 180 6 × 9 cm films.

If black and white negatives are to be contact-printed each printing of a 35 mm or 120 negative will call for one 10 × 8 in or A4 sheet of paper, and each 5 × 4 in negative for one quarter of a sheet, with a surplus of perhaps 25% to allow for test strips and mistakes. The number of contact prints needed from each negative might vary, however, depending on the system of registration in use. For example, contact prints of small finds recorded on 35 mm or 120 film might be needed for two copies of the register, for two copies of registration cards, and for conservation records, as well as for the ring binder holding the negative sheets. Thus each film would need to be contact-printed six times, and enough paper allowed for this. Given reasonably correctly exposed and processed negatives, only one grade of paper – Grade 2 – should be necessary.

Where it is proposed to make enlargements on site, clearly a wider range of sizes and grades of paper would be desirable. As was said earlier, variable contrast paper has great advantages where resources are limited; otherwise, a ratio of two boxes of Grade 2 and one of Grade 1 and one of Grade 3 is usually satisfactory. If any sort of line negatives are to be printed, Grade 4 is also useful. Even with a fairly experienced printer, it would probably be necessary to allow 100% surplus of paper to provide for test strips, wastage and mistakes.

In practice, development of prints is a good deal more flexible than film development. Since development is by inspection, exhaustion of the developer can, within limits, be compensated for by extending the development time. On the other hand, if only a few sheets of paper are to be processed, the developer will probably be discarded long before its full capacity had been reached. As a rough guide, one litre of working-strength developer should be enough for about twenty A4 sheets, and pro rata for smaller sizes. A similar ratio of twenty A4 to one litre can also be applied to working-strength fixer, although this can be extended by about 50%, and better fixing be achieved, if, as was mentioned earlier, a two-bath fixing system is used.

Handling and storage of equipment and materials
An attempt will be made here to sum up information on the use of equipment in different environments, and on the storage of sensitive materials both before and after exposure and processing. More information on these subjects can be found in Harp (1975), John (1965), Kodak (1985 a and b), and Keele and Inch (1990).

Were it not for the need to furnish a season-to-season budget, there would always be a strong temptation to order a great deal of material for the first season, and to carry the surplus over to subsequent seasons, topping up as need be. If circumstances permit, this can be a perfectly workable system, at least with some materials. Packed chemicals in powder form, for example, have a very long shelf life and can quite safely be stored from year to year (concentrated liquids do not keep so well); and although bromide paper does deteriorate with time, it could certainly be stored from one year to the next. Black and white film in sealed containers or boxes has a life of five to ten years, depending on the speed, but this only holds good given reasonable conditions of storage. If arrangements can be made to refrigerate the film between seasons, it can be relied upon to maintain its speed and contrast over its whole shelf-life; but if, for instance, it is left in direct sunlight, or over a radiator, it may deteriorate in a matter of months. Positive and negative colour films, and infra-red films, are best bought and used season by season. Although refrigerated storage for these is quite possible, it does represent something of a hazard.

Equipment
There are three climatic factors that can adversely affect photographic equipment: extreme cold, heat and humidity.

Rarely if ever will equipment be used for archaeology in the sorts of environment encountered in polar or high alpine work. There might well be times, however, when surveys and even excavations are conducted at temperatures close to or below freezing point, and a few precautions are necessary. At several degrees below freezing point, and particularly if a camera has been left in such a temperature for some time, lubricants can become more viscous and shutter mechanisms slow in response. This can happen with both between-lens and focal-plane shutters. For extreme conditions, it is necessary to have the camera stripped, cleaned and re-lubricated with a low-temperature oil before use; but under less severe conditions it is sufficient to keep the camera relatively warm when in use. It should always be carried in an ever-ready case, preferably inside one's coat. More of a problem, very often, is the effect of the cold weather on one's fingers. Manipulating the camera controls with bare hands might be difficult, and with thick gloves impossible. The best solution is usually to wear two pairs of thin gloves and to take off the outer pair immediately before using the camera.

Keeping the camera warmer than the surrounding air can, however, cause another problem, that of condensation. If a camera which is cold from having been used in a low-temperature environment is brought suddenly into a warmer one, as would happen if it were returned to a case or under a coat, condensation might well form on the lens, and perhaps even on metal surfaces within the body. The lens should always be checked for condensation – which can render the image misty or mottled – before each exposure, and the camera body dried over gentle heat after the day's work, otherwise parts may corrode.

Sealed alkaline batteries of the type commonly used for flash units retain their efficiency reasonably well down to freezing point and below. It is not until about $-20°C$ that they lose power to a really significant extent.

High temperatures, by themselves, should have little effect on equipment. Some of the earlier plastics can become soft and lose rigidity, and the lens cement on old lenses can also soften in extreme heat. Leather bellows can dry and crack in arid conditions, and should be waxed periodically, taking care to work the wax in thoroughly and to wipe off any surplus which might otherwise trap dust.

A more common effect of prolonged exposure to heat – although even this is rare – is for the camera lubricant to dry out. If there is even the slightest trace of dust in the camera body or in the shutter, this might have a disastrous effect, permanently damaging any moving parts involved. Even in moderately hot and sunny weather, cameras should never be left uncovered and facing the sun. The back-focus of the lens is, of course, usually left at or near the film plane, and the lens can very well act as a burning glass, quite powerful enough to burn a hole through a focal-plane shutter, through the film, and even through the back of the camera. Aluminium or white camera cases reflect a good deal more light and heat than do black ones, and therefore keep their contents cooler.

When high temperatures coincide with high humidity, much greater care has to be taken of equipment. Leather, fabric (including the rubberised fabric of which some focal-plane shutters are made) and stitching can easily become infected with various sorts of mould which can in time destroy the material. Equipment should be wiped regularly, and such things as camera cases and straps treated with fungicides or chlorine bleach. Some metals, particularly aluminium and uncoated steel, can start to corrode very quickly in this kind of environment, and should be kept lightly greased. Battery contacts are also vulnerable, and may have to be cleaned daily.

Materials

All unexposed emulsions, and exposed but unprocessed emulsions, deteriorate with time, resulting eventually in a loss of speed, loss of contrast, increase in background fog level and, with colour emulsion, a change in colour balance. Given reasonable conditions of storage, however, slow- and medium-speed black and white films can be used until well past their warranty dates without noticeable deterioration. Fast black and white, and positive and negative colour films, especially 'Professional' films, need more carefully controlled conditions of storage if consistent results are to be obtained, and infra-red films, both black and white and colour, are particularly vulnerable to poor storage, and have in any case a short shelf life.

Most 35 mm, roll and sheet films are supplied in sealed foil packets, and so long as the packets remain unopened, the film is protected against excessively low and high humidity, as well as against chemical fumes, although not against heat or radiation.

In cold climatic conditions, the storage of film presents few problems. There are only three hazards of any consequence. As with equipment, moisture may condense on the film surface if the film is cold and is brought into a warmer, moister, environment, although fortunately this rarely happens to films in cameras, since most camera bodies are almost airtight and the rate of ingress of warmer air should be almost matched by the raising in temperature of the film. Secondly, film base which has been cold for a considerable period tends to become brittle and more easily torn. 35 mm film is especially vulnerable in this respect, since in winding-on or rewinding strain is placed on the film. Except in extreme conditions, the only precautions necessary are to wind-on and rewind very gently, and not to kink sheet film when loading darkslides. The third hazard is of the build up of static electricity when relative humidity is low, as it tends to be in cold conditions. Not only can the discharge of static along the film cause fogging, but dust will be attracted to the surface of the film. Again, winding-on and rewinding a 35 mm or roll-film camera slowly and gently will guard against fogging.

In hot dry conditions also static discharge has to be guarded against, but the heat itself, and its effect upon film, is by far the greater problem. The effect of excessive heat on the unexposed film emulsion is to speed up its deterioration, the effect being particularly marked with colour film since the different layers of the emulsion age at different rates, resulting in a progressive change in the colour balance. The *Kodak Professional Handbook* (Kodak 1977a) suggests that both black and white film and amateur colour film such as Kodachrome, can be stored for a few months at room temperatures up to about 25°C; professional colour film and infra-red film should, however, always be kept under refrigeration. If temperatures are likely to be above 25°C, all film should be refrigerated, preferably at or below 15°C. It may well be, of course, that no refrigerator is available, although many digs in hot regions without electricity find it worthwhile to invest in bottled gas or kerosene refrigerators, despite their well-founded reputation for unreliability. In that case all that can be done is to keep the stock of film in as cool a place as can be found. If, for instance, a box is buried 50 cm or so beneath the surface of firm sand or silt, the fall-off of temperature between surface and box can be 10–15°C or even more. No more film should be taken from the cache than is needed for immediate use, and film and camera should be protected from direct sunlight and not left in such places as the boot or the dashboard pocket of a car, where temperatures can get very high indeed. Fortunately, in such conditions it is rarely if ever necessary to use high-speed film, the type worst affected by heat, whether black and white or colour.

If film has been refrigerated, it should be taken out of the refrigerator and left to reach 'room' temperature before being taken from its foil packing and loaded into the camera. This warm-up process might take an hour or two, depending on the temperature difference.

In hot and humid conditions, the same problems of accelerated ageing occur, and in addition there is the hazard of the growth of moulds and fungi on the emulsion. If the relative humidity is 60% or more, this can become a serious danger, although much greater for exposed than for unexposed films. While film is in sealed foil packets it is protected against such growth, and it should be left in these packets until the moment of loading. Unfortunately, in the humid tropics the night temperature and the humidity can be very nearly as high as during the day, without the nocturnal cooling which provides such a blessed relief in hot arid regions. Not only are unrefrigerated films thereby subjected to high temperatures for that much longer, but the cooling of liquids and water supplies which facilitates early-morning processing in hot dry climates hardly occurs. Refrigeration both of films and of processing chemicals therefore becomes almost essential. Although manufacturers do not recommend storing partly used packets of film under refrigeration, in these circumstances it is worthwhile, at least for sheet film. The foil envelopes in which the film is packed should be carefully slit open on first use, and resealed with pressure tape before being returned to the refrigerator, excluding as much air as possible.

There are two sources of contamination that can affect sensitized materials in all climates: chemical and organic fumes, and short-wave radiation. Films can be adversely affected by a number of vapour-producing compounds: sulphur dioxide, aldehyde and formaldehyde derivatives, hydrogen sulphide, ammonia and mercury vapour. While these are unlikely to be present in a dig headquarters, one or another might very well be found in a conservation laboratory, and unsealed film should not be left for long periods in such surroundings. In addition, motor vehicle exhaust fumes and the fumes from open fires can affect films, and a range of paint strippers and solvents can affect emulsions, both exposed and unexposed, very badly. These last are a particular hazard because of the chance nature of their occurrence. A perfectly safe cupboard, office or library store might be redecorated, and a jar of paint stripper or turpentine might be left unstoppered for a few days beside a negative file or a slide cabinet; the effect might be disastrous.

The second danger, for unprocessed film, is short-wave radiation, and by far the likeliest source of this is the luggage X-rays at airports. The effect of X-rays is to accelerate the ageing of the emulsion, resulting, if sufficient dosage is received, in fogging and loss of contrast. A typical effect on 35 mm film in cassettes is a 'venetian blind' pattern of fogging across the width of the frame. The effects are most marked on colour negative film, and especially on fast film of any kind. The effect is cumulative, so that although two or three passes through one of the low-dosage, conveyor-belt type of machines found at the major airports would probably not harm even a very fast film (1000 ISO or faster), several more passes might well do so. In some countries, moreover, older and higher-dosage machines are still in use, and an encounter with one or more of these, especially if the film is not passed through as quickly as it might be, can have serious results. If at all possible, unexposed, or exposed but unprocessed film, should be carried in a separate package and the airport security officials asked to hand-search it rather than use X-rays. Most are willing to do this, and even if an uncooperative official is encountered who insists on passing it through an X-ray machine, the fact that the package contains only film will be immediately apparent on the screen and should give no reason for halting the flow while the operator ponders on the contents. Film should not be packed in luggage destined for the hold, since such luggage often goes through high-dosage machines. The bags of thin lead foil advertised as 'X-ray proof' are of little value; no conscientious security man will disregard what appears on his screen as a solid block of metal – he will turn up the power until the contents *do* register, or perhaps even start a security alert.

The long-term storage of processed material

There is no doubt at all that the negatives and transparencies that form the record of many important digs are at present housed in conditions very far from ideal for their long-term preservation. Partly, of course, this is simply a matter of lack of facilities. Ideally, for long-term preservation films should be packed in sealed, moisture-proofed containers at a relative humidity of between 25 and 30%, and then stored in a freezer at a temperature between -18 and $-23°C$, and they should be protected from fire, flooding and extended power cuts. Although freezers are not at all uncommon in laboratories, and in many departments such storage could easily be arranged, there would often be problems of access. While an archive is 'live', that is while publication or research is still going on, such storage might be thoroughly inconvenient. When all the foreseeable post-excavation work on a site has been completed, however, it would be well worth considering such an arrangement. Post-excavation work of one kind or another can, of course, continue for many years, and during this time, while the archive is in continuous or occasional use, thought should be given to its conditions of storage from time to time. For a comprehensive account of methods of storage see Kenworthy *et al.* (1985) and Keefe and Inch (1990).

Colour negatives and transparencies will inevitably fade with time. This deterioration is greatly speeded up by heat or light, and transparencies used for many lectures, or for teaching, can become bleached in appearance quite quickly. If important transparencies are to be so used, they should be copied and the copies used for projection rather than the original (apart from the effect of intense light, there is always the possibility that a slide could be mangled by a faulty projector or a careless projectionist). Colour negatives are not so much at risk, unless they are to be used for printing a great number of identical enlargements, in which case it would again be worthwhile copying the negative and printing from the copy. Transparencies needed for occasional use or for reference are best kept in glassless plastic mounts. Slotted plastic or metal slide boxes (not wood) are probably the best means of storage, these in turn being kept in a metal cupboard or filing cabinet away from light and heat. Slides should never be stored in a container located under a window, over a radiator or against heating pipes. The ambient temperature should not be higher than 20°C and the relative humidity between 30 and 40%; at lower relative humidities film becomes brittle, and at higher ones the growth of moulds becomes possible (this problem is dealt with below). None of these figures is an actual barrier or threshold, but rather they indicate conditions to be aimed at; at all events, conditions should be kept as cool, dry and dark as possible.

Black and white negatives are inherently more stable, so long as they have been properly processed and adequately washed. Attention should, however, be given to packaging materials. Polyvinyl chloride should be avoided as corrosive, and even polyethylene, which is relatively stable and unreactive and which is often used for envelopes designed for 'archival' storage, should be treated with caution. Since the plastic is completely impervious, moisture can become trapped in the envelope without the chance to evaporate, with disastrous effects on the emulsion. Perhaps the most satisfactory envelopes are those made of acid-free, conservation grade paper. For sheet film they should be of the pattern with side seams, and it is preferable to use envelopes one size larger than the negatives, so that they can be slipped in and out without friction and without the chance of getting snagged on the envelope. The negative envelopes should be stored upright and not under pressure. For roll and 35 mm films, the type of A4 file sheets of similar material are satisfactory. They are best kept in box files rather than ring binders and, of course, the box should never be so over-filled that the sheets are pressed tightly together when it is closed.

Prints are obviously of less importance while the negatives remain, but again they should be stored in acid-free packing and, if mounted, on acid-free board. Dry-mounting is more permanent and less likely to stain the print than most mountants. Rubber solution is particularly to be avoided; not only do the prints lift off the mounts after a time, but they are also very likely to become stained. Prints intended for archival storage are better not mounted at all.

Storage in humid conditions
When the relative humidity is permanently or seasonally above 60%, and when temperatures are also high, permanent and access storage become very difficult indeed. High humidity enables fungal spores to grow and multiply (which high temperatures alone do not), and the resultant damage can be permanent and untreatable, particularly on colour transparencies and nega-

tives. Unless the material is stored in freezers or dehumidifiers, all that can be done is to make the film less attractive to fungal growth, and to inspect it regularly and clean off the growth before it can damage the image. Transparencies should be cleaned with a proprietary film cleaner, dried and mounted in plastic while maintaining a relative humidity well below 50%. The easiest way to contrive this is to mount the slides on a sheet of glass with a light bulb underneath.

For temporary storage, slides can be sealed in a metal or plastic container with silica gel (about 30 g of dry silica gel is enough to protect fifty slides). This is not recommended for permanent storage, however. Alternatively they can be kept in a cupboard or cabinet with a low-wattage electric bulb or heater to bring the temperature to 5 or 6°C above that of the surroundings, thus reducing the relative humidity. However, although this may be effective in inhibiting the growth of fungus, it would also mean keeping the transparencies at high temperatures for extended periods of time, and the cure might be worse than the disease. If a dehumidified chamber were available this, of course, would solve the problem. Finally, it is possible to use, with caution, a number of fungicides, not directly on the transparency or colour negative, but on its mount or envelope. Such treatment is discussed in detail in John (1965) and Kodak (1985a and b). If transparencies or colour negatives have been badly attacked, the fungus can be wiped off using a proprietary film cleaner (water or an aqueous cleaner should not be used as the emulsion may have been rendered partly soluble), but there is little that can be done to mask the characteristic branch-like tracks of clear film left on the emulsion. Cleaned transparencies should always be remounted, since the old mounts may well harbour fungal spores.

Black and white negatives are less subject to attack than are transparencies – or rather the effects of such attack are not so obvious – and they or their envelopes can be treated directly with an effective fungicide. If black and white prints have been adequately fixed in a hardening fixing bath they are not very subject to attack, and they can moreover be stored in a heated cabinet without great danger of deterioration.

Filing and cataloguing

Registering and filing the negatives and transparencies that record conservation work is a fairly simple business. Depending on how the laboratory work is organised, and for whom it is being carried out, they will either be attached to the conservation notes for the treated artifacts, or else form part of an archive which records all the work of the laboratory. Whichever method is used, there must be a register (either on cards or in a book, or in a computer file) of negatives and transparencies, which gives the date, the object's laboratory or museum number, its stage of treatment ('after preliminary cleaning', 'before treatment with solvent', etc.), the viewpoint ('close-up of spout', etc.), type of film, and any circumstances that may affect the appearance of the record ('axial lighting', etc.). With a black and white photograph it is particularly important to record whether a contrast filter was used, and if so, which one. It might also be useful to abstract from this register, as it is compiled, other categories of information; for instance, to note all the photographs illustrating a particular form of treatment, or those that might be valuable for teaching purposes, for public lectures, or for publicity displays. It is important, though, to establish and to stick to the principle that the primary purpose of the photographs of an artifact is to record its appearance and treatment, and that this archive should never be plundered of original transparencies or negatives for other purposes. If, for instance, slides are needed for public lectures about the work of the laboratory, or about the excavation from which the artifacts came, the archive transparency should be duplicated and the original retained in storage; better, of course, two or more transparencies should be made in the first place. It is all too easy for a transparency, and more rarely a negative, once separated from the archive, to remain so – there may be the probability of another lecture in six months' time, in anticipation of which it would be convenient to keep the slides together, and the importance of finding suitable slides always seems to outweigh the importance of putting them back afterwards.

Filing the negatives, prints and transparencies relating to an excavation or survey is rather more complicated. Usually during the course of the excavation, and during post-excavation work and publishing, the file of negatives and transparencies remains with, and is part of, the excavation records, and their registration is designed primarily to tie the photographs to the locus, artifact or stratum. Methods of doing this differ widely; there seem to be almost as many systems of registration as there are excavators (Dever (1978), Harp (1975) and Nassau (1976)). On some large and complex sites it has been found worthwhile to adopt a system of call-dockets and card registration whereby the photographer is notified of the need for a particular photograph by the site or area supervisor, takes and processes the photograph which is checked and approved by the supervisor, and supplies prints for the appropriate notebooks and artifact register against further dockets. On most digs, however, rather more informal arrangements have been found satisfactory, especially if the photographer has other duties and cannot be on call at all times. In the interests of comprehensive recording, however, it should be emphasised that whatever methods are used, it is primarily the responsibility of the supervisor to ensure that a particular feature is photographed, and to pursue the matter with the photographer, even to the point of harassment, until it is. A common sequence of events is that the supervisor notifies the photographer, the photographer points out that the light is wrong or the area insufficiently cleaned, the photograph is postponed until the objections shall be met, and meanwhile other features of interest emerge, or both supervisor and photographer are distracted by other concerns, and the photograph never gets taken. This hazard, and the need to guard against it, may seem so obvious that no warning is necessary, but a search through the photographic records of many important sites will reveal such lacunae. Very often indeed it is the really striking and important features that are under-recorded; everybody, including the photographer, is so keen to continue with the excavation and to reveal more of the feature, or to lift it, that time for proper recording is skimped.

When a site photograph is taken, certain information should always be recorded, preferably at the time and not hours or days later. Obviously this should include the site name, the level, locus or area designation, a brief description of the feature ('second town wall', 'amphora *in situ*', etc.) and the viewpoint of the photograph ('from the NW', 'facing south', etc.). In addition, a note of the lighting conditions may be useful ('in direct sun from the south', 'overcast daylight plus flash on camera'), together with a note of any filter used, and for the sake of future convenience, the type of film and format. All this is normally recorded by the photographer in a register, with a running number for the photograph, and the date. Very often this negative register number forms the basis for all future catalogues. If the excavation extends over several seasons it is as well to start each season's entries from number one, prefixed by the year. Not only will this avoid possible errors caused by overlap, but it will enable such things as transparencies delayed in processing to be allocated to the correct year. Similarly, with registers of site survey photographs, it is preferable to start each group of photographs pertaining to a particular site from number one, preceded by a letter or number for the site.

The basic information of site, year and running number should be transferred as soon as possible to the negative as well as to the negative envelope. On sheet film this is easy enough; the legend can be written in waterproof ink on the rebate of the film, preferably on the back – non-emulsion – side so that it would be legible on a print. It becomes difficult with 35 mm or roll-film, where the rebate is scarcely large enough to write on. For this reason many workers identify 35 mm frames by the manufacturer's edge-number, preceded by a letter or number for the whole film. This is satisfactory for many purposes, but it does interpose another number between the number in the register and the negative. A more important consideration is that if the film is identified only by a letter or number on the envelope or on the contact sheet, and the film is cut into lengths of five or six frames to fit into a standard A4 negative sheet, there is no way of identifying a strip that has become separated from the rest. It is wise, therefore, either to disregard the manufacturer's numbers and to write the register number on the film, which can be done by writing one numeral between each sprocket hole, or, if the film-letter plus frame-number system is preferred, to tag the end of each strip with a fragment of adhesive label bearing the film letter. It also has to be remembered that if

35 mm film is loaded from bulk, the edge numbering may not run conveniently from one to 36. Some bulk lengths are numbered in recurring sequences of one to 40, some one to 100, and some are not numbered at all.

By one means or another, then, the negative should be securely tied to its location, and by recording the register number in the site notebooks, object register, and registration and laboratory record cards, it should always be possible to recall the negative or transparency readily for reference or for further prints and copies. However, this may not be at all the most convenient system for post-excavation work or for publication. Occasionally – even frequently – authors, publishers and research workers ask for prints or duplicate transparencies from the archives of important digs – and indeed publication fees resulting from such requests can make a not insignificant contribution to institutional incomes. Rarely if ever will the request call for a photograph by its registration number; usually it will cite a previous publication, or ask for 'a view of the Roman road', 'the neolithic town wall', 'the royal tomb', or some such, and unless whoever deals with the order is very familiar with the archive, a deal of searching will be necessary. The most useful filing system for such purposes is a dual set of contact prints (of sheet film) or small enlargements (of roll and 35 mm film) printed to file-card size on double-weight paper. One set is arranged by area, square or locus, with the prints of each group ranged from the earliest to the latest phases. It would then be possible to see at a glance all the photographs of any part of the site, in reverse order of their excavation. The other set is arranged by subject, so that all the photographs of, for example, ovens, or doorways, or knapping floors, are brought together, and a research worker can see at once all that is available in their area of interest. Obviously it might be necessary to duplicate some prints from this series, when one photograph shows several features of potential interest. Every print should carry the register number and the rest of the information recorded about it.

The compiling of such a filing system may seem – and indeed is – a tedious business, but without a catalogue of this sort, using the archive involves an even more tedious amount of repetitive searching.

At the present time a good deal of research is going on directed towards the efficient storage of dig records on computer. It may well be that in future it will be possible not only to call up records of dig or laboratory photographs grouped according to different criteria, but to match these with computer-generated images of the photographs; the physical presence of the file would then no longer be necessary. More about recent advances in the registration and storage of images is given in Chapter 15.

Whatever catalogue system is chosen, it should be borne in mind that access to the dig archive may well be sought in the future by people who are not familiar with the circumstances of the dig, and any filing or registration system should be so designed that such knowledge is not necessary.

6

ARCHITECTURE AND STANDING MONUMENTS

A good deal of archaeological field photography might be considered to be, essentially, architectural photography. There is no clear dividing line between photographing an excavated stretch of wall two courses high and photographing a cathedral, although the wall could be photographed quite adequately with a 35 mm camera and a standard lens while the cathedral would need a large-format camera and several lenses.

Architecture, along with figure studies and landscapes, is often the subject of photography whose primary purpose is aesthetic, but this chapter is concerned entirely with the recording of architecture as artifact; recording, that is, the shape, texture, sequence of construction and of decay and destruction, and the setting of buildings. At times, of course, architectural photographs can be an accurate record and also aesthetically pleasing – in fact, that is the mark of a good photograph; but to regard a building principally as a pattern of light and shade, or as a setting for Gothick mystery, rarely yields an informative photograph.

An excellent account of the requirements of architectural photography for the Royal Commission for Historic Monuments is given in Buchanan (1983), and a similar account for America in Dean (1981). There are several books dealing with general architectural photography. A well-known example, with splendid illustrations, is Schulman (1977).

The essentials to be recorded are: the shape of the building from all elevations; the ground plan (insofar as this can be recorded without aerial photography); methods of construction and rebuilding, where evidence for these can be seen; materials of construction; interior features; and the setting of the building in its surroundings.

The shape of the building

If at all possible, there should be square-on views of all sides of the building taken preferably with a standard or longer lens. Very often, however, it is necessary to use a wide-angle lens, or camera movements, but nearly always these photographs, though showing the façade, will show little of the roof (Plates 8 and 9). These square-on views, although uninspiring, show better than any others the position and relationship of door, windows, roof-lines, exterior steps, etc., and may provide vital clues to the use of the building. The ideal light is hazy sunlight at about 45° or so to the face; enough to throw breaks in the façade into relief, but not enough to give hard shadows which might obscure details.

A vital consideration is that the photographs should show the junction of the building with the ground. With nearly all mediaeval and earlier buildings the surrounding ground level has changed, and the build-up or erosion of the surface is often apparent from alteration or rebuilding of door openings and approaches. To record this ground-line is not always easy; often there are all sorts of obstructions – plants or outbuildings, or, with ruined buildings, fallen wall make-up. If the building is in a town, there is often the added problem of a line of parked cars obscuring the view. Sometimes it may be necessary to work early in the morning or at weekends, sometimes the photograph can be taken not from ground level but from a height, perhaps a first-floor window across the street from which it is possible to see over the line of cars. This latter viewpoint has the added advantage of bringing the lens axis closer to the centre-point of the building (if it is of two or more floors) and thus giving a less distorted elevation. If the building is surrounded by trees or shrubs it is clearly better to take the photographs in winter or spring when the shape is not lost behind foliage (Plate 42).

Plate 42   Isolating a building. Even a building as dull as this looks more interesting when it is not obscured by cars or vegetation, and when its shape can be seen clearly.

As well as square-on shots, it is always useful – and gives a better idea of the overall shape of the structure – to have photographs that show two sides of the building. Not only do these give a clearer idea of shape, but they can record such things as the continuation of string courses and parapets, and changes of material between one side and another. It is not uncommon, for instance, for a building to have had its front façade refaced with ashlar while the sides still show an earlier or perhaps a cheaper material. Different parts of the building may also show different degrees of preservation; in this country, the westward side usually gets most attack from rain, while a north-east-facing wall would show relatively more frost weathering. Again, photographs taken from a corner often show the shapes of the roof to advantage.

The main consideration in recording roof shapes is viewpoint. By their nature it is rarely possible to choose an ideal viewpoint, and all too often the only one readily available shows an unintelligible jumble of surfaces. If the roof is steep-pitched, it is often possible to see both its surface and a gable-end from one viewpoint on the ground. Roofs with valleys, flat roofs, and roofs with domes, cupolas and towers are much more difficult, the more so if surrounded by a parapet. A higher viewpoint is the only satisfactory solution, and this may not be obtainable.

Flat or almost flat roofs supported by domes or arches are often slightly domed over their supports, and a low-angle photograph along the roof should show the extent and position of the sub-structure more clearly than one from a high angle. The angle of a pitched roof may be of importance as indicating the type of roofing material originally used. For example, thatched roofs are more steeply pitched than tiled or slated, and a steeply pitched tiled roof may well have been thatched originally. Similarly, lead roofs are commonly of very shallow pitch, and many church towers in this country show the marks of an original roof, presumably tiled, at a steeper pitch than their present leads.

It is quite often useful to be able to transfer details of masonry blocks, coursings, window surrounds, etc., from a photograph on to a drawn elevation with a reasonable degree of accuracy. The result is a compromise between a completely accurate theodolite or photogrammetric survey and a sketch drawing (although, of course, a measured sketch by a skilled draughtsman can achieve a high degree of accuracy). The method, known as 'rectified photography', is described in Dallas (1980). It is essential to use either a large-format camera with movements or a medium- or small-format camera with a shift lens, although the last two will be less accurate. The camera is set up exactly at right angles to the façade. This can be achieved either by using a theodolite, level or optical square working from a base-line parallel with the façade, or by laying out a 3:4:5 triangle from the façade. In the last method, the camera is positioned by plumb-bob on the apex of the triangle, and focussed so that the image of the tape that is at right angles to the façade runs exactly vertically through the centre of the focussing screen, or exactly bisects the centre of the viewfinder. The camera must also be levelled horizontally with a spirit level along both the line parallel with the façade and that at right angles to it. It is better to use a standard rather than a wide-angle lens, and to use no more than about 60% of the long dimension of the film.

A large façade will call for a series of such photographs with perhaps a 20% overlap between them. The factor that determines how many are needed is usually the height of the façade. If, for a given distance, the whole height of the façade is not visible on the focussing screen, it would be possible, in theory, to take two photographs from each station, one showing ground level and the other, with the rising front, or the shift, raised to its full extent, to show the top of the building. This is satisfactory for occasional chimneys or pinnacles, but if, as it were, a whole upper register had to be recorded, it would be difficult to ensure its accuracy; even a hairbreadth departure of the camera from the exact vertical would result in considerable distortion. If space permits, therefore, it is better to take in the whole height in each photograph.

Each photograph should include scales, at the façade, on both sides of the frame, and if possible top and bottom, positioned so that they do not obscure any joint or other detail. For short stretches, up to, say, five metres wide, two-metre ranging poles will serve. For greater distances than this, it is more accurate to mark off vertical and horizontal distances on the façade itself with crosses of black or white adhesive tape. Ideally the same camera distance should be maintained all round the building; in practice there are few buildings with sufficient flat, even ground all round, and usually it is necessary to move back and forth and to use the cross-front to get round obstructions. With flat façades the method works well, but with an interrupted façade which includes, for instance, buttresses, window bays or porches, it is important to determine whether the drawing is to be a simple elevation, in which case the camera distances should all be from a common base-line with the scales always on that line; or whether individual parts are to be treated separately, when the scales should be on the surface of the protruding or set-back element.

All the negatives must be enlarged to whatever is to be the scale of the drawing, preferably using an enlarger with a pivoted negative stage so that slight differences between the scales on the sides of the negatives can be corrected.

The method is sufficiently accurate for most purposes, and certainly a great deal quicker than plotting-in every block or every brick in the façade, but it is asking a great deal of the camera, and of the photographer, to expect a result completely without distortion or linear error from a large complex façade, particularly if the line of the façade is not straight and its elevation not completely vertical. It is wiser that the dimensions of the façade be measured and drawn independently, and such things as doorways and window spaces plotted in. The photographed detail can then be fitted into this framework with confidence.

A more exact and informative record can, of course, be obtained by the methods of photogrammetry, whereby distances and angles are measured and plotted from single or paired photographs; this method also makes possible the recording of contoured façades. In essentials this is a technique of surveying rather than of photography, and at present it calls for considerable precision in the field and much expertise and specialised equipment in plotting. With the development of increasingly sophisticated (and costly) computer-controlled analytical plotters, however, it may be that the need for such extreme accuracy in the field and for specially designed stereometric cameras will become less.

Apart from its primary purpose in aerial mapping, photogrammetry has been applied successfully to the recording of buildings, sculpture and architectural detail (a review of its use in these fields is given in Dallas (1983), and examples can be found in Parr *et al.* (1975) and Zayadine and Hottier (1976)); and it has even been used in the measurement of detail on a microscopic scale.

A description of the techniques is not appropriate here; a brief account of simple photogrammetry in archaeology can be found in Stewart (1973), and a more detailed treatment of applications of photogrammetry, including the graphical methods of plotting from single photographs, in Williams (1969). A general manual of theory and methods is Crone (1963), and an account of its use on monuments and urban sites is in Badekas (1975).

The ground plan
Occasionally, in very fortunate circumstances, it is possible to photograph the ground plan of a building – or more usually the wall stumps of a building – from sufficient height to provide a more or less accurate picture, given the use of camera movements. Perhaps the commonest case – and that is not very common – is that of the remains of the nave of a demolished church photographed from the still-standing tower. Apart from such rarities, and excluding vertical aerial photography, the recording of plans is normally the province of the surveyor and not the photographer. However, a photograph from a high viewpoint, even if it does not reveal a comprehensive ground plan, is often valuable, since it can suggest where completely demolished extensions of the building might have stood. The circumstances that can reveal buried features in aerial photography – differences in crop growth, drying marks and slight changes in soil colour, and changes in ground level visible in raking light – can be as valuable in this kind of photography. The drying-out and yellowing of the grass in lawns in hot weather can be particularly revealing.

Construction and rebuilding

Clearly the elucidation of the construction and history of a building is the prime task of the architectural historian, and no amount of careful photography will take the place of a thorough knowledge of building methods and materials and investigation of the building's history, whether textual or stratigraphical. Although a blanket coverage of every inch of a building should, presumably, reveal any visible clues, this is rarely possible or desirable and, in the way of such things, the single change of material or altered building line, or the anomalous detail that could reveal the existence of an earlier structure, is the one that will be overlooked. But, given a reasonable knowledge of the type of building, or good directions, it is possible to photograph a structure and be sure that at least the most obvious signs of different phases of building and alteration have been covered and the significant structural details recorded.

The viewpoints of the photographs have to be carefully chosen and informative in recording building details. Photographs of similar features should be as standardised as possible e.g. a number of photographs along the scarf-joints in a series of beams should, if possible, be taken from similar angles and under similar illumination, and photographs taken of areas of different brick coursings should all be printed to the same scale to make them easily comparable. Obviously there is a limit to this – no one could be expected to wait through the hours of the day and the seasons of the year just in order to have the sun shining from the same angle on to different wall faces; but the principle should be borne in mind.

If the foundation courses are revealed, either by deliberate excavation or by denudation, they should be photographed just as they would be on a living-site. The viewpoint should show the depth and thickness of the courses and if possible the shape of the foundation trench. If the two sides are different, both should be photographed; a dressed or mortared inner face may indicate a previous cellar, undercroft, or something of the sort. When the upper walls were built of material subject to weathering, like timber, clunch or mudbrick, the foundation courses usually stand above the ground surface as a plinth. Upstanding foundations are therefore not necessarily an indication of the exterior ground level having fallen. If foundations are of stone, they are likely to be undressed and no more than roughly coursed. They may therefore have deep and irregular joints. It is best to avoid strong cross light and to photograph them in diffused or shadowed light. Careful cleaning is also necessary. By their nature, foundation courses are likely to have all the interstices of their faces filled with soil material, giving the impression of mortared joints. There are two types that call for particularly careful cleaning. The first is the not uncommon case where the joints were packed with clay which may be of very similar or identical appearance to the neighbouring materials. The second is especially common in Mediterranean areas, where earthworms in hot weather do not come to the surface to cast, but seek out spaces below ground. Unmortared foundations can thus be packed solidly with wormcasts, and the excavator may have to choose between leaving them in position, where they look like mortar, or scraping them out and perhaps removing the only adhesive that is holding the stones in place.

Details of doorways and entrances are particularly valuable in providing evidence of alterations and of anything short of complete rebuilding. Steps, and the position of doorways, are also of interest, and again different types of photographs may be necessary; those showing details – rebates, bolt sockets, worn steps and so on – and those showing the setting. The most informative photograph of a doorway, for instance, may be one taken from the position of someone approaching it, perhaps from slightly off the centre line, so that the depth and material of the doorway's set-back is visible. If a large-format camera is being used, it is frequently possible to take one negative showing both detail and surroundings – the format is large enough to permit of the enlargement of one area of the negative. With small-format cameras, however, this is rarely advisable. Enlarging, say, 10% of the area of a 35 mm negative would certainly yield a very grainy result.

Materials of construction

Details of *stone* dressing are always important, and usually best shown in strong cross lighting (Plate 43). If the sunlight is not at a convenient angle, it may be possible to complement the ambient illumination by flash, angled to skim across the surface, preferably from the same direction as the sunlight. Light-coloured stones like limestone, marble and some sandstones, can be highly reflective, and it may be necessary to over-expose and under-develop to reduce contrast. The danger is that the lit surface will block in to white, revealing no surface detail at all. A yellow filter (for black and white) is often helpful, and with polished marble or dressed flint, a polarizing filter may be necessary. Dark, dull stone like basalt or undressed granite can absorb a great deal of light, and it may be necessary to over-expose by a factor of $\times 2$ or $\times 3$ to record any surface detail. Dressed blocks of good stone must always have been valuable, and may have been used several times in successive buildings; they may even have been carried long distances. This is even more common with column drums and capitals. It is always worth looking for and recording indications of past use – exposed mason's marks, lifting bosses, different and especially non-local types of stone, column drums of different diameters, anomalous types of dressing, etc. – and of course any inscriptions or cut decorations (Buchanan (1983) page 13, noted that inscriptions bearing dates might have been reused and are no certain guide in dating a building). For this sort of detail, it is important to photograph both the detail itself, preferably square-on, showing all its features, and to record its setting. It is, for instance, pointless to photograph a particularly large or carefully dressed block unless it is shown surrounded by the other and different blocks.

With *brick*, the tone, colour and surface texture of the bricks and of the mortar are important, as are the brick sizes, the pattern of bonding and the thickness and regularity of mortar joints (Plate 44). Such things as blocked entrances, vertical joints and relieving arches may be diagnostic, and since bricks are less likely to have been reused than stone, the use of different types of brick in a wall is likely to indicate alterations and rebuilding. The photography of mudbrick can present special problems (Plate 45). Sun-dried mudbrick, whether ancient or modern, is nearly always rendered with mud plaster to increase its resistance to weather, and often alterations and abutments are masked by this render. When ancient mudbrick is excavated this

Plate 43 Massive masonry. The details of the stone is best shown by strong cross-lighting.

render is often missing or so badly decayed that it cannot be distinguished from the fill against the wall surfaces. A greater problem, however, is that the bricks, the render, and the surrounding ground surface may be of a very similar colour, tone and texture, and especially in glaring sunlight the one can hardly be distinguished from the others. If, with black and white, a yellow filter is used, it can give a better impression of the surface texture, but there is a strong possibility that it will also render a cloudless blue sky as a light tone that may also be very similar to the tone of the building, thus adding to the confusion. Sometimes it is possible to rely on choosing a time of day when sunlight across the building will give enough light and shade to make the shapes intelligible; certainly to have the sun behind the camera is about the worst possible position. Often it is preferable to take the photograph early in the morning when the building is more or less entirely shadowed but slight overnight moisture on the surfaces enhances their texture.

Timber-framed, or entirely timber-built buildings represent, as it were, the other side of the coin. Many types of wood, especially when they have been stained, creosoted or painted, can appear very dark indeed, and may require considerable exposure – two or three times the meter reading to a neutral tone – to give reasonable detail in the wood. If, in addition, important parts of the timber are in shadow, it may be difficult indeed to obtain this detail without hopelessly over-exposing the rest of the building. The worst examples, from a photographic point of view, are buildings with dark timber frames and white

Plate 44   Brick. Normally a square-on view would show the details of shape and coursing more clearly, but the extraordinary degree of erosion of these bricks is best revealed from an oblique viewpoint.

Plate 45   Blocked mudbrick doorway. The plate shows how similar
mud-plaster, brick, blocking and floors can appear in tone, both in shadow and
in direct sunlight.

plaster in-fills, like some of the black and white buildings of Cheshire. For this sort of subject it may well be necessary to use a low-contrast developer (Jacobson and Jacobson (1978)). Fortunately this is a rather rare case, and most timber buildings are of very much lower contrast range. Oak, for instance, if untreated, weathers to an attractive silver grey. The difficulty then is to show the variations in the surface, which is rarely completely smooth. The ideal combination is diffused cross-light and, if the wood has any sort of sheen, a polarizing filter.

Interiors

Given a reasonably good wide-angle lens, and sufficient time to choose the most telling and informative viewpoints, the chief matter of concern in photographing interiors is lighting. With a very few exceptions, interior spaces are lit by daylight for much of the time, and it is important to photograph them in such a way that the presence and direction of the natural lighting is apparent. Sometimes it is possible to photograph by this light alone, provided that the room has no dark corners with important details in them. Usually however natural lighting is too directional and yields a range of contrast beyond the capacity of an ordinary emulsion, and it then becomes necessary to use auxiliary lighting. Three methods are possible; fixed tungsten light, moving tungsten light, and flash.

If stand lights are available, they are probably preferable for lighting spaces of moderate size – up to, say, 10 metres square. Obviously the lights themselves must be positioned out of sight of the lens, and their light directed to bring the level of illumination throughout the space to a little below that of the natural lighting. As a rough rule, a balance should be sought in which no important area registers more than two stops less than the best lit. In some cases this is far easier said than done – if the space is of complex shape, or with fittings and furniture casting shadows, and especially if the floor is dark. If there are doorways or other openings off the space, it may be necessary to light the rooms beyond them in order to avoid the appearance of 'black holes', but to a lower level than the room itself; there is something distracting in a photograph in which there are, as it were, brighter-lit areas just off-stage. A useful trick, if there are no stand lights available, is to replace existing light holders in the room with 'Photoflood' bulbs. These are bulbs that give a high light output at the expense of a short life.

Apart from overall illumination, light can also be used, of course, to show relief and to emphasise particular detail. So far as possible, strong under-lighting should be avoided, because it gives a thoroughly unnatural appearance to any feature, and lighting against the main direction of illumination can create distracting double shadows. If there are difficult and complex shapes or areas in the room, it is often better to use one or move moving lights – painting the space with light during the course of the exposure. The exposure must necessarily be long – very little movement can be achieved in 1/100 second – and other, fixed, light sources therefore low.

The use of flash in the photography of interiors presents no great difficulties, unless the space is so restricted that the flash unit can only be next to the camera and directed straight ahead, a situation that results in flat frontal lighting and considerable fall-off of light along the line of the lens axis. If space permits, it is usually better to bounce the flash from a ceiling or wall or from a reflector. Nearly always it is also better to use several flash heads, or if need be a single flash several times and, as with tungsten lamps, to complement rather than drown the natural lighting. Details of the use of flash will be found in Chapter 4.

The setting

It is as important to record the setting of a building as it is to photograph and survey the structure and detail of the building itself. In few cases is the whole architectural unit preserved. Those that are reasonably complete are usually religious or governmental buildings, or a more or less self-contained complex that has in some way retained its functions (a Georgian square or a mediaeval farm, a school or madrasa); or else they are so massive, like the fortifications of a walled town, or remote, like an isolated castle, as not to have been worth the knocking down. But even with the types of building most at risk, like urban houses or early industrial sites, there are very often traces of the building's contemporary setting still to be found in nearby wall fragments incorporated into later buildings, or in the layout of streets or, for instance, in the quays and tramways associated with early factories. Such fragments must always be sought out and recorded, although with a good deal of care and discretion. If the certainty of stratigraphic connection or documentary evidence is missing, it is all too easy to assume that the nearby presence of contemporary masonry must represent part of the same complex, while it may, in fact, be no more than a later re-use; or that a stretch of cobbled way must necessarily have led to the building under investigation, while it might, perhaps, have curved off to somewhere quite different.

That said, it is still well worthwhile recording all such traces. Taken together they may contribute to an overall picture of the area, and if any are anomalous, this usually emerges when all the evidence is set down and considered as a whole. If possible, of course, any such photographs should include at least a part of the main building – the cobbled way should show the factory at its end, or if an isolated fragment of wall lines up with a wall of the building, both should be seen. This may not be possible, especially in an urban area, but at least a careful record should be kept of the orientation and position of the fragment so that it can be considered in context.

As well as this artificial setting, the natural setting, if it survives, should also be recorded. Sometimes the building's position in the landscape is obvious enough, and the reason for it immediately comprehensible – the headland on which a castle stands, or the stream that powered a water-mill, for instance. Sometimes, however, the physical setting of the building may not be so easy to understand at first glance; for instance, farmhouses sited along a gravel ridge in a marshy area or an early smelter built not near an ore body but near a long-since-disappeared source of charcoal. Or indeed, the reason why a building is where it is may be historical or social, and comprehensible only in those terms; a fishing village built not on the coast but on the cliffs to be out of the way of raiders, or a church built well away from the nearest settlement because it was once part of a leper colony. In such cases, where the reason for the siting is not obvious, it is perhaps even more important that it should be recorded, in the hope that, sooner or later, it will become explicable, perhaps through other disciplines.

7

SURVEY PHOTOGRAPHY

Surveys take many forms, and a photographic record is always desirable. Whether field walking, looking for unknown sites or examining details of known ones, environmental surveying, studying or comparing buildings or building elements, or recording artifacts in museums or collections, it is unwise to rely on memory and notes alone. The features that it is necessary to record photographically, and the techniques for doing so, differ for these several types of survey, although they have much in common.

So far as equipment is concerned, it must be remembered that nearly all surveys involve walking, whether across miles of steppe or through endless museum corridors. It is never easy to strike a balance between minimal weight and an adequate range of functions. It would not be sensible to attempt, for instance, a survey of hill-top sanctuaries in Greece carrying a 5 × 4 in monorail camera and all its accessories; on the other hand, it is frustrating to discover a remote site and be without the means of recording it.

A minimum kit might comprise:

> Two 35 mm camera bodies, one for black and white, one for colour positive.
> *Either* 28, 50 and 200 mm lenses, *or* one or two zoom lenses to cover the same range; the weight difference is not so disproportionate as it might seem – three prime lenses would weigh 700–750 g, two zooms covering the same range about 850 g, or a 'super-zoom' 28–200 mm about 700 g. If the survey is of buildings, the 28 mm lens could advantageously be replaced by a shift lens; if of artifacts in museums, a 50 or 100 mm macro lens would be more useful.
> UV, yellow, red, green and polarizing filters, with adaptor rings if the lens diameters are different.
> Cable release, spirit level, compass, scales, lightweight tripod. It may be that a tripod is unnecessary for work in open countryside, but if there is any possibility of dark interiors, or need for detail and close-up photography, the slight extra weight is worth enduring. Alternatives, though less flexible, are a small clamp which can be fixed to a fence or bough or on to a survey pole, or a rifle-stock type of support, which is useful especially with long lenses, but which weighs very little less than a light tripod.

A padded or light metal shoulder-bag to hold everything, including spare film, is safer and more convenient than hanging the individual bits round one's neck. There are such things as 'photographic jackets', with pockets and straps to hold the entire outfit, but they are not to be recommended in hot weather.

Field walking

This covers the methodical examination, with surface collection, of a stretch of country, which may be a particular geographical unit or just the next square on the grid; the location and discovery of sites may be the prime purpose, or may be seen as a side issue to some grand scheme of statistical coverage. Unless there are groups of finds, or fragile or broken artifacts are discovered, the need for *in situ* photography will probably be small. A photograph of a sherd or flint in a ploughed field is not very informative. Photographers are likely to be more concerned with the setting – the type of country, soils, water, topography, vegetation, etc. It may be thought desirable to photograph every field or hillside covered, as a check to later identification if nothing else. If so, it is vital to record the compass direction, and if at all possible some point that can be identified on a map, in each photograph.

Photographs designed to show the type of country must be taken with a good deal of care. Some kinds are easy enough; the sweep of downland, alpine pasture or sand desert – given a wide enough vista such country is recognisable and speaks for itself. This indeed may be a danger. Our minds respond to clues in pictures, whether photograph or painting, and consciously or unconsciously fill in the details. A furze bush in the corner of a photograph, and we think 'heath-land', and assume the sandy soils and conifers; a marble column drum on a scrubby hillside, and our thoughts fly to the Mediterranean, especially if the sky is blue. These false clues apart, however, it is important to look for the vista, and especially the topography, which will characterise the country, and this means looking out for such viewpoints during the survey – a pleasant enough change from looking for sherds – and recording them as they are revealed. Sometimes the secondary effects are more telling than the shape of the land; it is difficult to show a low-angle valley in a photograph, since there is rarely anything that will give the eye points of reference of its angle, but a photograph of a meandering stream will certainly suggest it; or a stone-built village might indicate the type of bedrock when there are no quarries or exposures to be found.

It is important, even if obvious, to record the enduring rather than the ephemeral. The shape of the hills changes only slowly in nature (unless of course there has been glaciation or earthquakes), and usually they keep their general form through millennia. Shallowly incised streams, on the other hand, can change their course in a matter of years, sand-bars and earth-slip slopes in days. What should be recorded are features of a time-scale of the same order as that of the archaeology.

Site surveys

Probably the most familiar type of archaeological survey is the recording and comparing of known (and, with luck, of previously unknown) sites or some features of them; for example, examining the gateways of hill forts, or the mediaeval re-use of Byzantine farms, or the proximity of metal-working sites to ore bodies. Whether the primary purpose is the examination and location of sites or of some feature of sites, it remains equally important to, as it were, photograph the site into the landscape. The more completely the sites are put into their settings, the more valuable the record.

Two points must be made about this. Nearly everywhere in the world the face of the land is being rapidly changed, by mechanised agriculture, urban spread, man-induced changes in the natural fauna and flora, and from many other causes. Sites may or may not be protected, but their environs are often at much greater risk, and whatever can be recorded of this should never be neglected. It should also, of course, be published, or at least put into a known archive, but even piecemeal records are better than none at all. Although the purpose of the survey may be, say, the surface pottery on third-millennium tells in Mesopotamia, photographs of nearby wadi beds might be of inestimable value to some future worker (so long, that is, as their position is properly recorded). The second consideration is more short term, and less altruistic. It happens, not infrequently, in the course of a survey that at some point along its course it becomes apparent that, say, all Early Bronze sites were on hillside slopes, or all the farmhouses were on spring lines, or something of the sort. If the surroundings of the sites have been thoroughly recorded then, with luck, the environmental connecting thread has also been recorded, even if it was not recognised at the time. There is much to be said for the 'questionnaire' approach in these cases, even though it can be blinkering at times. This involves compiling a list, and ensuring that photographs (and if need be written descriptions) cover, for example, the immediate and the larger land-forms (not just the scree slope but also the mountain producing the scree); morphology (breaks of slope, river terraces, fixed dunes); water supply (streams and old stream courses, pools, lakes and man-made systems such as wells and cisterns); bedrock and geological structures, if there are exposures; any soils and buried soils that are visible; trees, natural vegetation and cultivation; natural routeways and tracks; other intervisible or connected sites (the next in a chain of fortlets, or the harbour of a cliff-top settlement). It will probably not be possible to record all of these, but any of them may later prove to be an important element in the total context of the site; it is disheartening to have to retrace one's steps to record the necessary data later.

Within the site itself, any standing structures should be recorded – assuming, that is, the more common type of unknown or unexcavated site, with perhaps a few wall-stubs above ground, or floors revealed by erosion, and not the lost city in the jungle, if there are such things. This is partly because the remains themselves, together with surface finds, might help to date the site, and partly because these occupation structures may be in the course of being eroded away, and may have disappeared altogether if and when the site comes to be excavated. If the site is large, and if there are considerable numbers of surface artifacts, it might well be sherded by some sort of random or stratified random grid system. It is useful in such cases to photograph each selected area, so far as possible from similar heights and viewpoints, in order to give an idea of its character. If possible, the site as a whole should also be photographed, showing the area of occupation insofar as this can be ascertained from the surface. For purposes of comparison, it is useful to take photographs from the cardinal points, and on a flat site to indicate in some way the spread of surface artifacts, perhaps by marking the area with sticks.

A most important consideration with this sort of photographic survey is to have a reliable record of the photographs. If the work is spread over some days or weeks, and if photographs are taken only occasionally, it is all too easy to lose track of what has been taken, and groups of working negatives are apt to become interspersed with snaps of local colour or of the survey team outside a pub. Obviously a note should be taken of each survey photograph – of location, compass bearing, purpose, date and time (e.g. Tell Marfee, facing west, floor levels exposed at eastern summit of tell, 2 June 1985, 12.00 h). The problem, however, often comes down to linking the description with the right negative. It is of little value to rely on the edge numbering of the film at this stage: winding on a film by one too many or one too few frames when the film is loaded, or taking an unrecorded negative somewhere along its length, may throw the system out entirely. In any case, if the film has been cut from bulk, each length will not necessarily start at one. Better far, though tedious and a little extravagant, to start each film with a photograph of a number or letter written on a notebook page (it is not sufficient to rely on numbering the cassettes – they may well get mixed up during processing), and then to start each group of site photographs with another shot of a notebook page carrying the name of the site, or its number in the survey, or some other means of clear identification such as Barbary Castle, or Site No. 17, or Hill-slope site grid no. 147832. When the films have been processed, each group can then easily be separated, contact printed on to a separate sheet, and the negatives matched to the notebook details.

Environmental surveys
Somewhere midway between field walking and site surveying are surveys that are not directly archaeology-oriented; for example, the tracing of river terraces

Botany

Botanical surveys normally call for three types of photograph: general views of the stretch of country being surveyed and of the collection area, e.g. the field of waving eincorn; photographs of individual plants or clumps of plants *in situ*, separated as far as possible from their background; and photographs of parts of plants or trees – heads of corn or individual flowers or leaves.

In the first, establishing, shots, the focus of attention is the type of country rather than the individual plants. Factors like the slope of ground, distance above water, presence or absence of trees and so on are of prime importance, and viewpoints have to be chosen with these in mind. Photographs of, say, a stand of wild cereals should show the plants clearly enough to be roughly identifiable, together with the other flora, the ground surface, and if possible the extent of the stand. The difficulty here is that plants like cereals and grasses tend to appear as an undifferentiated mass, especially if there is any wind at all; the slightest movement of the plants during the exposure will give a blurred image of their tops. This can sometimes be overcome by using a fast shutter speed – 1/500 or 1/1000 of a second – but this in turn can, depending on the light, necessitate a large aperture and thus a restricted depth of field, whereas a large depth of field from front to back of the stand would be desirable. Other solutions are to use a fast film, which could have other drawbacks, or to choose a time of day when there is no wind, in some parts of the world a virtual impossibility. The ideal viewpoint is one from which a few of the important plants can be seen to their full height in the foreground, but sufficiently elevated to include the whole area.

Photographs of individual plants or groups of plants should always be taken from close to ground level so that both top and bottom of the plant are clearly visible. It may be difficult to separate the plant from its background. Sometimes this separation can be achieved by differential focussing, using the largest possible aperture so that the plant is sharply imaged while the background is out of focus. In bright sunlight and even at the fastest shutter speed it may not be possible to open the aperture sufficiently, and a neutral density filter would then be called for. Another and perhaps better method is to erect a small screen behind the plant to cut it off from its background. The device can be quite simple: a rectangle of stout paper, or better of plastic sheeting, about 50 cm wide and 75 cm high, with four lengths of wire stuck on or in gussets behind it to act as supports and protruding by 10 cm or so at the bottom to hold it in the ground. If such a screen is arranged as a rough semicircle behind the plant, it will not only completely cut off the background, it will also act as a wind-break. Using a standard lens, and with the screen some 15 cm behind the plant, a 50 cm high plant can be photographed so that the whole of the frame is filled by the screen. This may be unimportant for black and white, but for a colour slide it looks better if the edges of the screen are not visible in the transparency. A 25 cm scale with a spike at one

and their contained artifacts, or the study of tradi
oases. Such surveys have their own expertise, and
established methods of recording. There are, howe
that can usefully be made for the sake of archaeolc
themselves involved in such surveys.

Geology and land-forms
Systems of terrain mapping and evaluation are many and
photography (apart from satellite photography) is rarely of mor
trative importance. Where archaeology impinges on these studies,
in such areas as Pleistocene studies and the examination of occupa
river terraces, it becomes important to relate the land-forms to sites, an
is sometimes best done by photography. Very often subdued land-forms
eroded terraces can be seen and photographed only in one particular light
usually by low morning or evening sun – and one must wait for that time.
Unfortunately, the range of tones and colours – greys to red-browns – likely
to be found in sediment exposures are those most distorted by the colour
changes of evening and morning sunlight. For colour photographs, it may be
necessary to use colour-correction filters (see Chapter 3, on Equipment), and
if the correct balance is important, to take several photographs through a
range of filters and to take note of the colour of the subject by neutral light,
using a Munsell chart, and choose the closest result after processing. It is
nearly always informative to record low-angle features showing the true angle
of slope. Obviously the camera must be set horizontally, using a spirit level,
but more than this, so far as possible the viewpoint must be chosen so that the
film plane is parallel with the length of the feature. For example, if the camera
is set up horizontally across the valley from a raised terrace, viewing it more
or less head on, the true slope will be apparent. If it views the terrace
obliquely, it may not.

Photographing small natural sections, buried soils and the like, is much
like photographing archaeological sections; viewpoints must be as square-
on as possible, and the section must be cleaned with care (unlike archaeological sections it is legitimate to cut back natural sections if need be to
show a fresh face). Open shade or veiled sunlight usually gives the best
illumination, perhaps aided by a white or silver reflecting sheet. Straight-on
flash is rarely helpful, and is more likely to blank out detail. Again, it is
important to set the camera horizontally, and it may be useful to stretch a
white string, levelled with a line level, across the bottom or the top of the
frame; this can be used to ensure that the final print or slide is exactly at the
right angle. A simple and useful accessory is a scale, perhaps 25 cm long,
with a small hole drilled through each end. This can be levelled along the
bottom of the frame and held in position by two nails pushed through into
the section.

end so that it can be driven into the ground to stand upright beside the plant is also desirable. Probably the best colour for the screen is a matt neutral grey. Not only will it not clash or give a colour cast to the plant, but a light-meter reading from the camera with this background should give a reasonably accurate exposure (perhaps with the lens closed down by half a stop if the plant is very light, or opened up by the same amount if it is very dark). The light from top to bottom of the frame may fall off considerably, especially if the soil is dark, and a small reflector – a piece of aluminium foil is quite adequate – can be arranged at about the camera position to reflect light down at the roots.

Separated leaves, flowers, ears of corn and similar sized specimens can be photographed flat on the ground, preferably against a white or neutral background, but in order to obtain an image of a reasonable size it may be necessary to work at magnifications of around 1:4 to 1:2, and sometimes larger. A macro lens or an extension tube will certainly be necessary, as will a tripod. It may be quite difficult to arrange for enough natural light in these circumstances, and another home-made device can give better results. This (Plates 46 and 47) is a length of rod attached at one end to a plate bolted to the camera base, and at the other to a bulldog clip. If the rod is about 25 cm long it will give a picture area of some 10 cm × 7 cm with a 50 cm lens. This is sufficient to hold something the size of an ear of wheat together with a scale. The device can be used without a tripod, given reasonably high light levels (although it is always better to use a tripod if one is available); at f8, a 50 mm lens will give a total depth of field of about 1 cm at this distance, enough to

Plate 46   Portable stand for photographing botanical specimens.

cover most likely specimens. The sky can be used to give an even, featureless background, but care must be taken with exposures. If a reading is taken against a bright sky, or if the camera is used on 'automatic', the specimen will probably be badly under-exposed, since the meter is reading mostly from the brighter background. This can be corrected by taking the reading with a grey card, or the palm of the photographer's hand, immediately behind the specimen. The advantage of the contraption, as well as its portability and light weight, is that it gives a standardised format with a minimum of adjustment, ensuring that all the photographs of this type for the survey will be readily comparable.

Plate 47   Ear of einkorn taken with the portable stand.

If the photographer is equipped with a rifle-stock support, this can easily be modified to hold a clip at one end, which will be just as effective as the device described above.

Finally, by using an automatic ring-flash (see Chapter 10) together with a frame of this type, lighting can also be standardised, and, by adjusting the power of the flash, a background of almost any tone from white to black can be arranged.

Buildings

Surveys involving buildings, as distinct from the photography of individual buildings (which is dealt with in Chapter 6) again require that the results allow of comparative study (e.g. the thirteenth-century churches of Suffolk, the truli of Apulia, examples of corbelling or of tool marks). For this reason, it is important to standardise viewpoints, elevation, scale and lighting, as far as this can be done. For example, a survey might be undertaken of a series of stone buttresses, either in one area or of one period. If in each case the photograph has been taken from the same angle, at the same height, and in roughly the same sort of light, the items will be far more easily compared one with another than if these criteria had been random. If the survey is long-term and intermittent – perhaps simply a matter of photographing such things whenever they are spotted – it is well worthwhile processing and printing one carefully considered example, and carrying a small print of it around to act as a guide for subsequent photographs.

Objects in museums and collections

If artifacts in study collections or on display can be moved and handled, and if working space is available in which to photograph them, then the methods employed are no different from those discussed later in Chapter 9.

Quite commonly, however, this is not the case. Museum authorities are, understandably, usually unwilling to open showcases or to move objects on display; and study collections may be stored, and their examination and photography restricted to corners of basements with little light and space. Moreover, there are few museums that will allow the unrestricted use of tripods in their galleries, although many more will give permission if prior application is made, sometimes limiting their use to certain times, or permitting only a certain number of applications. Similar restrictions may apply, though less commonly, to the use of flash. Whether a tripod is necessary, and whether supplementary lighting is needed for objects on display will obviously depend on the light levels, which may differ widely from one museum to another, and from one type of artifact to another. The practice of exposing organic materials only to low levels of light is commendable for their preservation, but it makes photography difficult.

Most people can hold a camera steady for about 1/60 of a second; longer than this, and there is a very good chance of camera shake. The result of shake is rarely a completely blurred or doubled image; it may be no more than a slight loss of resolution, a slight degradation of the finest detail. The picture is not 'spoiled', just a little less crisp and a little less informative than it could have been. As is so often the case, the smaller the negative the worse the effect. If it is not possible to use a tripod, all that can be done is to brace the camera as tightly as possible. It is best held with the hands completely enclosing the ends, the others pulled in, and, at the moment of exposure, the breath held. If it is possible, rest the camera against a wall or over a chair, or even over somebody's shoulder, or lean against a wall yourself, and if in doubt, take several exposures and pick out the best with an enlarger. Some museums will allow, or overlook, a monopod – a single telescopic leg – even if they will not allow a tripod. These can eliminate nearly all camera shake, although it can of course still sway. Another simple device that can be useful is a length of thin lightweight chain about 1.5–2 m long (depending on the photographer's height) with a bolt attached to one end. This is screwed into the bush on the camera base, and the other end held under the foot. By holding the chain taut a good deal of shake can be eliminated. Rifle-butt supports can also be helpful. Though intended primarily for use with very long lenses (with which camera shake is an ever-present problem), they are equally effective with shorter focal lengths.

Photographing into cases
Modern, internally lit, showcases may not be too difficult to deal with. Using a tripod, or one of the devices just mentioned, exposure should present no problem, and the tendency towards having fewer and better-displayed objects in each case reduces the problems of isolating the exhibits. The remaining difficulty may be reflections from the glass front. There are two ways of dealing with these; either to use a polarizing filter to eliminate or minimise them, or, often more effective, to hold in front of the case a piece of black cloth with a hole in the centre, positioned over the lens. This method is effective with internally lit cases, but of course if most of the light comes from outside the case, it will blanket out most of the illumination as well. Polarizers may be successful, but only if the incident light is at an angle of about 40° or less; and if there are reflections of several lights at different angles, then as one reflection is eliminated another will probably emerge. If it is necessary to use a flash unit, care must be taken that this does not produce an intense reflection. If it is on, or close to, the lens axis, then it certainly will. It is sometimes possible to hold the flash at the side of the case, or perhaps over the top if this is glass, and to hold a white or silver reflector against the opposite side. If a practice flash is let off with the eye to the viewfinder, it is usually possible to see, momentarily, whether there is an obtrusive reflection. The problem still exists, with crowded cases, of isolating one particular exhibit from those

behind it, and even from those overlapping it in front. Much can be done by careful focussing and by using a large aperture, only just small enough for its depth of field to cover the object of interest, and to throw nearer and farther objects out of focus.

Photographing collections

A fairly common requirement is to assemble an archive or catalogue of photographs of objects that are scattered through a number of museums and collections. Working conditions and freedom of access may vary widely, militating against the desirable end product of a series of record photographs directly comparable in quality and of similar scale, viewpoint, background and lighting. The solution is self-evident: always to use the same type of film and the same lens, the same working distance and the same background material, and if possible to carry one's own lights, either tungsten or flash. The most important step, however, is the first: before embarking on the survey, to set up an arrangement of camera, lights, stand and background, and, preferably using an artifact similar to those to be recorded, to take a series of test exposures at different speeds, apertures, and lighting distance and angles. When the film is processed it will establish the optimum combination, and the lighting angles and the position of the object against its background can be roughly measured. A print made of the selected negative or transparency, leaving in the whole frame, can then be used as a standard of comparison for future work. If the objects are too large or complex in shape to be lighted by fixed tungsten lighting or by flash, and if there is insufficient daylight, it is often possible to achieve quite adequate results using a single moving light, in the way described in Chapter 9.

8

SITE PHOTOGRAPHY

During the course of an excavation, photographs are taken for a number of purposes. Most important of these must, of course, be to preserve a record of the site and to provide illustrations for the published report, showing the appearance and relationship of walls, floors and buildings, and the details of constructions and of *in situ* artifacts. Ideally, photographs, plans and sections should complement each other, so that the position and measurements of each structure can be immediately matched to its visual appearance. Moreover, viewpoints should be chosen and the features excavated and cleaned in such a way that all the evidence on which are based theories of construction and chronology is revealed. This is a counsel of perfection, and such a display of archeological logic will probably never be achieved; but at least a serious attempt should be made to avoid the situation, all too common, where vital evidence has not been recorded and where, following the destruction of successive strata, assumptions and theories must go unsupported.

Two other aspects of site photography, of almost equal importance, should not be overlooked. Firstly, the dig must be placed in the landscape. Unless by good fortune a member of the dig staff has the rare talent of accurate landscape drawing, the photographer must be responsible for the recording of such things as the siting and aspect of the settlement in relation to communications, water, arable land, other sites, local topography, geology, flora and so on. Even today, site reports appear in which the site is located only as a grid number or as a dot on a small-scale map, and the reader can form little idea of its setting or why it is located where it is. Secondly, most excavations and some surveys will become the subject of illustrated lectures. For this purpose the more important black and white photographs are normally matched by 35 mm colour transparencies. Although straightforward, informative slides of the site's structure and stratigraphy serve very well for academic purposes, they may prove rather indigestible fare for public lectures, and a leavening of slides showing excavators at work, dig life, and local conditions is always a welcome addition. It needs some skill to produce a set of slides which display all the features a future lecturer might want to talk about and which are not just a procession of walls, floors and objects. General photographs, in colour and in black and white, may also prove to be of value in printed publicity material, particularly in nonspecialist journals, and for exhibition displays.

In spite of the obvious advantages of recording the site in colour, at present and for the foreseeable future printing costs will dictate that nearly all the photographs in site reports, whether in monographs or journals, will be in black and white. On some digs, all the photographs are taken on colour negative film, and black and white prints, as well as colour prints and slides, are made from these negatives. This technique can work very well, but it takes more skill and equipment than is usually available. Modern colour negative film gives far better results when printed in black and white than older material did. It must be remembered, though, that properly processed black and white film is more archivally stable than either colour negative or colour positive stock, although the difference may become less important if and when digitallised image storage is adopted. On some excavations, all photographs are taken on colour positive film, and black and white prints made via inter-negatives. The results of working in this way are rarely satisfactory, however, since they involve copying, and some degree of detail will be lost and tones altered.

For publication, then, the black and white negative is the most important record and, ideally, all dig photographs should be of publishable quality. Many excavators do find it of value to take series of quick, roughly prepared photographs, snapshots in fact, especially in Polaroid, to act as visual notes for future reference. This practice can be most useful, so long as they are not thought of as substitutes for properly thought-out and properly prepared photographs.

Increasingly the sort of visual diary of a site provided by sketches, Polaroid prints and quick, unprepared snapshots is being supplemented by video recording. How far such recording can in the future replace, rather than supplement, more conventional photographic records is discussed in Chapter 15.

Equipment

So far as black and white photography is concerned, a large-format camera will give better results than a small-format one. This statement is subject to all sorts of reservations, of course, but given equally good optics, films and processing methods, it is undeniably true. The degree of resolution that can be achieved on a negative is partly dependent on the lens – how far the inherent lens aberrations and flare will allow of the separation of fine detail – and partly on the film emulsion – the size of the grain structure and the degree of dispersion of light within the emulsion. Both these limitations are less serious the larger the image, and, in addition, since a large film has to be enlarged less than does a small one, the less noticeable they are on a print from a large negative. Moreover, the slightest blemish – dust-spot or scratch – on a 35 mm film will be bigger and more obvious on enlargement than will a fault of equal size on a larger film. This said, very few digs are in a position to buy the best or most suitable equipment for their purposes; most have to make do with what is available or what can be borrowed or bought cheaply. So an 'ideal' list of equipment would be no more than window-shopping for most excavations. For this reason, the list that follows is not a catalogue of necessities, but rather a number of suggestions and alternatives.

Cameras and lenses

The characteristics and uses of different types and formats of camera have been discussed in the chapter on equipment. For large format, a 5×4 in monorail or a technical camera with 90 and 150 mm lenses will be sufficient, with, for the monorail, a set of bag bellows. At least six double darkslides are advisable, together with a changing bag if no darkroom is available on site. Medium-format monorail and technical cameras will need 65, 100 and 150 mm lenses, the same number of darkslides, and a changing bag. For medium-format SLR cameras the choice of lens is wider, but probably 50, 80 and 150 mm lenses will suffice, with an 80 or 110 mm macro lens and, if possible, a shift lens, although these are prohibitively expensive.

Whatever other cameras are used, at least one 35 mm camera body will be needed for taking colour transparencies. Lenses of 28, 50 and 200 mm, or the appropriate zoom lens, will be needed for this, and perhaps a macro and a shift lens. If the dig is to rely on 35 mm alone, two bodies, one for colour transparencies and one for black and white, is the minimum. It is possible, just, to use one 35 mm camera only; this involves taking, say, half a dozen exposures of a colour film, rewinding it, replacing it by a black and white film, exposing and rewinding that, and going back to the colour film, and so on. It is not a method to be recommended, except in an emergency. Apart from being immensely fiddly, it entails the film passing through the gate of the cassette several times. If dust gets caught in the gate, likely enough if the business is being done on a dusty site, it will probably produce longitudinal scratches down the length of the film, which will show on every print. If there is no alternative, rewind the film slowly and stop before the lead disappears inside the cassette; films should never be rewound quickly in any case, since the friction can produce sparks of static electricity which will give spots of fog on the film. When the film is re-inserted, wind it on and press the shutter, with the lens cap on of course, until it reaches its previous position, and then allow one more frame before exposing it.

Black and white film can cope with only a limited range of contrast – a much shorter range than the human eye can deal with. With cameras using sheet film this presents no great problem. By manipulating exposure and development, even without resorting to the use of high- and low-contrast film and developers, reasonable results should be attainable from most subjects. 35 mm and roll film are a different matter, however; within one film exposures can be changed, obviously, but development cannot, and average development may give too high a contrast in a photograph of, say, a strongly sunlit group of buildings with deep shadows, and too low a contrast (although this is rarely so much of a problem) in the next frame of a shadowed section with little difference between its lightest and its darkest parts. It may be of great value, therefore, to have available two bodies for black and white; both can be loaded with the same type of film – it is a nuisance to have to keep several types of film on a dig – but one body is kept for scenes of high contrast, and the film developed to a lowered contrast level, the other for low contrast scenes, the film developed to a higher contrast. There is no need, of course, to keep two or three sets of lenses.

Accessories

Some camera accessories, including scales, are dealt with in detail in Chapter 3. They are considered here only in their application in site photography.

Tripods should extend to a height of at least 1.50 m, better 2 m, and they should be strongly built. The sort of lightweight tripod that is convenient for surveys might not last a season on a dig. The type with leg extension controlled by turn-screws or clamps is preferable to those with sleeve tighteners, which are too easily clogged by dust. For awkward situations those with legs that can be set at different angles are more useful (though not quite as stable) as those with legs that move out together. Pan-and-tilt heads are more convenient in use than ball-and-socket heads, and if the head incorporates quick-release devices or loose camera bolts it is important to make sure that there are spares to hand – such things get lost with dismaying regularity. The head on the centre column should be reversible for shots close to the ground, and a carrying case or strap is of great convenience.

Light meters are necessary when using a large-format camera, and although most 35 mm and some medium-format cameras incorporate built-in meters (for which spare batteries should be carried), there are many circumstances in which a separate meter is more reliable. The most accurate kind are spot-meters, with which a reading of 4–5° can be taken.

A spare *cable release* should always be carried; if they are trodden on they are usually rendered useless immediately. The thicker, plastic-coated type seems to be less vulnerable than the fabric-coated ones.

Lens hoods should be those designed specifically for the various lenses: too long, and they cut off the light from the corners of the negative; too short and they are ineffective. The most satisfactory for large- and medium-format lenses are the bellows type which can be extended to cut off extraneous light. It is always advisable to check before taking a photograph that no peripheral light is striking the lens surface. If it is, in spite of a lens hood, the lens should be shadowed with the hand or a notebook from 30–40 cm away. Front and rear *lens caps* and *body caps* should always be kept on whenever the lens is off the camera. Dust is a major enemy on many sites and it may be necessary to keep all lenses and bodies in plastic bags, as well as in a case.

Yellow, red and green *filters* for black and white, and light-balancing filters for colour, should be carried.

A small plastic *spirit level*, 5–10 cm long, or a line level, should be sufficient. A *compass* is desirable for establishing the direction of the photograph. Accuracy does not have to be very great, and a simple non-prismatic compass will do very well. A black *focussing cloth*, about 1 m or 1.5 m square is useful when focussing a large-format camera, and it can also be used for shielding objects from direct sunlight.

A *flash unit* may be needed, both as fill-in for shadowed areas and some-times to enhance detail or increase contrast (see Chapter 4). Two small flash units, one with a slave trigger, are often better than one large one. Better still, and by far the easiest to use, is automatic flash with through-the-lens metering.

For cleaning the site, soft *hand brushes*, *paint brushes*, *trowel* and *dustpan* are the most effective tools. Brushes on excavations always seem to be at a premium, and if opportunity presents itself, it is worth earmarking a couple for photographic use only.

A *changing bag* is not vital, but it is of great convenience for reloading darkslides, unjamming cameras, and even, if conditions are very dusty, for loading 35 mm and roll-film cameras. They are intended, and can be used, for the daylight loading of spiral tanks. The larger the better, and the black cloth variety are much better than those made of plastic, which become unusably clammy in hot conditions.

Reflecting sheets are used to reflect light into shadowed areas or to shade objects from direct sunlight. The most convenient are thin metallic sheets, some 2 m square, also known as 'survival blankets', which fold up into an amazingly small envelope; they are, however, rather flimsy. Some are made with a pattern of small holes punched in them, which not only prevents their being torn by the wind, but which, interposed in direct sunlight, gives a subdued illumination but not complete shadow.

Lens brushes should always be carried in the camera case. The most useful are those designed like lipstick cases, or those with a small puffer bulb attached. Small aerosol cans of compressed gas are also available for blowing dust out of camera bodies. They should not be used directly on reflex mirrors; apparently the gas can damage the surface. The glass surfaces of lenses should be touched as little as possible; optical glass is a good deal softer than window glass, and is quite easily scratched, and the anti-flare coating of most lenses is readily abraded. If there is dust on the front or rear element, it should be blown or brushed off. The safest lens-cleaning tissues, for use if lenses are smeared or finger-printed, are the throw-away variety supplied in individual sealed envelopes. On a wet or dusty site, a camera left standing on its tripod between shots should be covered with a plastic bag, removed only for the moment of exposure. In fact, on some Middle-Eastern sites photographers have found it worthwhile to keep their cameras in underwater housings as a protection against dust.

All this insistence on keeping dust away from cameras sounds, and is, tedious and time-consuming. Dust, however, is probably the commonest cause of spoilt films and jammed equipment on a dig, and it is worth going to a lot of trouble to combat it. Even if no disaster ensues, some departments and funding bodies insist, reasonably enough, that equipment used on expeditions be professionally cleaned before it is returned. If camera bodies have to be taken down completely, or lenses recoated, the cost may be very considerable.

The cameras, and all the above accessories except perhaps the tripod and the brushes, should be kept and carried in a *case* or *box*. Metal cases with clamp edges are both more robust and more dust-tight than are soft cases. The type with rubber or plastic sponge linings slotted for the various pieces of equipment are not only more shock-proof (an important consideration if the case is to be carried by vehicle over rough country) but act as their own check against leaving bits behind; if all the slots are full, everything is there. Many cases of this type come supplied with a solid sponge insert which can be cut to suit the particular outfit. If conditions are dusty, it is worth using a sheet of thin plastic as a lining. This is laid over the insert and pushed into the slots; at the end of the day, it is taken out, carefully, bringing with it any accumulated dust. For travel by plane, it is worth ensuring that the camera case is small enough to travel as cabin luggage.

Elements of site photography

The amount of photographic coverage required can differ greatly from one dig to another, depending on the personnel and equipment available and on the type of dig. On a rescue dig of strictly limited duration, all effort must be concentrated on retrieving a maximum of information in a minimum of time, and photography may have to substitute for much planning and drawing. Coverage has to be accurate and comprehensive, and since there may not be time to wait for film to be processed before removing a structure, methods and equipment must be entirely reliable. The size of the dig is also a determining factor. A large Middle East tell site might require a dozen or more well-prepared photographs every working day, and, if artifacts cannot be taken out of the country, photographs of them all to publication standard. On the other hand, a cut across a bank and ditch, or a small single-period site, might really warrant no more than before-and-after photographs, and perhaps a few close-ups of details. Nevertheless it should be emphasised that a full coverage of the site by photography is never wasteful. Photographs that record structures or levels from even slightly different viewpoints, distances or elevations, and in different lights, may well prove to be of great value in post-excavation work, even if only a small percentage are needed, or are suitable, for publication.

A host of man-made or man-modified features will be photographed in the course of providing a complete site record; walls and floors, pits and foundation trenches, banks and ditches, tombs, graves and buildings. They are the static artifacts which constitute the basis of all excavation. As far as photography is concerned, their recording requires a dual approach. Firstly their appearance – their size and shape, surface texture, tone and colour – must be recorded; and secondly their relationships – how a wall meets a floor, or the way in which the foundation of one building cuts through the remains of its predecessor. On both counts the most important consideration is usually the viewpoint. Very often a slight alteration in viewpoint, perhaps by only a few centimetres, will reveal or mask some feature; will show, for instance, an object silhouetted against a neutral background rather than against an obtrusive one, will show the levels connecting two structures or leave them unconnected, or will show the floor level associated with a wall rather than leave it apparently floating in mid-air. Of equal importance is the avoidance of viewpoints, and of photographs, which show false relationships. It can often happen that structures of different phases or periods are visible at the same time in a trench. Ideally, perhaps, this should not happen; each building phase should be completely excavated, recorded and cleared before the next is uncovered. But the exigencies of digging and the shape of the site may mean that, for example, a Roman hypocaust and the foundation of a Victorian warehouse which cut through it are both visible. It is vital to seek out the viewpoint which shows the cut rather than one from which both appear to form part of the same building.

Viewpoints should also be chosen so that, if possible, the front-to-back depth of the structure is revealed. This may seem obvious enough, but it has to be borne in mind always that a photograph is a two-dimensional image of what is usually a three-dimensional object, and it is all too easy to forget that while someone on the spot can walk around a structure and can view it with binocular vision, a photograph will show one aspect only. The depth of a doorway, or the separation between two walls, immediately apparent on the ground, may not be at all obvious in a photograph unless the return of the doorway is shown, or there is some indication of the space between the walls. The first step, then, is to view the structure, whether a small pit or a group of classical buildings, from all sides and from all possible elevations, and to choose those best showing the overall shape and setting. The excavator, obviously, is in the best position to say what is of importance and what is not; but the photographer (if indeed they are not the same person) should be better able to decide what will yield a clear and informative record, and what will fit best into the limitations of the format. A typical problem might be a wall running diagonally across a trench. The obvious viewpoint would be from one corner, looking down from the baulk. But this would result in a photograph half of which, in area, was occupied by four triangles of blank space at the four corners of the format, and which could not be cropped to give a square or rectangular print for publication. Better, probably, to take the photograph from halfway along one side, giving an angled wall but a less wasteful print.

On some excavations the viewpoints of all site photographs are standardised; each structure is photographed from the cardinal points no matter what its orientation is (Wright (1978); Levin (1986)). One can see the reasoning behind this; it greatly simplifies the comparison of photographs one with another and with the site plans. But so often when photographing a site, moving the camera a few degrees one way or another will reveal or mask elements of a structure or will simplify or confuse its relationship with other structures. This flexibility of approach is at times so useful that perhaps it should not lightly be abandoned. If time and facilities permit, of course, it is preferable to follow both procedures.

If details of structures, or of surfaces, are worthy of being recorded separately (tool-marks on a stone wall perhaps, or stained areas on an occupation surface) it is vital to record also the entire wall or the whole floor in order to locate the detail in its proper position.

The factor that can make or mar the effectiveness of site photographs is the strength and direction of the natural lighting, modified occasionally by the use of reflectors and subsidiary flash. Direct strong sunlight, particularly if it falls across the scene diagonally, is probably the worst possible lighting. Not only will it raise the contrast to unacceptable levels, giving solid black shadows, or burnt-out highlights, or both, but the pattern of light and shade may be strong enough to overwhelm the shape of the structure. Assume, for instance, a series of wall stubs standing at the bottom of a trench; with strong cross-lighting, the shadows cast by the walls, and by the side of the trench, may form an outline of black stripes and masses far more obvious to the eye than the shape of the walls themselves. It might seem that it would be better to choose a time of day when the sun is behind the camera and shadows therefore cast behind the structures; but this would mean that any surface facing the camera would be in direct, straight-on light, and its surface texture would therefore be lost. There might also be a problem with the shadow of the camera itself, and of the photographer, filling the foreground. Or it might even be possible to work when the sun is at its zenith and shadows thus reduced to a minimum, although in these conditions, anything sticking out of the sides of the baulk, a stone or even a peg, will cast a very long shadow indeed, as would something like an overhanging brick at the top of the structure. In other ways also this is a bad time of day for photography. Sections of wall faces will have had all the morning to dry and become dusty, and depending on the material of the site, a morning's digging may have filled the air with dust. In general the best natural illumination is sunlight with a thin cloud cover – common enough in summer in temperate latitudes, but virtually unknown in some parts of the world – with enough direction in the light to emphasise texture on surfaces and to cast soft, light shadows, giving depth to structures. Often, however, there is no 'ideal' light by which to photograph a structure; different angles and intensities of the light may reveal different aspects, and the subject should be observed at different times of day, and photographed when one or other feature is best lit. It is possible to work out the angle of altitude of the sun at any time at any point in the world, and thus to predict when its light would be from a suitable direction. This can be done, with a certain amount of algebraic calculation, from the Smithsonian Meteorological Tables, published by the Smithsonian Institute in 1951; or solar location diagrams for some northern latitudes can be obtained from the Royal Greenwich Observatory for a modest price. This is probably not worth doing on a dig, where a few days' observation should provide the same information without the need for mathematics; but if a trip were planned to photograph, say, a hill fort or a rock inscription, it might be of great value.

If strong sunlight during the day is inevitable, then it may be necessary, or preferable, to take photographs in the early morning or in the evening, when the light is subdued or out of the trench altogether, although the photographer may be hard put to it to take all the necessary photographs during these short periods. Probably the best time of all is in the early morning when overnight moisture remains to enhance the colours and tones of surfaces and atmospheric dust is at a minimum. It must be remembered, though, that the colour of the light in the morning and evening is distinctly redder than at midday, and it may be necessary to use light-balancing filters with colour film (see Chapter 3).

For structures or objects up to about 2 m square it is often of great value to use a reflector to bring light into shadowed areas or, particularly if the object is at the bottom of a deep trench, to lighten its base. Silver foil is the most effective reflector, but failing that a bed-sheet will serve. It is also possible sometimes to shield the subject from direct sunlight if the sun is at a fairly low angle, although on a large scale it can be a difficult and at times ludicrous business, with the whole staff lined up along the edge of the trench trying to block odd rays of the sun with their clothes. A large fly-sheet or, better still, a 2 m wide roll of sacking is far more effective.

In some circumstances it is possible to use fill-in flash lighting to bring light into the shadows or to emphasise the texture of a surface. The techniques for doing this are discussed in Chapter 4. The method is particularly effective for objects or surfaces square-on to the camera, but less so for structures of any great depth, owing to the rapid fall-off of light away from the flash source. If, for instance, a stela was positioned so that strong sunlight was just raking down across its surface, the inscription might show in strong relief, but also in too great contrast with the surface of the stone. By using a small flash on the camera, the surface could be lightened, thus reducing the contrast. Or if the side of a block-like structure were strongly lit by the sun, the face towards the camera could be lit to a comparable tone by flash. (It should be emphasised that in this sort of situation the flash must be as close as possible to the lens axis, otherwise two sets of shadows may be produced, one from the sun and the other from the flash.)

Sections of baulks and wall-faces

Most excavators would consider photographs of sections to be of illustrative but rarely of interpretive value. The prime record is the section drawing, and stratigraphic interpretation stands or falls on that. Certainly it is rare indeed for a photograph of a section to reveal anything that the eye cannot see in the section itself (with the possible exception of UV photographs of cave sections), and chance shadows, slight surface irregularities, and the inability of the camera to distinguish subtle changes in colour or texture can lead to results that are deceptive. Nevertheless, a good photograph can give a useful general picture of a section even if the minutiae are missing, and for some features such as piled turf or tip lines, a better impression than a drawing can. The two should, of course, be complementary.

The basic formula for an acceptable section photograph is simple: a square-on viewpoint, as long a lens as space permits (to avoid linear distortion at the edges of the field), and a clean section. The degree to which the first two can be achieved depends mostly on the size of the square or trench – a 5 m length of section can just about be covered from 4 m away, using a 28 mm lens on a 35 mm camera, while a standard lens at the same distance would cover only a little over 3 m. So far as cleaning is concerned, few sections retain a pristine appearance for very long and almost none for more than one season. In wet or temperate climates they become eroded and runnelled, and the lower part coated with wash from the top; in arid conditions they dry and crumble and become dusty. Most sections can be made clearer by scraping with a trowel or brushing, and many can be improved by spraying, gently, with water, although this is a waste of time with dry open-textured sediments, in which the water will sink or evaporate more quickly than it can be sprayed on. There is a strong line to be drawn, however, between cleaning a section, gently or vigorously, and 'improving' it – undercutting horizontal lines, or outlining features with the point of a trowel. Most archaeologists would, rightly, be suspicious of a photograph of a section so treated. It is all too easy to *create* the stratigraphy, or by emphasising one line to suppress another. The stratigraphy of a section should be apparent through differences in tone, colour, texture and moisture content. If the section is fairly smooth and flat, sunlight falling across it at a steep angle will emphasise texture, but if the section includes protruding rocks or bricks, they may cast long, distracting shadows. Colour differences can sometimes be enhanced, on black and white film, by means of contrast filters, and slight differences in tone by underexposure and overdevelopment, although this is a dangerous road, since it is quite possible to lose detail in the darkest parts of the film.

Walls

Walls are normally photographed as part of structures, but if the emphasis is on the wall itself, either to illustrate its construction or to show the position of rebuilds and so on, the wall is best photographed in the same way as a section: square-on viewpoint, and as long a focal length as possible. A brick wall, whether baked or unbaked, is best shown in strong raking light; in fact such light can show an amazing amount of detail, unless the joints are deeply recessed, when an appearance too like a chequer-board might result. Large masonry blocks respond better to this sort of lighting than do small ones.

Pise and mudbrick walls are a special case as far as cleaning is concerned. The ability to 'articulate' mudbrick is a source of much pride among Meso-potamian archaeologists, and is not a matter for non-specialists, so they will tell you (Plate 48). Walls, whether of brick or stone, which have been buried, may present problems in cleaning. Unmortared joints are likely to have

Plate 48   The hazards of cleaning mudbrick. The lower left-hand part of this wall has not been cleaned back to the brick, the upper part has been adequately cleaned, while the lower right-hand part has been inexpertly cleaned so that the mortar is standing proud of the bricks, giving a honeycomb effect.

become filled with soil, collapse material or wormcasts, and their removal may lead to collapse.

Whenever possible, walls should be photographed from very slightly above, or to one side, so that the thickness of the wall is apparent and, as with all such site photographs, a part at least of the floor surface with which they are associated should be included.

Pits

Pits, silos and, for that matter, the walls of small soundings, are not at all easy to photograph, partly because of the difficulty of the steeply angled viewpoint, and partly because, unless the pit is cut in chalk or some equally light-coloured material, the light falls off sharply from top to bottom. What is needed in most cases is a photograph showing the rim of the pit, in as true proportion as possible; the section down one side; and the shape of the base. How far all three can be recorded in one frame depends on the relative width and depth of the pit, but if possible some part of the rim should always be included, even if the proportions are those of a well. If the photograph is taken looking down a hole, whatever its size or shape, without including a part of the ground surface, it gives a strange impression of tunnel vision; the eye can find nothing to relate to and cannot judge the proportions.

The steeply angled viewpoint will result, inevitably, in a strong perspective effect, with the side section foreshortened. This can be modified, if not entirely overcome, by using camera movements or a shift lens, but even without these facilities shallower perspective can be attained by using a long lens rather than a standard one, and taking a more distant viewpoint while still taking in the rim, section and base. For example, if a camera were pointed diagonally into a pit, at such an angle that the distance from the lens to the top of the pit were 1 m and to the bottom 1.5 m, the ratio between the two would be 1:1.5, and this would also be the ratio in the photograph between equal horizontal lengths along the base and the rim of the pit. If the camera were moved back on the same diagonal line by 2 m, and a longer lens used (or, of course, if the same lens were used but only the centre of the negative were enlarged) the ratio would become 3:3.5, about 1:1.15, and therefore the apparent difference between equal horizontal distances, top and bottom, would also be proportionately less. There is obviously a limit to what can be done in this way, not only because of lowered resolution but also because the necessarily elevated and distant viewpoint might not be attainable within a trench.

The fall-off in light to the bottom of a pit can sometimes be counteracted by a reflector on the wall opposite the one being photographed, but this may still be insufficient, and it may be advantageous to use flash. What is needed, of course, is light from the flash unit to illuminate the bottom of the pit but not the top, so there is no point in using the flash on the camera, which will merely reinforce the fall-off. With most small flash guns it is possible to use an extension lead, so that the flash can be at the bottom of the pit while the camera is at the top – assuming, that is, that the flash gun and reflector can be positioned so as not to be seen in the frame. This unfortunately entails having a cable leading over the lip of the pit, and it would be better if the flash were triggered by a slave unit responding to another small flash linked to the camera shutter but directed away from the pit itself. Direct flash would probably give too harsh a light, but if the flash were facing a reflector on the near-side wall, it should be possible to produce a soft spread of light.

Graves

Depending on the depth of the grave, photographs should be either vertical or from very slightly to one side, so that the depth of the grave is visible on one side. The photograph should be taken so as to include a rim all round of the surface from which the grave was cut. Admittedly this may not always be possible; in silt-grade material especially, the compacted backfill of the grave and the material in which it was cut may be indistinguishable, and all that can then be done is to avoid a false stratigraphy. The skeleton should of course be cleaned so that all the bones are clear and, if practicable, the fill removed down to the floor of the grave. On some excavations skeletons are plotted in position in the grave and on the site grid by drawing and measuring in the skull, pelvis and long-bones, then taking an exactly vertical photograph which is enlarged to the scale of the site-plan and traced off on to it (Spence (1990), 3.5.2).

The use of scales and information boards is discussed in Chapter 3. It may also be necessary to photograph, from different angles, grave goods *in situ*, and perhaps to record details of the bones. If so, it is valuable to include in each photograph enough of the skeleton to allow the close-up shot to be related to the overall photograph. The chief difficulty in recording skeletons lies not in photography, which should be simple enough, nor even in drawing them, which a skilled draughtsman using a frame can manage fairly quickly, but in cleaning them. This can take an inordinate amount of time and attention, and in hot dry weather the bones cleaned first can dry out and practically crumble away by the time the last are attended to, despite spraying and covering. In large cemetery areas, therefore, when the skeletons themselves are not of great archaeological interest, it may be sufficient to clean them only roughly and to clean fully only extremities and skull and enough of the rest to show orientation, before recording and lifting. Rarely, if ever, is it practicable to leave the skeletons in a large group of graves exposed for long enough for a photograph to be taken of the whole cemetery, and this is therefore a case where the fitting together in a mosaic of a series of vertical photographs taken as the graves are excavated would be of great value. To achieve this, it is vital to grid and photograph the whole cemetery, otherwise there will be blanks in the areas between the graves. If subsequently graves are found in what was first thought to be undisturbed ground, these can then easily be fitted into the mosaic.

Tombs and other subterranean chambers

Shaft and chamber tombs can present very considerable difficulties in photography, as can some built tombs and underground and rock-cut cavities generally. Access, viewpoint and lighting are the common problems, and there is usually a need to work quickly, either because of the danger of roof fall or collapse, or because the act of opening the tomb and thus altering the temperature and humidity and the composition of the atmosphere can start irreversible changes in any organic material present.

For all its drawbacks of negative size, the 35 mm camera is undoubtedly the most useful in this sort of photography. Not only is it compact enough to be held or positioned in small spaces, but the additional depth of field given by the shorter focal length of lenses can be vital. Quite often it is not possible to focus through the viewfinder, either because of lack of light or because, in order to gain sufficient working distance, it is necessary to hold the camera flat against the tomb wall. All that can be done is to focus the lens by the scale on the lens barrel and rely on the depth of field to give a negative sharp from front to back of the tomb. If a 28 mm lens is set to 2 m, it will yield a reasonably sharp picture from 1 m to infinity at f16, while a 24 mm lens at 1.5 m will give from 0.75 m to infinity at the same aperture. It may be worth setting these distances in daylight, and fixing them by a piece of tape round the lens in case the focus is accidentally moved in the tomb.

Viewpoint depends entirely on the size and shape of the chamber; a large chamber with a single skeleton may present no problems at all, while a low domed chamber with a maximum headroom of perhaps no more than 1 m or 1.5 m and a jumble of multiple or secondary burials across the floor may make an overall photograph virtually impossible. If a vertical photograph or one from an oblique viewpoint high enough to show the whole extent is not attainable, it may be possible to take a series of close-up vertical photographs which can be fitted together as a mosaic. Ideally, the floor of the tomb should be gridded with strings, and height and focus kept constant throughout. However, this may not be possible in the time available, nor may the fragile material on the floor allow of it. But if the camera is positioned, pointed downward, on a tripod (an offset arm is useful here, carrying the camera clear of the legs) set as high as the roof allows, and focussed to a little above floor level, perhaps to a point roughly half the depth of the highest object on the floor, then, by using the smallest possible aperture and photographing the whole floor with at least 50% overlap between frames, a reasonably standardised set of negatives should be attainable which could be printed and mosaiced together.

The shaft and door-blocking of the tomb should be photographed before unsealing, and details of tool-marks, etc., as the tomb is emptied.

Occasionally it may be possible to photograph a tomb using only daylight, and good photographs have been taken of tombs opening from shafts by reflecting light through the entrance with mirrors. More frequently, though, the illumination has to be light from a generator or battery-powered video lights, or by flash. When continuous lighting is available, and if the heat of the lamps is not judged likely to be harmful to the tomb contents, it has great advantages. By moving the light during the exposure, hard shadows can be eliminated and the tomb lit quite evenly. The necessarily long exposures mean that the camera must be on a tripod or other support, and the yellow cast of low-voltage lamps may mean considerable colour correction of slide or negative colour film, but these are minor drawbacks.

Although flash is not the ideal form of lighting for tombs or caves, it is more often than not the only type available, and perfectly good results can be obtained, given a few precautions. If space permits, the main flash head should be positioned to the side of, and above, the camera, so that the direction of light is not wholly frontal and so that some at least can be thrown to the back of the tomb. Two flash heads are preferable to one, and if there is room it is more effective to bounce the flash rather than to use it direct. With limestone or other light-coloured rock, light can be reflected off the walls or roof of the tomb, although a sandy, yellowish stone will, of course, reflect a yellowish light which may need filtering; if the rock is dark, it may be possible to bounce the light off a square of foil stuck on the wall of the tomb.

Very similar considerations to the above apply when photographing such things as cisterns and small caves, except that, with cisterns, it is rarely of much value to photograph the contents, and the most important photograph is usually one taken after it has been emptied, upwards from a corner to show the entrance, the shape, and the cutting or constuction of the walls. A difficulty common to deep cisterns and wells, as well as to shafts, rock-cut stairways and long passages, arises from the fact that it is usually possible to light both ends but it may be virtually impossible to light the centre part. So, for instance, looking along a tunnel, the far end could be lit by daylight and the nearer end by flash, but unless there are rocks or side passages on the way along which could shield small flash units, the length of the tunnel would be in darkness. There is a method that can overcome this problem, although it depends very much on the configuration, and it can only be used when there is virtually no ambient light at either end. The camera is set up on a tripod facing along or down the shaft, focussed about halfway along and with a small enough aperture to render both ends sharply. With the camera lens open, a light in a fairly narrow shade is dragged or lifted along the shaft from the far end, towards the camera. The light is directed towards the far end, and the shade must allow absolutely no light to shine back towards the camera.

As can be imagined, it is not at all easy to do this successfully; the lamp cable must be pulled from behind the camera, and at no time can the lamp be stationary within sight of the lens. If the photograph is of a vertical shaft like a well, the light must be hauled close against one wall; if it is pulled up centrally, the silhouette of the shade will be visible in the photograph. Fortunately shafts, wells and so on are unlikely to be demolished or made inaccessible in the course of a dig, so there should be the chance to make several attempts at the photographs.

Archaeological photography in caves, as distinct from speleological, so often akin to underwater photography, usually suffers from similar restrictions of space and light. In addition, caves are apt to be wet and muddy, or else dry and dusty, and considerable care may have to be taken to protect the equipment. The type of lightweight flexible plastic bag made for shallow-water photography can be of great value. These incorporate a disc of plane glass or plastic which fits over the lens and a waterproof, and therefore dust-proof, sealing. The camera can be manipulated through the bag.

Since most cave excavations take place in or near the mouth of the cave, the lighting problem is not so much that of a complete lack of natural light as of a fall-off of light away from the entrance. A section or floor running back into the cave may call for many times greater exposure at one end than at the other. It may be possible to balance the lighting using tungsten illumination at the darker end, but the amount of light that can be produced by a generator is unlikely to be sufficient if the area is of considerable size, unless portable quartz-halogen lamps are available. In any case, such lighting almost rules out the taking of colour photographs because of the difference in the colour temperature of the two light sources. Flash lighting can be used quite effectively, although if the cave is large several flash heads may be necessary. It is usually better not to photograph caves when the sun is shining fully into the entrance, when the subject contrast will be far too high.

In any sort of photography involving film and lenses underground or in very confined spaces, care must be taken to avoid condensation on either the film emulsion or the glass of the lens. This will almost certainly occur if a camera is moved from a hot dry atmosphere into a cool damp one. Condensation on the lens will result in an overall foggy or mottled effect on the negative, and on the print will show as light patches. The only safe solution is to allow the camera to acclimatise itself to the new environment for half an hour or so before taking any photographs.

Overall site photographs
Photographs of larger areas – entire squares, or the whole of a building phase, or the excavated quadrant of a barrow – need a good deal of preparation, perhaps even some days of cleaning, and a most careful consideration of viewpoints and of the state of the site beyond the area in question. It is also

worth considering in advance the most suitable time of day, and trying to time the cleaning to be finished at that time. If, for instance, the cleaning were finished by midday, but only the morning or evening light were suitable, the area would be effectively immobilised for the intervening hours. The square or area to be photographed should itself be cleaned, of course, but attention should also be paid to more distant parts. It is easy to overlook extraneous objects, such as wheelbarrows, which are beyond the square but still within the frame of the viewfinder, and which might therefore appear in the final print.

Similar overall photographs are usually thought necessary at the end of each season of a multi-season dig. These not only show progress from season to season, but can be of great value when work is resumed. A site left alone for months nearly always suffers from erosion, sedimentation or vandalism, and sometimes all three, and even with extensive notes and retentive memories may appear as a series of unfamiliar humps and hollows at the beginning of a new season's excavation. Photographs taken from the four corners or from the centres of the four sides of the squares should greatly aid orientation.

Overall photographs, particularly if the site has a complex ground-plan, should include photographs taken from a higher viewpoint than that provided by the side of the trench. The same very often applies to site photographs of lesser extent. Even the two metres or so provided by a stepladder or the top of a vehicle may show, for instance, the shape of a floor or the outline of a room. If the design of the stepladder permits, it is preferable to clamp or rope a tripod to its top rather than try to hand-hold a camera; to be standing on a small platform above the ground looking down through the viewfinder of a camera is a vertiginous business that does not make for a steady hand. It is possible to rope a ladder upright to the back of a vehicle like a Landrover, to a height of four or even five metres with reasonable safety, although the ladder would have to be solidly built to be sufficiently vibration-free for any but the shortest exposures. The camera can be mounted on a G-clamp fixed to the top rung, and if the photographer is also anchored by a safety belt or some similar attachment, both hands are left free for the camera.

Many devices have been used to achieve high oblique viewpoints on various digs; the bucket of a JCB (make sure the braces are down), the type of extending or jack-knife platform used for cleaning street lamps, which can be hired at considerable expense or, given good local contacts, borrowed from a local authority; even Fire Service rescue ladders have been used. The most widely used devices, however, are builders' scaffold platforms, built up from rectangular frames. They can be moved and erected quite easily by a couple of people, and the only necessary, and obvious, precaution is that the feet must be firmly based and levelled. On a soft surface they are best rested on a pair of scaffold planks at right angles to the edge of the trench. Safety regulations state that towers should not be higher than 9 m, and that at heights of more than 4 m they should be fitted with stabilizers.

Without the use of such structures designed or adapted to take both photographer and camera, it is possible to take high oblique photographs by raising the camera alone to a calculated height and angle. A metal 4 or 5 m telescopic survey staff is strong enough to bear the weight of a 35 mm camera and, given a fairly windless day, a couple of people could hold it steady and vertical for long enough for short exposures. The difficulty lies in calculating the angle of the camera atop the staff. If surveyors' tables are available, or a calculator with trig facilities, then the calculation is straightforward enough: the length of the staff H is known, and angle A is a right angle; measure horizontally a distance L to a point B midway across the area to be photographed; the angle at C will be found from the formula Tan C = $\frac{L}{H}$, as illustrated in Fig. 8.1.

As a rough guide, Table 2 lists the angles at C, given a 4 m staff.

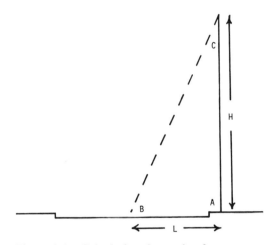

Figure 8.1   Calculating the angle of a camera on a staff.

Table 2. *Angles at C, given a 4 m staff*

Values of L in metres	Values of C in degrees
1	15
2	26
3	37
4	45
5	52
6	57
7	61
8	64
9	67
10	69

Plate 49

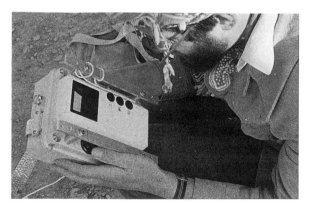

Plate 50

Telescopic carbon fibre mast for overhead and oblique site photography, designed and built by Mr T. L. Martin. Plate 49 shows the mast being pivoted up to raise the camera, Plate 50 the monitor screen and controls, Plate 51 the camera and video viewfinder, and Plate 52 a vertical photograph taken with the apparatus.

Plate 51

Plate 52

A greater height, and therefore a larger area or a steeper angle, can be achieved by using a telescopic mast of the sort supplied for mobile radio transmission and emergency lighting towers. Lighter models extend up to 10–12 m and will safely carry a load of 2 kg, more than enough for an average camera. They are erected pneumatically by hand pump and need only light guys to hold them steadily upright. Heavier models can be obtained which extend up to 20 m or more and can be mounted on a trailer or on the roof of a vehicle.

The most sophisticated of these masts incorporate a tiny video unit which is attached to the eyepiece of a reflex camera and is connected to a small monitor at ground level (Plates 49, 50, 51 and 52). The camera can be tilted and panned by remote control, and also the shutter fired and the film wound on. The cost is formidable, but such masts can be hired on a daily or period basis (*British Journal of Photography* (1986)).

Photographs taken of sites or parts of sites from *directly* above may serve four purposes: for illustration of the area's ground plan; as an aid in drawing such things as pavements or cobbled floors; for stereo-pairs; and for photogrammetry. The same photographs, of course, can be used for different purposes. For an area of the size of a 5×5 m square, rigid or dismantleable quadripods, bipods or inclined masts will give sufficient height and rigidity. Areas much larger than this can be covered by cameras attached to balloons, kites and aerofoils, until the field of low-level aerial photography is reached.

The requirements of a tower or mast for such photographs are stability (best achieved by a quadripod), mobility (for which bipods and single masts are far better), and accuracy of centring the camera and ensuring that the lens axis is vertical (which, with care, can be achieved with all three types). For the sake of good resolution of detail, the larger the camera format the better; and in order to minimise linear and perspective distortion at the edge of the field, the longer the focal length the better. There is, however, a limit to the format size and focal length that can be realistically managed; the bigger the camera the heavier and more unwieldy it is, and the longer the focal length, the higher the tower has to be. The relationship between the height, the focal length and the dimensions of the area covered can be worked out, approximately, from the basic optical formula:

$$\text{the height of the camera} = \frac{\text{the length of the area}}{\text{the width of the format}} \times \text{focal length}$$

or,

$$\text{the length of the area} = \frac{\text{the height of the camera}}{\text{focal length}} \times \text{width of the format}$$

Thus, to calculate the necessary height to cover a trench of 5 m sides (plus

0.5 m to define the line of the baulk) with a 35 mm lens on a 35 × 24 mm camera:

$$\frac{600}{2.4} \times 3.5 = 875 \text{ cm}$$

or, with a 65 mm lens on a 6 cm^2 camera:

$$\frac{600}{6} \times 6.5 = 650 \text{ cm}$$

Or to calculate the length of side of the area covered by cameras and lenses of these sizes at a height of, say, 10 m:

$$\frac{1000}{3.5} \times 2.4 = 686 \text{ cm}$$

and

$$\frac{1000}{6.5} \times 6.0 = 923 \text{ cm}$$

All the measurements must, of course, be in the same units.

Since nearly all excavations are based on square grids, whether or not standing baulks are retained between the squares, a square-format camera has great advantages as far as black and white photography is concerned. The ideal camera would be a 6 cm^2 single lens reflex with motorised drive, radio-controlled shutter release and aperture-priority automatic metering. Few if any digs could afford anything of this sort, but perfectly adequate photographs can be taken using a twin-lens reflex with a 65 or 75 mm lens, the shutter fired by means of a pneumatic release (these can be obtained with tube lengths up to about 25 m). Their chief disadvantage is that the camera has to be lowered from the top of the tower for the film to be wound on, and the shutter re-cocked between each exposure.

Details of the construction of quadripods are given in Cooke and Wacher (1970); of bipods in Whittlesey (1975) and Fleming (1978); of a bipod with an extended boom in Nylén (1963); and of monopods in Graham (1981). Some of these, such as those in Whittlesey and in Nylén, would need the resources of an engineering shop, while others, like the bipod described by Fleming, could be cheaply and simply constructed of locally available materials in most parts of the world. A summary of the different types and of their use, together with a bibliography, is given in Sterud and Pratt (1975).

It would be supererogatory to restate all the details given by these authors, but since some digs might want to design and build their own apparatus to their own plans, it is worth outlining the more important features of the different types, together with their use.

Quadripods are pyramidal frames built of wood, slotted angle-iron, alloy scaffolding or telescopic poles. They should be dismantleable, or light enough to be carried by four people around the site. Lightness of construction is important not only for mobility but also because the heavier the tower the more it can damage the site. In plan they must be large enough to cover a square, or whatever is the standard area of excavation, plus 0.5 m or so all round so that their legs can rest out of the square. To cover a 5 m square, therefore, they should measure 6 × 6 m and, using the formula given earlier, for a 6 × 6 cm camera with an 80 mm lens, the camera height will be 8 m; or with a 35 mm camera with a 35 mm lens, 8.75 m. The ends of the legs should be adjustable by about 1 m to allow for uneven or sloping ground, and they should terminate in flat plates or rubber feet to minimise damage. The number of braces and cross-struts will depend on the rigidity of the legs (since the four sides are triangular in shape they should be inherently rigid laterally), but the more struts there are the greater will be the number of shadows thrown across the site in sunlight. Such shadows may be unavoidable unless there is overcast weather or unless flash guns can be mounted on the legs. If the photograph is to be used as a basis for drawing, shadows are relatively unimportant, but if it is intended for publication, they may be distracting and unsightly.

The most important part of the tower is the turret that carries the camera. There has to be a cradle into which the camera, attached to a base-plate, is raised by means of a line passing over a pulley at the top of the turret: the cradle which will hold the camera in alignment with the base of the tower. The base-plate, an L-shaped plate with a slot to take a bolt to the camera bush and a shackle for the lifting line, must be so designed that the camera is held firmly in position; if the shape of the camera permits, it is as well to have it held in addition by a strap or an elastic strainer, partly for safety's sake and partly to relieve the strain on the camera bush. Given a tower made to very close specifications and exactly levelled at the base for every shot, it might be possible to rely on the rigidity and alignment of the cradle and base-plate to ensure that the lens axis is perpendicular. It is safer, however, and calls for less precision if between the base-plate and the cradle, or between the cradle and the top of the tower, there is a self-aligning device so that the camera hangs vertically by its own weight. This can be either a system of gimbals, stirrup-like carriers one inside the other similar to the mountings of a boat's compass, or a universal joint, or a ball-and-socket head. Whatever the device – and the choice would probably depend on availability – it should not be so free-swinging that the camera could be set swaying by the wind. If something of the sort is used, it is necessary to have the shackle attachment on the back of the base-plate adjustable, so that the camera points exactly downwards under its own weight. A valuable addition would be a double base-plate, so that two cameras could be lifted at once and thus colour and black and white photographs could be taken at the same time. If the two base-plates are separated by about 30 cm, it is possible to take stereo-pairs, which when

Site photography 143

printed and viewed with a standard stereo-viewer will give a useful three-dimensional image, while being close enough to the centre point to be used as single negatives.

When the quadripod is set up, it is positioned over the square, levelled by using a spirit level on the lowest cross-struts, and the centring and levelling checked by lowering the base-plate and measuring the distances from it to the corners of the square. For a simple photograph or slide of the excavation within the square, these preliminaries should be sufficient, with the addition of survey poles as scales on two sides of the square at the excavated level. But if it is decided to make a mosaic of the whole site, or of more than one square, more preparation is necessary. The site should be gridded, if this has not already been done, and the corners of the squares marked with white crosses, large enough to be visible in the photograph. This ensures that any slight differences in the size and shape of the squares on the negatives can be adjusted in the enlarger. The run of photographs should be made with a 40–50% overlap between them. This is not so much to counteract distortion at the edge of the field as to give a reasonably vertical view of standing remains. Because the view of the lens will be oblique at the edge of the field, a feature such as a wall will only be seen vertically if it is immediately under the lens, or if it runs radically across the field; if it runs across the field transversely, then both the top and the base on one side will be visible, and the higher the wall the more it will appear displaced. Obviously this cannot be remedied completely, but by taking short steps, and using only the centre of the field in each exposure, it can be minimised.

At these heights and using the focal length of lens in the examples given earlier, depth of field should present no problem if apertures are kept to f8 or smaller. Complications arise if the site is steeply sloping or undulating. For straightforward planning or for viewing, the height of the camera is best kept constant relative to the excavation surface, so that a boulder measuring 1 m across in one part of the site will be recorded at the same scale as another of the same size in a different part. In an area of even slope this means that, strictly speaking, the camera axis should not be vertical but should be perpendicular to the centre point of the slope – a thing very difficult to arrange. Even on a 10° slope, if the boulders were at the top and bottom of a 5 m square, then from a height of 8 m they would register as being about 10% different in length. This discrepancy can be reduced by taking shorter steps until the difference becomes unimportant. For photogrammetry, however, it is necessary to keep at an even height, not above the ground surface, but above a horizontal datum, and to position scales on the highest and lowest points of relief in each square.

At first sight it would seem that a *tripod* or three-legged tower would be lighter and more manoeuvrable than a quadripod, and since any structure built up in triangles is inherently stable, more rigid than a bipod. Unfortunately, however, unless one could be designed with no cross-struts at all, such a stand would have to be so widely based as to be quite unusable. Each side would have to be about 12 m wide to cover a 5 m square; anything less and the cross-struts would cut across the corners of the squares.

Bipods are essentially a pair of legs, joined at the top and wide-spread enough to span the square or trench. Consideration of height, focal length and the requirements of the camera cradle are the same as for quadripods. The legs are raised to the vertical by first lifting and, when the position of moment is reached, hauling with two or four lines fore and aft to the cross-axis of the legs. When raised, the bipod is held in position by guy-lines. The advantages are mobility, lightness and simplicity of construction. The lines do not cast distracting shadows, although the legs may, and by tilting the legs by a set amount it is possible to take high oblique photographs or stereo-pairs. A bipod does not have the stability of a quadripod, and setting up can be a lengthy business, needing six or eight people. Since there can be no cross-struts between the legs below camera level, stability depends entirely on their strength, and a compromise has to be sought between weight and mobility. If the legs bow unduly in use, not only is there a danger of their snapping, but exact positioning may not be possible.

Another variant is an *inclined mast*. The turret described by Nylén consisted of a tripod with legs about 9 m long, with a boom extending one leg to a height of 16 m. The legs were of telescoped steel tubes, hinged to a top-plate and strong enough to stand without cross-struts. The 6 cm^2 camera was lifted to the top of the boom (also of steel tubes) and fired by means of an inbuilt delay mechanism. As the boom stood well out from the tripod, there were no problems with shadows, but the fishing-rod-like construction led to a good deal of sway and wind movement, so much so that the author recommended the use of exposures of 1/250 sec or faster. Some really excellent photographs were taken with this device, including mosaics of one hundred prints and more. The drawbacks are the need for precision engineering, with consequent high cost, and the weight, 63 kg, easily transportable by car but not very practicable for carrying over rough ground.

It is also possible to take vertical photographs by means of a camera fitted with a *shift/(PC) lens*. A 28 mm PC lens on a 35 mm camera will move the mid-point of the frame by about 22° at its maximum extension. Thus if the camera is clamped to the top of a 4 m survey staff, it will give an apparently vertical photograph of an area of 3.4 × 5 m to one side of the staff. Such a photograph, however, would only really be satisfactory across a flat site. The increasing radial obliqueness of viewpoint which occurs with a centrally-placed camera would here be replaced by an increasing obliqueness from the lens axis, perpendicular over one side of the square, to the far edge of the picture.

Graham (1981) describes the construction and use of a simple *monopod*, which can be managed by one person, inclined to take vertical photographs. The construction is simple and the cost low, and in the hands of an experienced operator, very satisfactory photographs of tesselated floors were taken.

One other fixed-height stand that might be of considerable value when excavating a cemetery is a *quadripod of rectangular base*, large enough to cover a single grave. Using a 35 mm lens on a 35 mm camera, a height of 2.25 m will cover an area of 2.1 × 1.7 m, certainly enough for most graves. Such a stand could be built of wood, slotted angle-metal, or alloy or plastic tube. At this height the camera would not need to be hauled up into position but could be set up from a stepladder or, given a tall photographer, from ground level. There would also be no need for a levelling mechanism behind the camera since the whole frame could be levelled easily enough – graves, after all, are rarely found on steep slopes.

Above about 15 m towers become unpractical, and vertical photographs of whole sites can only be taken with the aid of balloons, kites and aerofoils. These have been used for many years – excellent balloon photographs were taken in the 1920s and 1930s, especially in the Middle East – but it remains a specialist business, requiring considerable equipment and expertise. Accounts of the various methods are given in Whittlesey (1974), Sterud and Pratt (1975), Myers (1978) and Myers and Myers (1980).

Aerial photography
If a programme of aerial photography is contemplated, especially if the intention is to record elusive evidence such as crop- and soil-marks as well as the appearance and setting of sites, it is advisable to enlist the aid of an experienced aerial photographer, or at least to gain experience with an established aerial survey unit. Even for more modest projects some practice and instruction is desirable. The expenses of flying time are high, and in many parts of the world ideal weather is rare, so mistakes due to inexperience or unfamiliarity with the equipment are costly indeed. It is not uncommon, however, for opportunities to occur for photography of a site with a hand-held camera from an aeroplane belonging to a member of a flying club, for example, or through the goodwill of a flying unit engaged on some other project in the area. Observance of a few basic rules should enable a photographer not experienced in this type of work to obtain reasonable results. A comprehensive account of the subject, including details of methods of matching oblique photographs to maps, can be found in Riley (1987).

When photographing in this way – with a hand-held camera from the cabin of an unmodified aircraft – oblique photographs are very much easier to take than are verticals, and for many purposes obliques are indeed the most useful. The most suitable type of aircraft is a high-winged monoplane, since the view from the cabin is relatively unobstructed, and the most suitable flying height is between 300 and 700 m. Higher than this, atmospheric haze becomes a serious limitation, as it is of course at any height if the weather is not clear. Helicopters are in many ways ideal, although the older types are subject to vibration, and the cost of flying time is higher than with fixed-wing aircraft.

35 mm cameras can give adequate results, and they have the advantage of being small and easy to handle – an important consideration in the cabin of a light aircraft. A standard lens is usually sufficient, although a longer lens, up to 200 mm, may be needed to record small areas. A motor drive is valuable, as is a camera body with an automatic exposure control. This is one of the few instances in archaeological photography when a shutter-priority mode is preferable, since consistently short exposure times are more important than control of the depth of field, which is usually quite adequate at the distances involved, even with large apertures.

Medium-format reflex cameras with similar facilities can also be used, and these would, of course, yield a better rendering of detail. However, many are limited to 10 or 12 exposures on 120 film before the spool is changed – a distinct disadvantage when flying time is short and expensive.

Exposures should be of the order of 1/500 or 1/1000 sec, partly to minimise the effect of aircraft vibration and partly because some displacement of the image is inevitable in a photograph taken from a fast-moving platform, and this is naturally reduced if the exposure is short. Except in the brightest weather, a fairly fast film is therefore necessary, 125 ISO at least for both colour and black and white. For black and white, a yellow filter is usually advisable (Wratten 6 or 8), both to filter out the ultra-violet and therefore reduce the effect of water-vapour haze (although it will have no effect on haze caused by dust in the atmosphere), and to lighten the green of vegetation, thus increasing the contrast slightly. If the country surface is sand or rock, however, a yellow filter might well flatten contrast, and a haze filter alone (Wratten 2A or 2B) would be preferable. Colour film, whether positive or negative, should be exposed through a UV barrier filter (Wratten 1A or 1B). Aerial photographs commonly appear rather flat, owing to the overall lighting, and slight under-exposure and over-development is often beneficial. Infra-red film, both black and white and colour (so-called 'false-colour' film), is used extensively in ecological aerial surveys, and has some applications in archaeological work. This is discussed further in Chapter 11.

Photographs taken at angles between 30° and 50° to the horizontal are usually the most informative, giving a reasonable stretch of country and showing the morphology of the ground. These can be taken easily enough from a high-wing aircraft with little banking, while a low-wing plane has to bank quite steeply for angles of this kind to be achieved without the wing tip appearing in the frame. If possible, photographs should be taken approximately at right angles to the direction of flight rather than being angled forwards or backwards. Features in photographs taken at acute angles are difficult to fit on to a map or plan. The direction and angle of the sun is often the primary factor in recording crop-marks and low structures, and the season of the year is also frequently important. The use of aerial photography in such recording, with many examples, is described in Muir (1983), Wilson (1982) and Riley (1987).

The uses of vertical photographs

Used as illustrations, either in publications or as lecture slides, vertical photographs can give an excellent 'feel' of the site. They can convey an impression of size, texture and layout in a way that plans cannot, and photographs of successive layers of an area, printed side by side, can give a better idea of a site's stratigraphy than section drawings can. If, as is often the case, the excavation of different squares is proceeding simultaneously but at different rates, a particular phase in one square can be photographed and matched by photographs of other squares when, perhaps weeks later, they have reached the same phase. Needless to say, this calls for carefully recorded positioning of the tower, and for absolutely reliable stratigraphic control; it would be a terrible gaffe to publish a mosaic of what were really different periods. It would also be desirable to keep note of weather and time of day, so that direction of the light and the subject contrast were similar. There are illustrations in Sterud and Pratt (1975) of the construction of mosaic groups, and they, and other authors, insist on the need for information panels in each photograph showing the position in the grid of the area represented by each photograph. When there are no identifiable structures visible, one stretch of floor can look very like another in a photograph. Vertical photographs can also serve as base maps for plotting the position of finds. A useful technique is to print the negative, whether a single negative of a square or a copy-negative of a mosaic covering several squares, very lightly to give what is almost a ghost image on the bromide paper, against which find-spots marked in ink will be visible.

For some types of surface – cobbles, stone, brick and tesselated pavements, and low wall stubs – tracings from vertical photographs can provide plans as accurately, and a great deal more quickly, than can surveying. This is particularly the case with such things as cobbles, where there is often a dilemma about the degree of accuracy that can be justified in limited time and with limited personnel. Perhaps there might be times when it would be necessary to survey in, for instance, every stone in a five metre-square cobbled courtyard, but it would certainly be a long and tedious operation. The three requirements for a reliable tracing are, firstly, that corner points should be accurately plotted and the print accurately enlarged to scale and fitted to these points. Secondly, two or three points in the square should be surveyed in from a datum line and angles and measurements taken to points plotted in other squares, especially if the photographs are to be mosaiced (the problem is not so much that of not trusting one's own corner points as that small errors can easily accumulate across a wide area from such things as mis-matching parts of the mosaic, the bromide paper stretching or shrinking, or complementary lens aberrations in the camera and in the enlarger lenses; measurements across the whole grid will show only that errors have occurred, while a second web of surveyed points should also show where they have occurred). Thirdly, the surface must be well cleaned and the photograph should not be taken in strong cross-light, otherwise it may be difficult when tracing to tell which is the edge of a stone and which is its shadow. If it is not possible to work when the light is hazy or the sky overcast, it is better to take the photographs with the sun as nearly overhead as possible; then at least the shadows will be distributed evenly round the stones.

Obviously there is a limit to what can be tackled in this way. On sites where a phase might involve height differences of several metres between surfaces, or run across steeply sloping ground, or include standing remains many courses high, the difficulties of perspective and oblique viewpoints, as well as the sheer labour of manoeuvring the tower about the site, might more than counterbalance the saving in surveying time.

The photography of objects *in situ*

On most excavations, finds of any significance are plotted and photographed *in situ*, lifted, and then registered, drawn and re-photographed after whatever field conservation is necessary. The definition of significance, however, varies widely from one type of dig to another; on a small upland site with acidic soils the discovery of a few sherds could be a matter for celebration, while on a large tell site nothing less than whole vessels still in their original position might be thought worth photographing. At all events, the final photograph of the find after cleaning and restoration is the one that will be regarded as the find record, for study and publication. The *in situ* photograph has, however, another role that is equally important. It reveals the find in its setting and in its association with structures and with other finds. The emphasis that has been placed in recent years on the importance of studying finds as com-ponents of assemblages, and on spatial analysis both of finds within settle-ments and of the settlements themselves, has increased the value of *in situ* recording.

Another aspect to be borne in mind is that some finds, apparently intact, and some materials, such as wood, should be photographed as soon as possible after excavation, since they may warp, shrink or change colour on exposure to the air. In addition, a record of the object's appearance in the ground could be of great value to the conservator, and on some excavations a Polaroid photograph of every artifact is taken when it is excavated, and remains with it thereafter (Levin (1986), p. 36). A further class of artifacts, like the impression of timber or textile, or tool-marks on bedrock, might never be lifted at all, and the *in situ* photograph will be the only record.

Perhaps the most important general rule of *in situ* photography is that the find must always be photographed on the surface on which it originated, and on, or in, no other. For example, if an almost unbreakable artifact like a large quern were left on the floor of a house, and the walls and roof then collapsed, the quern would first emerge, when the house was excavated, in the collapse levels above the floor, levels with which it was unconnected. Not until the floor was cleared would it be truly *in situ*. Even in quite recent excavation reports it is sometimes possible to find photographs of artifacts sitting on columns of soil, the remains of levels taken away from around them; or apparently at the bottom of small pits, the photograph having been taken before the proper floor level was reached. Such photographs are, of course, a reproach to both the excavator and the photographer (Plates 53 and 54).

It is nearly always valuable to take two sorts of photograph of finds *in situ*; one (or perhaps several) showing as much as possible of the shape of the object and its immediate position, e.g. standing on a bench or fallen on to the floor; and the other showing its position in a room or how it is grouped with other artifacts. It may well be that both purposes can be served by one negative, and often, of course, it would be pointless to photograph individually every smallest find; perhaps every hand-axe, for example, though not every scrap of debittage; a necklace certainly, but not every bead.

Viewpoints can never be as standardised as they should be when making the final object photographs, and they are usually a matter of common sense. For example, a pot that was found inclined, leaning on a stone, should be photographed from the side to show the inclination; or a group of flakes should be photographed from above so that the overlap of one tool over another is apparent. Finds should of course be clean, but except in very rare cases it is not advisable to remove, wash and replace them as is sometimes done. The contrast between the find and its setting is too great, and such photographs look contrived.

It is often useful for this sort of work to use a tripod that will hold the camera securely 40 or 50 cm from the ground, and use of a reflecting sheet can give detail on the shadowed side of the artifact.

Cleaning of sites
Throughout this section it has been taken for granted that any site, square or artifact will be cleaned properly before the final photograph is taken, and reference has also been made to the cleaning of sections, walls and skeletons. Cleaning can be a tedious and time-consuming operation, and it is worth considering any methods that might speed it up. On sites that are entirely of stone, water hoses have been used for cleaning, as have air hoses and wet-and-dry vacuum cleaners. On most excavations, however, the basic tools are still the trowel, dustpan and brush. The main requirement is always the same; to reveal the original surfaces without any masking of mud or dust.

There are only two, very elementary, points that have to be remembered. One is always to work from the top down and to clean back from the edges of the trench before cleaning a baulk section. This may seem entirely obvious, but it is all too easy to clean, say, the face of a wall and then realise that the top of it remains uncleaned. The other requirement is to select viewpoints and check through the camera viewfinder exactly what the photograph will include before starting to clean. There is no point in cleaning both sides of a wall if only one is to be photographed, nor in meticulously cleaning a whole square if only half of it will be visible. It is, of course, a basic tenet of excavation that the working area should be reasonably clean and free from detritus at all times, but there is a deal of difference between this degree of neatness and the almost obsessive cleanliness necessary for a good site photograph.

Most soft or fine-grained surfaces, like ash or clay, respond better to careful scraping with a trowel than to brushing, which tends to smear the surface, and on stone or brick, a coarse, hard brush is usually the most effective (taking care not to brush out the mortar). Cleaning should be from

Plate 53 and Plate 54   Recording artifacts on the correct surface. Plate 53 shows a house-altar photographed standing above the ground surface, not upon its surface of deposition; while the fireplace in Plate 54 has been recorded only after its accompanying surface had been cut down by nearly 50 cm. Both are misleading records.

the centre outwards, and shoes with studded soles, which can leave a pattern on soft surfaces that is impossible to disguise, should never be worn. The corners of sections and baulks should be trimmed square, partly just for the sake of appearance but primarily to lessen the chance of their being mistaken for structures. If there are working surfaces in the photograph that are not floors but simply the levels at which digging has stopped, they are best roughened in some way so that they will not look like stratified levels. Very minor flaws – an odd root trailing down the baulk, a footprint, a line of labels at different angles down a section – can look surprisingly obtrusive in a published photograph, and it is worth standing back just before taking the photograph and trying to look at the scene with fresh eyes, to make sure that some distracting detail has not been overlooked.

Photographing people
As was said at the beginning of this section, there is always a need for a few photographs showing people as well as photographs of stratigraphy and artifacts, and such photographs are surprisingly difficult to take. Without

Plate 54

seeking to emulate the highest standards of travel photography, the sort of thing found in the *National Geographic Magazine*, good interesting photographs can be achieved of diggers and local people, but they need thought and a certain amount of time. To rely on a few snapshots taken when other work is slack is rarely sufficient. There are really only two approaches, one concentrating on the people and the other on the tasks.

Photographs of people at work, whether singly or in groups, require that a lot of attention be paid to the backgrounds, and to the position and lighting of the figure or figures. A group of people trowelling the floor of an empty square, for instance, is likely to be quite uninteresting, if not unconvincing, especially if it is in colour and all the participants are wearing dust-coloured clothes. At the least, try to have activities going on at different levels or at different distances, and make sure that most of the faces can be seen, and that it is reasonably clear what everybody is doing. It is usually better to have too few people at work rather than too many, and the working area should, of course, look clean and efficient, without luncheon bags or coats strewn about. Because someone is bound to blink or sneeze at the moment of exposure, take several shots from several viewpoints. This is a very mechanical way to take a photograph, but it should yield some usable results. Many people become self-conscious when being photographed, but this rarely lasts after the first one or two shots.

Photographs which concentrate on the tasks, or on the locale, can be either of a director directing, or of a surveyor surveying; single shots designed to show how a dig works; or they can be of an instructional type showing, for example, how a skeleton is lifted, how samples are taken for carbon-14 dating, and so on. In each case, it is necessary to plan the work carefully, to seek out the typical or meaningful image from among all the activities (which does not necessarily mean having the director pointing imperiously, or the surveyor peering through a theodolite) and, for serial photographs, to plot the course of work. If, for example, it were decided to take a series of photographs showing the lifting of a skeleton (the same principles apply whether the series is of still photographs or a cine or video camera is being used) it should first be decided what are likely to be the significant stages; discovering and clearing the top of the grave, excavating down to the burial, disclosing and cleaning the skeleton, drawing and photographing it, possibly measuring and conserving it, dealing with grave goods if any, lifting and transporting the bones, clearing the grave itself, later treatment or examination of the bones. For the sake of interest, viewpoints should be varied, but it is probably better if the scale of the photograph, and the number of people involved, are quite restricted; perhaps a couple of establishing shots to show the grave in the whole site, and then only two or three different scales. All the excavating photographs should be from a distance sufficient to show the whole of the grave, for instance, and detail shots of cleaning, measuring, and so on, from close enough to show only the part being worked on, the tools, and the heads of the excavators. The reason for this restriction is that if photographs are taken from many different distances and viewpoints it may be difficult for the onlooker to relate one to another. For a similar reason, it is better if the same person or persons are shown in each photograph (unless it is felt to be valuable to emphasise that, for instance, the conservator or the osteologist was called in for one particular stage), and also if the people concerned look more or less the same every time. The viewer may realise very well that the process extends over several days and that the people working there do not really wear the same shirt for a week (even if they do in fact) but to see them wearing quite different clothes, or with and then without a beard, in subsequent shots, can be confusing.

Tact is always necessary in photographing local people and local settings. In some places, of course, it is thought highly offensive, and nearly everywhere, quite rightly, it is considered impolite to take photographs as if a local village or farm or café were merely a sort of tourist attraction. Except where there are strong religious objections, however, photography is possible nearly everywhere once the photographer has become known and accepted locally, but it is important to wait for that acceptance. If local people become irritated by having cameras pointed at them, that irritation is as likely to be directed against the whole dig as against the individual concerned, and no dig can operate for long without local goodwill.

9

PRINCIPLES OF OBJECT PHOTOGRAPHY

This chapter is concerned mainly with the photography of movable artifacts, neither so large that they have to be photographed *in situ* nor so small that they need the techniques of close-up photography (this is dealt with in the next chapter). For all such objects the same principles of lighting and arrangement apply, and the same sort of information should be recorded by the camera.

The aims should be to record the maximum amount of accurate information, and to avoid distortions of shape, proportion, texture and colour. Ideally, it should be as informative to compare photographs of two objects as to compare the objects themselves, and although this ideal may be unattainable, differences between the photographs should at least reflect real differences between the objects and not just vagaries of the photographer. A further requirement is that photographs of artifacts, and particularly of artifacts which in some way constitute a group or assemblage, or 'before and after' photographs of objects undergoing conservation, should be as standardised as possible. If all are lit in approximately the same way, taken from similar viewpoints and against similar backgrounds, the images will be the more easily comparable and the eye will not be distracted by differences that are not related to the objects themselves.

Equipment
Cameras
The advantages and drawbacks of different camera formats are discussed in Chapter 3; they apply equally in object photography as in the field. Large-format cameras can record finer detail, films can be processed individually, and foreshortening can be prevented by the use of camera-movements. Small-format, including 35 mm cameras, are readily available, the film is comparatively cheap, and by using longer-than-standard focal-length lenses, foreshortening can be reduced, although not eliminated. One other advantage of large- over small-format cameras concerns not the image of the object itself, but its background. If a photograph is to be published, there is a strong possibility that the proportions of the print will not be those needed in the published plate; it is nearly always necessary to crop one dimension or the other. With a large-format negative, it is quite reasonable to allow a wide margin of neutral background all round the object, but with small-format,

154

because the image is necessarily so much smaller, it is important to fill the frame with the object as completely as possible, and the possibility of cropping the background is lost.

Lenses

For a large-format 5 × 4 in camera, a standard 150 mm lens will be adequate for most work. Of the different lenses on the market, some show better resolution when focussed to infinity, and some are better at a magnification of 1:10 or more. The differences, however, are very slight and since most cameras used in archaeology will have to serve both in the field and for photographing objects, it scarcely seems worth differentiating. Although a standard lens is adequate, a lens of longer focal length, 210 or 240 mm, does have advantages, the main one being that, for a given size of image, the

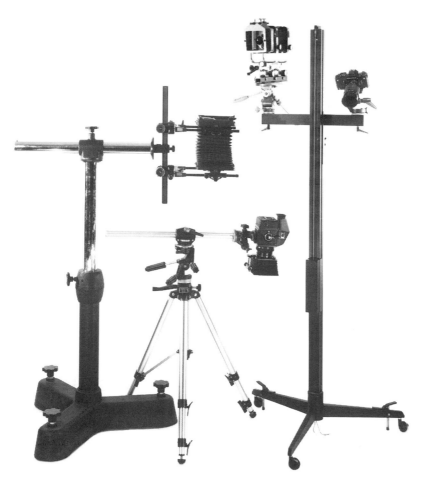

Plate 55 Tripods and camera stands. From left to right these are: heavyweight vertical support, tripod with cross-arm, light-weight column stand.

working distance – the distance between the camera and the object – is greater, making the placing of lights, reflectors, etc. easier.

For medium-format, 6×4.5 to 6×9 cm cameras, the advantage of a longer lens is proportionately more, because of both its flatter perspective and the longer working distance.

The range of choices for 35 mm cameras is much wider, and because of the need to fill the frame, a longer lens is much more necessary. For most purposes a lens between 85 and 135 mm will serve (a 100 mm macro-lens is particularly suitable) but it is of advantage to have a choice of two or three. Although a standard lens of 50 mm is usable for objects of 50 cm or more in height, if the full frame is used for objects very much smaller, foreshortening may become obtrusive. Certainly a photograph of something about the size of a teacup, taken with a standard lens to fill the frame, will show grotesquely steep perspective.

Tripods

Any strongly built tripod that can be adjusted in height between about 75 and 175 cm will serve. It should have an adjustable centre-column, and the type that can be wound up and down is preferable, though not essential. A pan-and-tilt head is more convenient than a ball-and-socket one, and rubber feet are better than spiked, if only for the sake of the floor. A cross-arm that will carry the camera well clear of the tripod for vertical shots is often useful, although unless the tripod is very heavy it may be necessary to hang a counterweight or sandbag on it to prevent it overbalancing. For use in a studio, but not outside it, column-stands have advantages over tripods. These are tubular or square-section columns set in heavy bases which move on castors, usually with a locking device to hold them steady once in position. A counterweighted arm extending from the column holds the camera, on a pan-and-tilt head. These are more stable, and take up less floor space than a tripod, and the camera can be raised from close to floor level up to the full height of the stand, usually 2 or 3 m (Plate 55).

Filters

Contrast filters may be necessary for photographing some types of artifact in black and white, and colour-correction filters for obtaining a correct record with colour film. Polarising filters and screens may be used for both. Their use is discussed in the section on filters in Chapter 3.

Light meters

In the field, and for occasional use, the built-in meters of 35 mm and roll-film cameras are adequate for object photography. There are many circumstances, however, when separate light meters are more accurate and easier to use. Of these, spot-meters are the most convenient although rather expensive, but incident and reflected light meters are almost as reliable, given careful use. An 18% grey card (e.g. a Kodak Neutral Test Card) is also useful. The use of light meters is also discussed in Chapter 3.

Stands

The basic arrangements for photographing objects are horizontal, with the object standing on its base and the camera recording a profile, or something close to one; or vertical, with the camera pointing down at the object. Pottery, figurines and similar free-standing artifacts lend themselves to the first method, and coins, beads, tablets and sherds to the second. Occasionally some other arrangement is preferable; a pendant on a chain, for example, is best shown against an inclined board so that the links of the chain are correctly spread, and such things as garments may be better displayed if suspended by a horizontal pole through the arms. Horizontal and vertical set-ups are, however, probably suitable for more than 90% of objects.

The simplest horizontal stand is a shelf or table 40–50 cm deep and 1 m or so wide, standing against a wall, with a single sheet of background paper or cloth running down the wall and across the horizontal surface without a break. In many cases, however, a clearer picture results if the object stands on a sheet of glass or perspex supported on blocks above the shelf, so that the base of the object is not lost in its own shadow (Plates 56 and 57). This arrangement can sometimes result in rather unnatural-looking photographs, with the object apparently floating in mid-air, but at least all the detail is clearly shown. Stands of this sort can be cheaply and quickly arranged anywhere – in a site hut on a dig, or in a museum basement. If object photography is going to be undertaken regularly, however, it is worth buying or constructing a framework on castors, holding a sheet of opal perspex curved up from a horizontal bench-top to a vertical back. A couple of equipment manufacturers do supply such things – at a price – but they can be built easily enough from 4×2 cm hardwood strip or from slotted angle-metal. A suitable construction is shown in Plate 58. With a stand like this,

Plate 56, Plate 57   Plate 56 shows a bowl on a sheet of white paper, with its base obscured by shadow, Plate 57 the same bowl on a sheet of translucent plastic. Notice, however, the slightly increased underlighting.

lights can be positioned below and behind the perspex to give an opaque shadowless background (it is important that it is built in such a way that there are no cross-struts to throw shadows on the perspex). One snag with any glass or perspex surface is that metal, stone or pottery artifacts, no matter how carefully handled, will sooner or later scratch the surface, and these scratches will be visible in subsequent photographs. It is as well always to stand the objects on small sheets of clear or frosted acetate, which can be frequently and cheaply replaced.

Vertical photographs with 35 mm or medium-format cameras can be managed with a heavy tripod and a counterweighted cross-arm, although this is not a very convenient arrangement. It is awkward to adjust, the tripod legs can get in the way of the lighting, and it can be unstable. For light cameras a

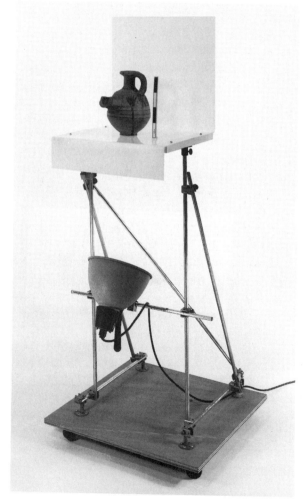

Plate 58   Object stand constructed of laboratory scaffolding and 5 mm Perspex sheet.

Plate 59   Vertical object stand: heavy wooden base with bolted-on copy stand. The lighting arms are made of laboratory scaffolding and the light-box has been fitted with a rheostat.

copying stand is better; a vertical column with a horizontal arm of adjustable height, preferably counterweighted. There are many makes of these on the market, at widely different prices. The heavier the construction the better. Bright-metal components should be avoided, because of possible reflection, and fixed-position lights, which some copy-stands are equipped with, are of little value. If such a thing is available, an old enlarger can be readily adapted for this purpose (Plate 59). They are best mounted on a solidly built low bench, 50–60 cm high, which can be moved about so that lights can be positioned all round the stand. For 5 × 4 in cameras, a heavy column stand or some form of gantry are the only reliable supports (Plate 55), but if these prove too expensive – as they well might – a rather clumsy but usable alternative can be contrived by mounting the camera on a bracket extending from a solid wall by about 50 cm, and placing the object to be photographed on a horizontal board beneath it. A number of blocks, 10 or 15 cm thick, can be used to raise the board, and, with a monorail camera at least, finer adjustments in the size obtained by moving the camera body up and down its rail.

Minor items of equipment

A comprehensive list of all the bits and pieces that could prove useful in object photography would fill several pages, and would probably still be incomplete. Camera accessories would certainly include:

> cable releases; 20 or 25 cm are the most convenient lengths, with perhaps one long release – 50 or 75 cm – for use when the camera is less accessible;
> lens hoods and caps for all lenses, just as important here as in the field;
> focussing cloth;
> loupe magnifying glass, × 6 or × 8;
> spirit level.

A minimal list of other useful items would be:

> reflector material; 3 or 4 pieces of board, white on one side and covered with crumpled and resmoothed aluminium foil on the other;
> diffusing material: either white fibreglass web or heat-proof acetate;
> a supply of cheap mounting board that can be cut up for masks and backgrounds;
> tape, both double-sided and masking type, together with a roll of strong canvas tape (gaffer tape);
> a few blocks of wood, about 5 × 10 × 25 cm, black-painted, and an old drawing board, for use as temporary stands;

pot stands; the traditional stands for round-bottomed pots, made of wire with legs soldered on, are rather obtrusive. Short cylinders of perspex in various diameters are better, especially if the front 120° or 130° is cut out to show the base of the pot. A length of stiff but bendable wire can be useful for making temporary supports;

laboratory stands or laboratory scaffolding, for holding baffles and reflectors and sometimes objects;

plasticine, blue-tack, bulldog and crocodile clips, drawing and map pins, all needed at times for holding things up or pinning things down;

white nylon line, for suspension;

rules, scissors, plastic tweezers and small brushes.

Backgrounds

For standard record photographs in black and white, the most effective background is itself either black or white. Any other tone will result in grey on grey, detracting inevitably from the clarity of the object. Obviously it would be pointless to photograph something very light in tone – an alabaster head or a silver brooch – against white, or something very dark – a basalt axe or a jet necklace – against black. But the majority of artifacts are, after all, of a fairly middle tone, and if there is a choice then, for two reasons, a white background is preferable to black. Firstly, unless the lighting is very skilfully arranged, the edges and thus the shape of objects are apt to get swallowed up by a black background; and secondly, object photographs are likely to be published, and plate-making processes rarely produce smooth areas of solid black – they are inclined to appear muddy and sticky. White background material can be the opal perspex mentioned earlier, ordinary cheap cartridge paper, or flexible matt-surfaced white plastic. For use on a dig, and for uncleaned objects, plastic is much to be preferred, being washable and less likely to tear. Black cotton velvet (not nylon) or black flock paper are about the only materials that will give a solid unreflective black, for ordinary black and white photography of objects. Unfortunately velvet is all too easily marked, and apparently innocuous materials like plasticine can leave a virtually indelible patch. It is worth preparing a few scales for use on velvet, by sticking small magnets to their bases so that they will stand upright over a thin piece of steel (a steel rule will serve) placed under the velvet.

Very occasionally, it is advantageous to use a background graded from light to dark. This can be achieved either by lighting white paper from one end only, or more easily by using a sheet of graded background paper (some photographic suppliers stock them) which needs no special lighting.

For colour photography white backgrounds are best avoided. If the photography is for colour slides, white backgrounds are apt to glare on the screen, although they do act as a useful check on the colour balance of the film – if the white is reproduced as truly white, then it is reasonably certain that the colours are correctly recorded. A black background is often effective, and since the contrast of the picture involves colours as well as tones, a lower degree of subject contrast between the object and its background is often acceptable. Usually, however, a coloured background will give a more pleasing, if not a more informative, picture. There must, however, be a certain care taken in the selection of the colour. Very intense saturated colours distract the eye from the object itself and, especially if there is a large area of such a colour, produce a carry-over effect to the eye, and reflection from the background can tinge the artifact with its colour. For aesthetic reasons, if no other, it is preferable to avoid eye-catching colours like jade green or mauve. Ideally perhaps the background colour should be a desaturated version of the colour complementary to the main colour in the object, but the subtle effect of such precision would make no appreciable difference to the picture. A few sheets or rolls of unobtrusive coloured paper is usually sufficient; chrome yellow, rusty brown and olive green would cover most situations.

This chapter has been concerned so far with photographs for record purposes, where the clarity of the object is the paramount consideration. But when photographs are taken for publications other than site reports – for displays, for nonspecialist publications, or for public lecture slides – more interesting backgrounds may be appropriate. Textured or natural backgrounds, or the inclusion of a piece of equipment or a laboratory bench in the frame can, if handled with discretion, make for more interesting pictures. Certainly to the general public, and often to the specialist for that matter, a tool or weapon becomes more understandable if it is pictured gripped in someone's hand, and jewellery is often best shown round a neck or wrist. As with human scales in site photography, the model should not appear more interesting or attractive than the artifact.

Backgrounds for close-up work are dealt with in the next chapter.

Types of lighting

Objects may be photographed by natural light, by continuous tungsten light, by flash, or by a combination of these. Colour photography under mixed lighting should be avoided, however, because of the different colour temperatures involved.

Direct undiffused *sunlight* is normally too harsh a source for object photography, while photographs taken in shadow may be too softly lit to show texture. In addition, light reflected into a shadowed area from a blue sky or from a nearby surface may well give a colour bias to the light which would register on colour film although almost undetectable to the eye. The human eye and brain have a considerable ability to, as it were, discount the colour of ambient light; the pages of a book will be thought of as white, even when viewed under a bright yellow, blue or red light, but film emulsion has no such ability, and a colour photograph of an object taken by yellow light will appear yellow-tinged. On a site without electricity, or without lighting equipment, it may be necessary to photograph by daylight, and two simple structures can be of great value. These are a light but steady table or bench that can easily be turned and slightly tilted to bring the light to the right angle and direction (an old plane-table can be ideal); and a frame a metre or so square covered with white gauze or butter muslin which can be held or propped in a position to diffuse direct sunlight. A couple of pieces of card covered with crumpled aluminium foil are also useful as reflectors, and if the work has to be done in the open, a wind-break is often necessary. It should be added that for some sorts of material, such as silver and glass, reflective metal or polished stone, diffused daylight is unsurpassable. A photographer with access to a room with a north-facing skylight is fortunate indeed.

Continuous *tungsten lighting* is in many ways the most effective light source for object photography. The direction and intensity of the lights can be closely controlled and, most important, the effect can be seen before the photograph is taken, which is not the case with flash. Both tungsten bulb and tungsten-halogen sources can be used and both can be set in a variety of flood and spot holders, giving diffused or concentrated beams of light. Bulbs are comparatively cheap and their housing simple. They have the disadvantage that as they age their light output is reduced and, more important, their colour temperature drops, which may necessitate the use of colour-correcting filters for colour film. The slight loss of light with ageing is not usually a problem except for lighting plans or other flat copy with four or more bulbs, when it is important to have the same output from each bulb (see Chapter 13). Ordinary domestic lamps of 100 200 watts are really too low-powered for anything but close-up work, and their colour is too yellow for colour photography. Far better, though not so cheap nor so easily obtainable, are 500 watt photo-lamps (e.g. Philips Arga photo B), which have a long life and retain their colour temperature, more or less, throughout. For occasional use, it is worth having 'photoflood' or 'overrun' bulbs, which, by using a thinner filament, have a much higher light output than their nominal wattage suggests. They are designed to be used with tungsten-balanced colour film, although filtration may be necessary (see Chapter 5). Both photoflood and ordinary tungsten bulbs can be obtained with internal reflectors, giving either a wide or a narrow beam. These again are valuable for occasional use or when proper lamp housings are not available. Fluorescent tubes can be used for the illumination of large plans or drawings for black and white photography but for little else. Since they emit light that is not of a continuous spectrum, their effect on colour film can be very strange.

Tungsten-halogen lamps have a high output of light which remains almost constant in amount and colour throughout their life, which is much longer than that of tungsten bulbs. They are relatively expensive, although this may be more than offset by their longer life, and they can be housed only in holders designed for them. They are rather fragile while alight and immediately afterwards, and they run at high temperatures, so nearly all housings incorporate a fan-cooling device. Most projectors and spotlights are now built for tungsten-halogen lamps.

Both tungsten bulbs and tungsten-halogen lamps give out a considerable amount of heat during use, and if 4000 or 5000 watts of light are left trained on an artifact for more than a few minutes the rise in temperature can be considerable. For many organic objects, and even for some glass and metal, this may be quite unacceptable. In such cases it would be better to use flash, or to wire a half-power switch into the lighting circuit so that full light, and heat, is switched on only for the moment of exposure. In extreme cases, it may be necessary to use lights fitted with heat-retarding filters (e.g. Chance glass Type HR1).

There are a great many types of *lamp-housings and supports* on the market (see Plate 38), and as with lenses, it is always worth looking for secondhand equipment For temporary use, portable folding stands, of which there are two or three brands aimed at the amateur market, are quite adequate. None of these are very stable used at their full height, and their folding tripod legs can be obstructive around the work bench, but they are cheap and lightweight, and three or four stands can easily be carried by one person. For more permanent set-ups, lights on pillar stands with castor bases, or overhead tracks, are far more convenient. A group suitable for most work would comprise two pillar-stands extending from about 1 m to 1.75 m in height, fitted with bowl reflectors 20 or 25 cm in diameter, and with side-arms so that the lights can be taken down to floor level; one pillar fitted with a saucer reflector of 50 or 60 cm diameter, which will give a broad soft beam of light; and a boom-light, a tall pillar-stand carrying a long cross-arm so arranged that a 20 or 25 cm reflector can be used from overhead. For use on site or on location a couple of clamp lights are useful (these are also known as 'gaffer-grips'). Some are made with a grip wide enough to be used on builders' scaffoldings.

All these types of fitting can be matched, rather more expensively, by tungsten-halogen units. Of particular value is a tungsten-halogen 'broad light', which gives a broad beam of light rather more effectively than a saucer reflector does. A small spotlight – about 500–600 watts – may be useful to show texture on an object or to give a 'rim-light', a bright halo outlining an object against its background. Spots are often best used with snoots, tubular front extensions which restrict the width of the beam; and both spots and floods with 'barn-doors', flaps that can be used to cut off part of the beam.

On any lights that are to be used outdoors, the fittings should be weatherproof and designed for the purpose. Ordinary care must be taken to ensure that all electrical equipment is properly insulated and that circuits are not overloaded. When, as is often the case, equipment is not bought all at one time but built up as finances allow, it is all too easy to overlook the load that is finally being imposed on the circuit. If, in addition, the number of electric outlets is inadequate and reliance is placed on extension leads and adaptors, the result may well be a breach of the law and a real fire hazard. In areas liable to voltage fluctuations it is worth installing a voltage regulator (for some purposes, for example colour printing, this is essential). A mere 5% increase or decrease in the voltage will result in a 20% change in the light output, together with a change in the colour of the light. A tungsten lamp operating on a voltage of 5% above its rating will also have its working life reduced by almost 50%.

Most commercial studios, and many museum departments, now use *electronic flash* as the only form of lighting. The advantages are: light output is very high, and consequently exposure times can be shorter and slower-speed films can be used; heat production is negligible; and, most important, light is of a colour that does not change and for which daylight-type film is balanced. The disadvantages are the high initial cost and the difficulty in seeing the effect of slight changes in the direction and distance of the different lights before the exposure is made (although most large flash units incorporate small tungsten bulbs – so-called 'modelling lights' – for this purpose). The different uses of flash are discussed in Chapter 4. Studio flash units come in a wide, even bewildering, variety of sizes and shapes, but the commonest types are flash-heads mounted on a column or tripod stand, which can either be used directly with a bowl reflector or through some sort of baffle, or directed against an umbrella to give a softer beam.

Positioning and lighting objects

When an artifact is set up to be photographed, there are three criteria to be borne in mind. The first of these is the shape of the object. The overall shape is often the most characteristic of its attributes and, particularly with pottery, the basis of classification. This must therefore be clearly shown in any photograph, whatever else is not. If there is a conflict between showing, say, the decoration in the bottom of a large bowl and the profile of the bowl including its base, then two photographs are called for (Plates 60 and 61). Not only should the outline of the object be clear, with no part of it lost in shadow nor melting into the background, but its three-dimensional quality should also be apparent. For example, a picture of a box should show two sides and the top even though only one of the faces may be complete or bear a surface decoration. The portrayal of the object's shape is mainly a matter of viewpoint, and it cannot be stressed too strongly that the first step towards a good photograph is a close examination of the object and a careful consideration of the best viewpoint. A specialist knowledge of the class of object concerned may or may not be helpful. The specialist will know, for instance, that the position of rivet holes, or the wheel-marks, or the absence of ear lobes, are important and must be shown. At the same time, familiarity with types of artifact can lead to a disregard of what seems too well known to require display. The specialist will know – or think – that all this class of cooking pot are round-based and therefore not bother to record it, or that the inscription is important but the tool-marks are not; but someone looking at the photograph later will want to see them. This is not, of course, a plea for ignorance in photographers, but rather for the consideration of the artifact as a whole, at least so far as the primary record photograph is concerned.

The choice of viewpoint is often a matter of quite fine adjustment, and particularly with an object like a statue or figurine a slight change in viewpoint may disclose the shape of one feature or obscure another. A portrait bust, for example, would normally be photographed straight on and from both profiles, but a viewpoint of a little less than three-quarters full face will often give a better idea of its shape and character. The viewpoint should always be considered first, before bringing the camera to the eye's position; if the object is put straight in front of the camera and immediately focussed through the viewfinder, one usually assumes that the viewpoint presented is adequate, if not ideal, without further adjustment.

The effects of perspective and camera movements are discussed in Chapter 3, but other considerations, e.g. of solidity and three-dimensionality, are functions of lighting (Plates 62, 63, and 64). In general, the main light should always come from the top. We are all accustomed to seeing the world lit from the sky, and even a face we know well can look strange and even unrecognisable when lit from below. As a matter of convention, objects are lit from the top left (when facing the object). It is really quite unimportant whether the light comes from top left or top right, but if a series of photographs are to be compared, unnecessary differences in the direction of the main lighting can be

Plate 60, Plate 61   Viewpoint. Quite often, as with this bowl, there is no single viewpoint which would show both the base and the detail of the interior. The only satisfactory solution is to take two photographs.

distracting. With some two-dimensional or shallow objects this one key light is sufficient, but if the artifact is three-dimensional then either a reflector or a fill-in light will be needed on the other side of the object. This raises another important general point: the human eye can detect detail in a far wider range of tones than any film emulsion can. If you look along a street lit by strong cross-light, or at a pot lit from one side only, it is usually possible to see detail

Plate 62

Plate 64

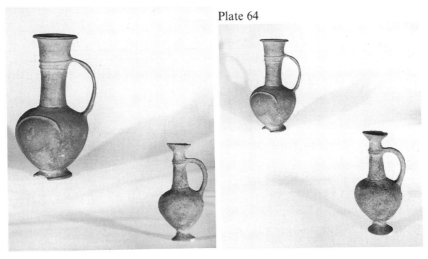

Plate 63

Apparent size differences. Plate 62 shows two jugs side by side, Plate 63 the same two jugs with one 60 cm behind the other, photographed with a long lens (240 mm) on a 5 × 4" camera. Plate 64 shows them in the same position as in Plate 63, photographed with a wide-angle lens (90 mm). The shadows add to the distortion.

in both the most strongly lit and the most shadowed parts. Take a photograph, however, of either the street or the pot, and even at optimum exposure either the shadows will reproduce as completely black or the lighter tones as completely burnt out, or both. This fact must be constantly borne in mind when lighting objects, and the difference in the level of light between the two sides should not be more than about one stop. This is not to say that the level should be exactly the same across the object, or from top to bottom. If it were, the object would probably look flat and one-dimensional. A cube, for instance, viewed from one corner, would need different light levels on each of the three visible faces.

Having arranged the main lighting, it is then necessary to look at the object carefully again to see if there are any parts of it that should be emphasised by a little extra light (very often a small reflector is all that is needed), and also to make sure that there are no hard-edged shadows across its surface. A slight soft shadow within the rim of a pot can emphasise its shape, or along the line of an incision can show its depth, but a hard-edged shadow can be obtrusive and, if the photograph is black and white, may be indistinguishable in the final print from a stripe of colour or something of the sort.

Finally, set the background lighting. Against black, of course, no further light is necessary, but if the background is to be white, the level of light should be at least two stops above the light on the object. If there are enough lighting units, a couple can be arranged to throw light only on the background (or through it, if the background is an opal perspex sheet); if not, the front lights can be moved back after the object has been exposed, and a second exposure given of the background only, leaving the object as a silhouette. This is much easier to do with a Compur or similar shutter, where all that is needed is to re-cock and re-fire the shutter, than with a focal-plane shutter, where the shutter must be re-cocked by operating the wind-on lever while keeping the film stationary by holding down the rewind button.

There are some problems that can best be solved by using a 'moving light'. There are occasions, for example, when the photography of an artifact or of an interior calls for a large amount of tungsten light but such light is not available or cannot be used (as might well be the case in a museum). There are also times when an object of irregular shape, like a statue, cannot easily be photographed by stationary lights because of the intrusive shadows cast by various parts of it. In such cases, acceptable photographs can often be taken by means of a single light, moved during the exposure to, as it were, paint the object with light. Prerequisites are that the camera is on a tripod and that the level of ambient light is low, although it is not necessary to work in total darkness. It is easier, but not vital, to have two people present, one to open and close the shutter, and one to manipulate the light. The technique is simple enough; one person opens the shutter and times the exposure and the other sweeps the light over the object or space, keeping the light moving throughout but making sure that it is never directed towards the lens. As can be imagined, the difficulty lies in determining an exposure since it can never be guaranteed that any single part of the object will receive a controlled and exact amount of light. The whole operation is in fact rather hit and miss, and it is wise to make several exposures.

The light used can be any sort of lamp-holder with a shade on it, preferably a fairly narrow one, with enough cable to enable the operator to walk around the statue without getting the cable entangled with it or with the tripod. Holding the lamp to point at the centre of the statue, from about a metre away and to the left, a meter reading is taken of the centre. The indicated exposure should be of the order of 5–10 seconds. Usually this means using a low-voltage bulb of about 100 watts. Assuming that the indicated exposure is 8 sec, the top of the statue would need a little more – say 10 sec – so that the main light appears to come from top left, and the base a little less – say 6 sec. The right-hand side of the statue should receive less light, but in the same proportions, perhaps 8, 6 and 4 sec. However, it is not possible to light one part of the statue without having the light spilling over on to the other parts, and if the statue were indeed given these exposures, with the lens open for a total of 42 sec, it would certainly be overexposed, quite apart from the effect of any ambient light. Trial and error has shown that if these indicated exposures are halved, giving in this case 5, 4 and 3 sec on the left, and 4, 3 and 2 sec on the right, the total exposure will be of the right order. It is as well to rehearse the procedure before actually making the exposure, one person holding the lamp at the top left of the statue and, while the other person opens the shutter, moving the light down the statue, counting off the seconds, then walking behind the camera while the camera operator holds his hand in front of the lens, and lighting the other side. If it is possible to hang a sheet behind the statue, this can be lit separately by playing the light upon it after the main exposure, while avoiding lighting the statue itself. The background exposure should be about twice as much as that received by any part of the statue.

The same sort of technique can be used to light interiors – rooms, or tombs, or caves – either as the sole lighting or as a supplement to natural light, as was described in Chapter 6. A similar technique using flash is discussed in Chapter 4.

There may be occasions when, no matter how carefully the lighting has been arranged, there are details of shape or texture which cannot all be recorded in the same photograph. A technique can be employed (Nylén (1978), p. 90) whereby several photographs are taken, all from the same viewpoint but using different lighting to record different details. One print is used as a base and details from the others are drawn on to it. In skilled hands this might give very good results, but it does call for a high standard of draughtsmanship, combined with an expert knowledge of the class of artifact.

In the near future it might be possible to achieve a similar result by combining different digitalized images.

After shape, the second main consideration is texture. This is of particular importance since the shape can be recorded as well by drawing as by photography, while texture cannot. A skilled draughtsman can give some indication of texture by means of dotting and hatching, but it can never be more than a generalisation, and written descriptions, 'hard, sandy ware' and the like, are notoriously imprecise.

The depicting of texture, given a lens and an emulsion capable of recording it, is again almost entirely a matter of lighting. Acutely angled lighting will emphasise texture and frontal lighting flatten it (Plate 65). But the angle of lighting has to be related to the fineness or coarseness of the surface. For instance, if a light is just skimmed across the surface of a flat piece of limestone, it may show the grain of the stone very clearly; light at a similar angle across a deeply incised bronze plaque or a heavily wheel-marked pot may give the impression that the plaque is pierced with slits or the pot ridged, especially if the light is not balanced by a fill-in. To over-emphasise texture is as deceptive as to suppress it (Plates 66 and 67). There are some sorts of texture that are particularly difficult to show correctly, for example, glazed wares, dark wood or leather, and cast bronze (see Chapter 12).

Plate 65   cross lighting. The strong crosslighting of this fragment of stone bowl was effective in revealing the grouping of chisel marks.

The third consideration, which is coupled with texture, is tone and colour. So far as tone is concerned, there are both the difference of tone within the object and the overall tone to think about. Both are more of a problem with black and white than with colour photography. If, for instance, a terracotta figurine is unevenly lit, so that the head is much lighter than the base, on a colour film the colour of the terracotta should still be apparent, and the fall-off of light should be seen for what it is; but if the same object is recorded on black and white film, the fall-off may well appear to be a difference of tone in the original. A greater difficulty is posed sometimes in recording the overall tone. Many artifacts, including most pottery, are of a fairly medium tone, with neither solid blacks nor solid whites. If such an artifact is photographed against a white or a black background, there may be very little indication on the negative of its proper tone, and it would be easy to print the negative to give a very light- or a very dark-toned image. If the object itself is still available, by far the best check is to match the print with the original for likeness of tone; if it is not, then the photographer has either to rely on visual memory (which can be very accurate), or to include in the frame some key to the tones. The best key is a graded scale of grey tones (e.g. the Kodak Q 13 scale), which can be positioned to lie along the edge of the frame to be matched with a similar scale when printed. In fact, it is unlikely that a perfect fitting of tones between the original and the printed scale will be achieved, but so long as the middle tones are similar, the image of the artifact should be reasonably faithful.

Plate 66, Plate 67   Texture. Both the over-emphasis of texture in Plate 66, resulting from a single top-light just skimming the surface, and the under-emphasis of Plate 67, caused by too-flat frontal lighting, are deceptive. The truth is somewhere in between.

If the object has colours of any significance, the requirements of black and white and of colour photography need different approaches. For successful colour photography, the colour temperature of the light must match the film type fairly closely, otherwise there may be an overall colour bias to the result. This is relatively unimportant with colour negative stock, since slight overall casts can be compensated for at the printing stage, but correction is barely possible with colour positive film. It is also necessary to prevent reflected light from the background material affecting the object, if the background is itself coloured. It is as well to position the object well in front of the background, and not to over-light the latter. Reflectors, diffusers and baffles can similarly change the colour of light and affect the colour balance. In this respect, foil reflectors are more reliable than white card, which is likely to reflect a slightly yellowish tone.

If it is important to achieve a close match of colours between the object and a print from colour negative film, it is advisable to include a colour scale in the frame (Kodak sell one that has a grey scale alongside it), as a guide for printing.

The use of contrast filters for emphasising the difference between the colours of an object when these colours are reproduced as tones on black and white film is discussed in the section on filters in Chapter 3. Very briefly, some colours, particularly reds and greens, may record on black and white film as virtually identical grey tones. Sometimes they can be separated by means of filters which lighten or darken the tones given by one colour or the other. While this can be a valuable technique, it does entail a distortion of tones and it has to be used with discretion. It is quite easy, for instance, to reproduce a red-ochre decoration on a buff-coloured pot so that in the print the decoration

Plate 68, Plate 69   Tonal differences. The difference in tone between a buff ground and red ochre decoration is shown reasonably correctly in Plate 68, using panchromatic film (FP4) without a filter. In Plate 69, similar film with a green contrast filter (Wratten 54) shows the decoration more clearly but falsifies the difference. The decoration appears to be almost black.

appears to be black (Plates 68 and 69). If there is a choice in the matter, it is better to change the tone of detail, and that no more than is necessary, and to leave the body of the artifact unaltered.

The various types of lighting unit, and their use in commercial photography, are discussed in Evans (1984) and Kodak (1978). Many of the techniques mentioned can equally well be applied in archaeological and conservation photography.

Scales

Types and sizes of scales are discussed in Chapter 3. There should normally be a scale included in any object photograph, except in some cases for photographs intended for exhibition or something of the sort, or unless the size of the object is unimportant or self-explanatory. As with site photographs, it should be a properly drawn or printed scale and not, as is still sometimes seen, a penny or a match box. In colour slides, scales may be thought obtrusive or distracting, and if there is such doubt, it is best to take two slides, one with and one without a scale, so that lecturers can make up their own minds. For black and white photographs, it is preferable always to include a scale, but in such a position that it can be cropped out of the print if need be. If many objects are to be published together, it is better to include scales in all the negatives, print the results to a common enlargement, given in the caption, and crop out the scales themselves. A page of small object photographs, each of which has a scale attached, but all reproduced at different sizes is as unintelligible as one without scales but with a legend stating that 'Figs 1 and 2 are at 1:1, 3 and 4 at 3:5 and 6 at 18:25'. In neither case are the objects easily comparable one with another. The scale should be clean, upright or horizontal, and of a size to match the object. It should also lie or stand in the same plane as the object – a scale well in front of or behind an object is positively deceptive.

There is a further value for a scale correctly placed in relation to the artifact. When a point in front of the lens is focussed upon, the depth of field extends in front of and behind that point. If the camera is focussed so that the image is the same size as the object, then the depth of field extends as far behind the focussed point as it does in front of it; or if it is focussed at the so-called hyper-focal distance (the distance at which the rear depth of field just reaches to infinity), the depth extends twice as far behind the point as in front. It is scarcely worth working out the proportions of the depth of field for intermediate distances, but if the scale is placed between one-third and one-half back in the visible depth of the object, front to back, and focussed sharply, then there is the best chance of depth of field covering the whole of the object.

Finally, the scale should be neither so close to the object as to overlap or appear to crowd it, nor so far away that it cannot, without wasting space, be included in the print.

An illustration in Di Peso (1975) p. 221, shows a type of scale developed for recording stone objects. The object is photographed as if in a corner formed by two walls and a floor, with the intersection of the three faces centred in the photograph. The three faces are gridded into 1 cm squares, and by means of tapes stretched across the object its length, breadth and thickness can be read off on the grids. The arrangement is an effective method of recording objects of similar size and shape in a standardised way and of including their dimensions. The background is rather obtrusive, however, and so are the tapes if the object is small; and since all objects have to be photographed from the same three-quarter viewpoint, shape and detail may be lost.

Exposure and resolution

Modern black and white film has a considerable exposure latitude – a negative can be under- or over-exposed by a factor of two or more and often still yield a reasonable result. Colour film is much more restricted – usually × 1.5 at most. Although the result of deviation from correct exposure may be usable, it will not be of the best attainable quality. The denser a black and white negative is, the larger the grain and the more difficult to retain a correct balance of tones in the print; the thinner it is, the more likely are the dark tones to disappear. It is always preferable to aim for the correct exposure, and then, if there is any doubt about it, or if any imponderable factors are involved, to bracket the exposure. For black and white film, this means making two additional negatives, one at twice the indicated exposure and one at a half; for colour, to be absolutely certain, the steps should be of half a stop, i.e. × 1.5 and × 2, × 0.75 and × 0.5. This rather wasteful insurance may not be necessary if the film is to be developed at once, or if the object can easily be re-photographed, but otherwise the cost of the extra film is well justified.

Although exposures can often be estimated correctly, i.e. without a meter, given a familiarity with the film and the lighting, it is not a method to be recommended. The eye is a poor instrument for estimating levels of light because of its powers of compensation, and it is preferable always to rely on a light meter. Using a meter is simple indeed – set the film speed, press a button, and read off the results in terms of exposure and aperture. What is actually measured takes rather more consideration. An ordinary reflected-light meter accepts a cone of light at the cell with an angle of about 45°, roughly the same as the angle of a standard lens. The light is integrated and the dial calibrated on the assumption that an averaging of all the tones in the scene will result in an acceptable reading. In many cases this is true; a group of people or a landscape (provided that too much of the sky is not included) will probably contain an average distribution of light and dark tones, and an integrated reading will be satisfactory. If, however, the photograph is of a small dark object against a large white background, a reading taken from, or behind, the camera position will comprise mostly white background. The meter, averaging across the field, will record a high reflection, and therefore indicate a short exposure. So the background, instead of a dense white, will print close to a mid-grey, and the object itself will be very much underexposed. Similarly, a small, light-coloured object against a black background will be very much over-exposed.

The first rule, then, is to confine the reading to the object itself, or to something of a similar tone. Take the meter, or the camera if the meter is built in, close to the object, perhaps 30 cm from it, and take the reading from there, making sure that the shadow of the meter or camera is not falling on the object. If a camera with automatic exposure control is being used, it may be necessary to operate the exposure lock – if the camera has such a thing – after the reading is taken, otherwise the meter will revert to an overall reading when the camera is moved back. If the meter has an incident-light dome, it can also be used to take a reading of the light falling on the object, by holding it close to the object and taking a reading with the meter pointing back towards the camera. A similar type of reading can be taken with an incident meter by taking a reading on a grey card with an average (i.e. 18%) reflectance, held at the object's position. This method is particularly useful when photographing an object too small or too interrupted (for example, a piece of open-textured cloth on white background) to allow of a direct reading. However, this also assumes an average reflectance in the object, and if it were very dark or very light it might be under- or over-exposed. Ideally, perhaps, there should be available half a dozen or so cards of graded levels of reflectance – very light grey to very dark grey – one of which could be selected after matching with the object. Easier to use, and more reliable, is a spot-meter, which incorporates a viewfinder and an angle of acceptance of only one or two degrees, so that from 2 m away, a reading can be taken on an area no more than 3 cm across.

If the artifact has a wide range of tones, as might be the case with a piece of furniture or a brass and iron instrument, the most reliable method of exposure measurement is to take a reading on the darkest part and another on the lightest part, and place the exposure midway between the two. This ought perhaps to be modified to the darkest and lightest *significant* tones; if the object included, for instance, a solid black or a solid white line, this could safely be disregarded. Light meters are discussed more fully in Chapter 3.

Unfortunately, there are three other factors that may have to be taken into account in determining exposure. The first is magnification, which is discussed in more detail in the following chapter on close-up photography. If the photograph is taken at a magnification of more than about 1:5 (for black and white) or 1:8 (for colour), allowance must be made for the increased distance between the lens and the film; this does not apply if a camera with a built-in meter is being used. Secondly, for exposures longer than about 2 sec (for black and white) or ½ sec (for colour), extra exposure may be necessary to

photographed is three-dimensional it is often necessary to sacrifice some degree of definition in order to render the object in sharp focus front-to-back.

If a large-format camera is to be used, a monorail type is easier to manipulate than a technical camera. Since the back panel of the monorail camera can be adjusted, the camera can be focussed without changing the lens-to-object distance, whereas the front-focussing movement of a technical camera means that as the camera is focussed, the distance between the lens and the object is also changing, thus changing the magnification. In fact, at magnifications beyond 1:1, focussing by this means may become impossible, and the only effective method is to focus the camera roughly (e.g. if the distance between the film plane and the lens centre is set at twice the focal length, the magnification will be approximately 1:1), and then to move either the whole camera or the object back and forth until the image is sharp. For larger magnifications than this, the camera is then racked out a little more, the image made sharp by moving object or camera body again, and the process repeated until the desired degree of magnification is reached – a time-consuming process. Even with a monorail camera, however, or with a 35 mm camera fitted with bellows, it is preferable to make the final, fine, adjustment by moving camera or object, since at 1:1 and above the depth of focus becomes considerable, and it is not at all easy to adjust the lens-to-film distance critically.

Most single-lens reflex cameras, whether 35 mm or medium format, can be used satisfactorily for close-up work, while twin-lens reflex cameras need some device fitted whereby the taking lens can be moved into the position of the viewing lens after focussing; and range-finder cameras need quite elaborate, and expensive, fittings (such as the Leica close-up device) enabling the object to be focussed through the lens first, and the camera body then to be moved into position on the lens.

Close-up attachments
On the majority of 35 mm and medium-format cameras a standard lens will focus down only enough to give a magnification of 1:8 or 1:10 on the negative. This is often inadequate for black-and-white work if fine detail is involved, and for colour if the object is small. For instance, a coin of 2 cm diameter taken at this sort of magnification and projected would fill only about 1/15 of the width of the screen. Some device is usually necessary, therefore, either to produce a larger image for the same lens extension, or to increase the amount of lens extension possible.

There are several such devices in common use. *Supplementary lenses* are extra lens elements designed to be screwed into the front of a standard lens. They act by reducing the focal length, thus enabling a greater magnification to be achieved for the same lens-to-film distance. They are simple to use, but have the disadvantages of shortening the working distance – the space between lens and object – which might make it difficult to light the object properly, and of adding another thickness of glass to the lens, thus increasing the possibility of aberrations. This last is not a serious problem with supplementary lenses designed by the manufacturers for use with specific lenses, but cheap, unmatched, supplementaries can give serious problems, particularly in colour photography. For the best results they should be used with a small aperture and with the lens set to infinity.

Extension tubes are the simplest, and certainly the cheapest, close-up attachments. They are short tubes (usually sold in sets of three that can be used singly or together to give different magnifications), which can be fitted between the camera body and the lens, thus increasing the distance between the two and allowing magnifications of up to 2:1 or 3:1. The more expensive models incorporate a matching pin system whereby the lens's automatic diaphragm (the device that enables the camera's reflex viewing system to be used at full aperture up to the moment of exposure) can continue in use. Tubes are somewhat vulnerable to internal reflections which can result in a 'hot-spot' – a patch of reflected light in the centre of the negative. Care has to be taken also to mask off any extraneous light that might reach the lens from outside the object area.

Most 35 mm cameras and some medium-format cameras can be fitted with *bellows units*, designed to carry the camera body at one end and the lens at the other (see Plate 72a). The lens is focussed by moving either it or the body along a supporting rail. Many bellows units have a second rail below the focussing rail by which the whole unit can be moved backwards and forwards for fine focussing. They are more flexible, although heavier and bulkier, than extension tubes, and the bellows act as a baffle to the spread of light inside the unit. Fitted with a standard lens, most will give a magnification of 4:1 or 5:1. Some include a device – either a rod mechanism or a double cable release – which operates the automatic diaphragm, but any sort of mechanical movement in the camera or lens at the moment of exposure increases the risk of camera shake, and it is safer to disconnect the mechanism and to rely on opening up the aperture for focussing and closing it down before exposing (although it is all to easy to forget to do the latter).

Optically, the best results can be achieved by using *macro lenses*. These are designed for close-up work, giving noticeably better resolution at the edges of the negative than do other lenses when used at short distances. Typically they have a rather small maximum aperture, usually about f5.6, and close down to f32. Most will focus down to 1:2 without accessories; beyond this they can be used with extension tubes or bellows units. For the 35 mm format they are available in 50, 90 and 100 mm focal lengths; for medium format, 80 or 120 mm are the commonest focal lengths. In addition, there are specialist photomacrographic lenses available of shorter focal lengths, e.g. 12.5, 16 and 25 mm in the Leitz Photar and Zeiss Luminar ranges, but the price is high.

Quite satisfactory work can be carried out with a 25 mm *cine lens* for extreme close-up, and good quality *enlarging lenses* (which are also designed to give a flat field) will give reasonable results. At 1:1 and above, macro and enlarging lenses will give a larger angle of coverage than is used by the format for which they are designed. It is therefore possible to use them in a larger camera and to obtain sharp definition across the whole, or most, of the larger negative size. At 2:1, for instance, a 50 mm macro lens will cover a 5 × 4 in negative, retaining both sharpness and even illumination to the outer edges.

A number of *zoom lenses* can be extended to give an enlargement of 1:2 at their shortest focal length, but although such lenses are called 'macro-zooms' by their manufacturers, most are not true macro lenses, and their resolution at close distances is no better than that of a standard lens with an extension tube.

Whatever lens is used, a certain loss of resolution may occur at the edges of the field when the magnification is greater than 1:1. For most photography, the lens-to-object distance is greater – usually many times greater – than the lens-to-film distance, and the lens elements are so arranged as to give their best resolution in these conditions. At a magnification of 1:1, however, the two distances are equal (both twice the focal length), and at magnifications above 1:1 the lens-to-object distance is less than the distance from lens to film. To restore the optimum resolution it is therefore advantageous to reverse the lens in the camera, thus returning it to a position with a greater distance in front of the lens than behind it. This is done with a *reversal ring* which is screwed or locked into the camera body and the front thread of which screws into the filter thread of the lens. When a reversal ring is used, the automatic diaphragm mechanism is inoperative, except that in some bellows units it can be operated by the double cable release.

For occasional use, extension tubes and a standard lens are perfectly adequate, together with a reversal ring for magnifications above 1:1. For a more permanent arrangement, bellows and a macro lens are preferable. Apart from the optical superiority, bellows units carry a tripod bush, enabling the camera to be supported at its point of balance; a camera body plus several tubes and a long lens can be very front-heavy and unstable. Unfortunately even the more widely used macro lenses are relatively expensive – usually about twice the price of a standard lens – so that only regular use would normally justify their purchase.

Stands and tripods

As in any object photography, close-up photographs may be taken horizontally or vertically (i.e. from above), but a vertical arrangement is nearly always more convenient. The exceptions are either for objects best shown standing on their bases, like small figurines, or objects best suspended, like pendants. For horizontal photographs, a scaled-down version of the type of stand described in Chapter 9 would be quite suitable. A stand a metre or so high to the platform is more convenient and less stressful to the back than one that is lower. Vertical stands for large-format cameras need to be formidably rigid and heavy, but a wall-mounted appliance of the sort mentioned in the previous chapter should serve. If a monorail camera is being used, the rail should, if possible, be supported at both ends to minimise vibration and to relieve the strain on the bush. Vertical stands for 35 mm and medium-format cameras can be smaller and lighter, although they must be just as rigid. There are a number of such stands on the market which work well enough. The points to look for are: that the column should be strongly bolted to the baseboard and itself rigid and non-vibrating (box-section columns are usually stiffer than circular ones); that the vertical adjustment mechanism should be smooth and not likely to work slack with time, and that it should have a position-locking device to clamp it in position; that there should be some

Plate 70   Macro 2000 close-up stand.

degree of horizontal adjustment on the arm that carries the camera so that different formats of camera can be used; and that the plate on to which the camera bolts should be short enough that the rewind button of a 35 mm camera can be reached. Preferably the whole unit should be black-finished rather than bright metal, and it is of advantage that the camera-carrying head should incorporate a fine-focussing movement.

Quite a satisfactory stand can in fact be built using an old enlarger column and laboratory scaffolding. For temporary use, or for use in the field, a stout tripod with a reversible head or column is adequate. The pan-and-tilt head is attached to the bottom of the column, or the whole column reversed, so that the camera is slung beneath the tripod and points downward. Such an arrangement is always more stable than merely tilting the head down through 90° or using a cross-arm.

One manufacturer makes a vertical macrophotography stand (Macro 2000, made by Industria Fototecnica, Firenze) (Plate 70) incorporating pinpoint quartz lamps of a colour temperature suitable for tungsten-type film; most other lighting units supplied with vertical stands are really intended for copying and are too diffuse and too inflexible for photographing objects. Another useful device for close-up photography of *in situ* detail is a stand of the 'Copipod' type (Plate 71). These consist of a collar which screws into the front of the lens mount, tapped to take four telescopic legs, the spread ends of which define the field of view. They are intended for copying documents, and the marked positions of the leg extensions cover different sizes of paper from A4 upwards. The legs can, however, easily be replaced by shorter struts to give standardised, close-up views of smaller areas, using a macro lens. They are particularly useful for the routine photography of such things as textiles and basketry undergoing conservation.

Whatever device is used, it is important to ensure that camera and object are motionless at the moment of exposure. As well as camera-shake due to a flimsy support or shutter vibration, there are often floor vibrations from various causes in all but the most solid buildings. If a choice exists, it is advisable to work at ground or basement level, and it may even be necessary to operate at night or at weekends when traffic and building use are at a minimum. If a shutter is particularly noisy or violent, and always for extreme close-up work, it is preferable to expose by switching the light on and off with the shutter locked open. Exposures for close-up photography are rarely shorter than about a second, so timing them should present no problem; to ensure accuracy an enlarger timer can be wired into the circuit. Vibration or camera-shake, even if quite slight, may produce an overall degradation of the negative's resolution, not as obvious as a doubled image, and perhaps not readily identified.

Because of the shallow depths of field involved in close-up photography, it is essential to ensure that the film plane and the main plane of the object are parallel. A simple way to check this is to lay a small mirror in the object plane and focus the reflection of the lens. If the image is centred in the viewfinder, the two planes will be parallel.

Backgrounds and mounting
Assuming that the primary requirement is the recording of clear, accurate information, with aesthetic considerations a long way second, black or white backgrounds are the most suitable for black and white photographs, and black or white, or subdued unobtrusive colours, for colour photography.

A shadowless white background can be contrived either by photographing

Plate 71   Copipod stand.

over a light-box – a rather inflexible arrangement unless the box is fitted with a dimmer switch – or by placing the object on a sheet of non-reflective glass or clear plastic raised above a white independently-lit background. The glass should be sufficiently far above the background that shadows thrown by the object are clear of the format area. It is also important that the background area should be neither too large nor too brightly lit. A large, brightly lit background will over-light the edges of the object, giving a halo effect, and may, by directing strong peripheral rays into the lens barrel, result in flare, an effect that degrades image detail and contrast. For the same reason it is always advisable to use a lens hood for close-up work. The lit background should be masked off to an area only a little larger than the picture size, and the level of illumination should be just sufficient to kill shadows on the glass and to ensure a white background in the print.

A solid black background is a little more difficult to achieve. Black cotton velvet is probably the most non-reflective material, but even this may show a distinct texture if glancing light catches it, and if it is within the depth of field of the focussed lens. For objects of the size of coins or brooches, it is usually possible to contrive a way to support them one or two centimetres above the surface of the material, and thus to throw the background out of focus. Plasticine or modelling wax is not very suitable, since velvet marks so easily, but if short, black-painted, lengths of dowel or of hard-setting moulding material are prepared with pins set in one end, they can be pushed through the velvet into a piece of fibre-board beneath without marking the cloth. The object is then balanced on the upper end. This works very well with single objects immediately beneath the lens; but if a number of objects are photographed together, it is difficult to avoid the supports of the objects at the edges of the frame appearing in the photograph. Another and slightly more elaborate method is to use a topless box, each side about 10 or 15 cm square, black-painted on the inside. The base of the box has a number of holes drilled in it and vertical dowels or wires are set in these holes and support the objects just above the rim of the box. So long as light is not directed down into the box, this gives an excellent solid black background, but there is always a danger of a fragile object overbalancing and falling to the bottom. As a general rule, fragile objects, even of metal or ceramic, should never be fixed to a support with adhesive or plasticine; the possibility of staining or of lifting off the surface is too great. In special cases, the support can be shaped to fit the object.

These methods, or some variation of them, will serve well enough for discrete, solid objects down to 0.5 cm or so across. Smaller than this, however, and for such things as small beads, grain, or fragments of textile, a flat surface is necessary. No material is completely satisfactory, most being either too reflective or, like velvet, having too deep a nap. Perhaps the best available is black carbon paper of the sort used for typewriters. This is reasonably satisfactory, and cheap enough that when it becomes marked or creased, as it does very easily, it can be replaced. Some workers use black silica beads as a background for photographing grain. These can be obtained in very fine grades, and although they are not reflectionless, they are regular enough in shape and size to give an unobtrusive background and cradle the grains effectively.

Both black and white backgrounds can be used for colour photography. Black is achieved by any of the methods just described, but a light-box fitted with fluorescent tubes will not give a white background on tungsten colour film, but a rather unpleasant green-blue. This can be neutralised to white with a sheet of amber acetate, but achieving a pure white may take some experimentation with different strengths of colour. Strongly coloured backgrounds should be avoided as distracting, and close proximity of a coloured background can result in a colour-cast on the object. If the object is on a sheet of glass above a coloured, and especially a dark-coloured, background, reflections can be a problem, and they are often not easily noticed in the focussing screen or viewfinder. A sensible precaution is to interpose a sheet of black card between the camera and the object, with a hole cut in it large enough to admit the lens. This will at least cut out reflections of the camera itself.

Types of lighting
Lighting is by far the most important element in close-up photography, and is therefore dealt with in some detail here. The arrangement of the apparatus, the exposure, and the processing of the film can all be standardised easily enough, but the intensity, direction and balance of the lighting can make or mar the final result, and must be adjusted quite finely.

Close-up photography can, if necessary, be undertaken by natural light, either shadowed daylight or even direct sunlight. Obviously the direction of the light can be altered only by rotating or tilting the object. Direct sun gives too harsh a light for most purposes, but hazy sunlight, or sunlight diffused by a sheet of gauze or muslin, can give quite satisfactory results. However, artificial light is certainly easier to control and more flexible in use. Fortunately, the area to be covered by the lights is never more than a few centimetres across, and quite low-wattage lights are sufficient. For temporary use, a couple of desk lamps with 100 watt bulbs can be used, with, if possible, a third to light the background. Internally silvered reflector bulbs can also be used, but care must be taken to mask the lens from stray rays of light (see Plate 59). Such lights, however, are only really suitable for black and white photography. For colour photography, on tungsten-balanced film, they would give a decidedly yellow cast to the result. It might be possible to overcome this by using a bluish conversion filter (Wratten 80D or 82A) over the lens, but the colour of light from low-wattage bulbs can vary considerably depending on their age and on the mains voltage, and the results may be unpredictable. It is better, if possible, to use low-voltage tungsten-halogen

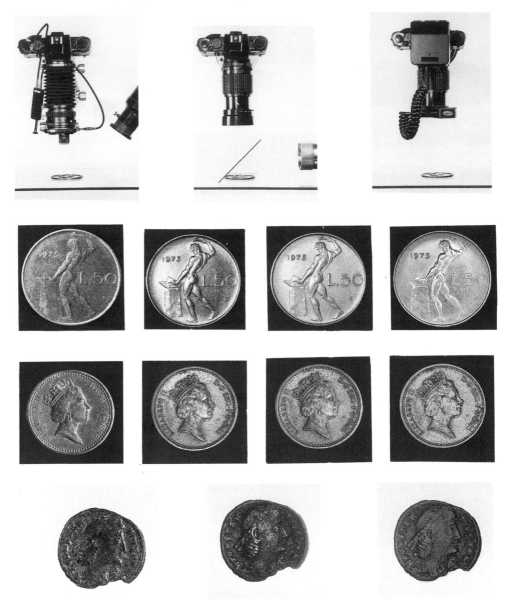

Plate 72   Oblique, axial and ring-flash lighting. The upper row shows firstly a
35 mm camera fitted with bellows, a reversed 50 mm macro lens and oblique
microscope lamp; secondly, a 35 mm camera with a 100 mm macro lens and
axial lighting by a projector and 45° plane glass; and, thirdly, a 35 mm camera
with 100 mm macro lens and ring flash. The second row shows a very bright
metal coin lit by oblique, direct axial, baffled axial, and ring-flash lighting; the
third row a medium-tone coin similarly lit; and the fourth row a very dark coin
with oblique, direct axial, and ring-flash lighting. The light coin is probably best
shown by baffled axial lighting, the medium-toned by oblique, and the
dark-toned by ring flash.

lamps (lamps intended for colour enlargers, e.g. Osram 8v, 50 w Bellaphot lamps), which maintain a constant colour temperature and, if properly housed, give out little heat. Either kind of lamp will give reasonably well-resolved detail at magnifications up to about 2:1. At higher magnifications, though, the fineness of detail that can be recorded is largely dependent on the resolution of 'point lights' – the reflections from minute irregularities on the surface of the object – and the size of these reflections, in turn, is a function of the size of the light source; the smaller the source, the smaller the reflection and the better the resolution. At these magnifications, then, the ideal light source has the smallest possible filament with a minimum of spread. Either microscope lamps, or small projector bulbs with the filament turned end-on to the object, can be used.

There are three basic arrangements of lighting for close-up photography: oblique, where the strongest light falls against the sides of the relief and the face of the object is darker in tone; axial, where the light is along or parallel to the lens axis, and the face is therefore lighter than the relief; and diffused, where the light is thrown almost evenly over the object (Plate 72).

Plate 73   Direction of lighting. The eye will generally assume that the light is coming from the top of the picture. The lower of the two photographs gives the correction impression – the stamp is in the bottom of the bowl. In fact, both prints are from the same negative; if the picture is turned top-to-bottom the effect is reversed.

Oblique lighting

For objects of low relief, which includes most coins, fragments of surface-decorated material, beads and seal impressions, one lamp at an angle to the object of 20–50° will suffice for the main light. It is important that the main light comes from the top (if indeed the object has a top and a bottom). There is a well-known optical illusion whereby the eye assumes that objects are top-lit. If the lighting comes from an unfamiliar direction, a dome can appear to be a hollow and vice versa (Plate 73).

A single oblique light will usually cast strong shadows and give too great a contrast in the negative. Nearly always it is necessary either to use a second, fill-in light, or to reflect light back into the shadows with a mirror, or a curved 'wall' of aluminium foil. The latter alternatives are preferable, since a second light, if not carefully controlled, can throw a second shadow.

If the surface of the object is at all shiny, such an arrangement will probably still give too high a contrast level. The edges of the relief of a silver coin, for example, may be rendered as hard white lines. In such cases much better results can be obtained if the main light is somewhat diffused. Sections of white plastic bottles and funnels make excellent diffusers when placed between the main light source and the object. They are rarely completely white, however, and for colour work new white acetate or fibre-glass web is preferable. If various combinations of distance and angle of light, and distance and position of reflector and diffuser, are tried and the results observed through the viewfinder, it is usually possible to find one particular combination that will show the relief detail without undue harshness, and will render the body of the object in somewhere near the correct tone.

A variation of this method of lighting – peripheral lighting – entails positioning three or four lamps around the object so that their light is just skimming across its surface. This can work very well for flat, light-coloured objects with crisp, unworn relief. With domed or concave objects this lighting is likely to be too uneven, and with dark objects there may be too little light reflected from the surface.

A method has been described in Buchanan (1986) for achieving peripheral lighting using either a ring-flash or an ordinary small flash unit. The object is placed on a stage within a plastic cylinder, the flash is so positioned that peripheral light is reflected from the inner wall of the cylinder across the object, and the camera is clamped to the top of the cylinder. The purpose of the device is to act as a simply-constructed, compact and portable unit for photographing such things as coins in museums or on a site with a minimum of setting-up time, and giving well-lit and standardised results.

Axial lighting

For objects of high relief, where oblique lighting would give a jumble of shadows and reflections no matter how carefully arranged (and, oddly enough, for objects of shallow but thinly incised relief, for example a scratched initial on the back of a brooch) lighting is better arranged axially, as if the main light were directed down the lens barrel. By this method the main surface of the object receives most of the illumination and the exposure is therefore based on the light reflected from this surface. This has the advantage that the tone of the surface is correctly recorded (with oblique lighting, because the main surface is necessarily always darker than the relief, it is rarely of the correct tone). The method is suitable for flat objects – coins, medallions, the flat surface of scarabs and so on – but is not always successful with domed objects or with objects of relatively great vertical height. This is because all the methods of achieving axial light entail having a light source, direct or reflected, close to the lens, and with such a short throw of light, fall-off, top to bottom, can be considerable.

Near-axial light can be achieved by means of a ring light, which encircles the lens and throws an even, fairly soft, light straight down on to the object. Such ring lights can be contrived using a ring of small tungsten bulbs, but the heat produced will certainly do no good to either the lens or the object. Small ring-shaped fluorescent tubes are obtainable, effective for black and white, although they can give strange results with colour film. Their light is very soft indeed and really closer to diffused light than to axial, but for things like matted-together fragments of textile they can be very effective. There is a type of illuminated magnifier with a fluorescent ring-tube surrounding a magnifying glass, mounted on an 'Anglepoise' type of arm and base. With the magnifying glass removed this can be most conveniently used as a fluorescent ring-light. Care must be taken to use a lens hood long enough to prevent light from the tube affecting the lens.

Ring-flash units can give excellent results over a limited range of magnification. They can be used successfully for most non-shiny objects, including some coins, although they suffer from the same problem of fall-off as do other axial sources. By far the easiest to use are those with automatic control – the duration of the flash being set either by a photoelectric cell on the flash or by the camera's meter. It is difficult to use a manually controlled ring-flash since neither of the two variables normally used to control a manual flash unit's output are available. Distance cannot be adjusted since the flash has to be positioned on the lens, and the aperture, although still adjustable to control the amount of light within limits, has also to be set in accordance with the requirements of depth of field. Ring-flash has the advantage of complete portability, so that the photographer is not dependent on the lights available in, for example, different museums. He is limited, though, in both the type of object it can be used for and the degree of magnification. With coins or other objects that are at all shiny, it often gives unacceptably hard reflections, and if the lens, and consequently the flash, is closer than about 20 cm to the object, the effect of a parallel-sided beam of axial light is lost, and the object is simply flooded with harsh light from all directions, and shape and texture merge.

If the object is markedly convex or concave, and therefore the overall shape might well be lost by straight axial lighting, it is sometimes effective to block off one quadrant (other things being equal, it should be the lower right quadrant) of the ring with black tape. This will give a slightly directional quality to the light. As well as ordinary ring-flash units there are also available a few units consisting of small separate tubes or heads, arranged like a ring-flash but which can be independently switched to give the effect of light from a quarter, a half, three-quarters, or the whole of the ring. With some, also, the units can be moved slightly away from the lens axis to give more oblique lighting.

An alternative method of axial lighting can be arranged by setting a piece of plane glass between the lens and the object at an angle of 45°. A beam of light is directed at the underside of the glass, which reflects part of the light down on to the object, and the photograph is taken through the back of the glass. This method works very well if a few precautions are taken. The glass must be optically flat and the beam striking it must be even and, preferably, parallel-sided, and coming from a direction at right-angles to the lens axis. A small spotlight or a microscope lamp will serve as a light source, but a slide projector is particularly suitable. The condenser system of the projector should ensure an even beam, and a masked-down slide in the projector will serve to restrict the beam to just the area needed.

There is an upper limit to the size of object that can be illuminated in this way, since the size of the beam, and of the glass, must obviously be big enough to cover the object; and a limit on magnification dictated by the lens-to-object distance, which must be sufficient to accommodate the inclined glass. For very small objects – seeds or the like – a microscope slide cover glass can be used for the inclined reflector. One other precaution is necessary: the glass must be shielded so that no light or reflection can reach its upper surface and be reflected into the lens and cause flare. For objects of a light or middle tone, plane glass, even though it will reflect down only about 10% of the light, will serve. For dark-toned objects, however, this limited amount of light may result in inordinately long exposures, and even then the darkest areas may not be recorded; it is worth trying a semi-silvered mirror with a 50% reflectance. Obviously the mirror must be of very good quality, otherwise the quality of the image will suffer. As with oblique lighting and flash, the relief edges of very shiny objects can show burnt-out highlights with axial lighting. This can be modified by means of a piece of lightly frosted glass or plastic held between the light source and the reflecting glass; this spreads the light slightly and spills some obliquely onto the object. By adjusting the angle of the frosted glass while watching the effect through the viewfinder, the ratio of axial to oblique light can be varied, and a quite remarkable degree of control over the rendering of detail of tone can be achieved.

Diffused lighting

For some objects of simple shape where relief needs no emphasis, or of very complex shape where emphasising one aspect of relief entails suppressing another, and for objects like jewellery where spots of highlight or shadow might obscure or distort the appearance of the surface, it can be effective to employ completely diffused lighting, coming more or less evenly from all directions. There are several ways of achieving this sort of lighting. The object, or the object and the camera, can be surrounded by a wall of white paper or fabric, and light directed either through it from the outside or against it from the inside. The top half of a large white plastic bottle or the bottom of a funnel can be used in the same way for small objects. One quite effective method is to stand the object on a light-box and over it place either a truncated funnel covered on the inside with crumpled aluminium foil or, if one can be obtained, a hemispherical mirror with a hole in its apex for the lens (a car headlamp reflector from the days before sealed-beam units is one possible source). Care must be taken with this sort of arrangement to avoid too strong an effect of back-lighting, which may give lens flare or may degrade the edges of the object by penumbral light. If, with the same arrangement, the object stands on a disc of black velvet of about half the diameter of the funnel, diffuse lighting can be obtained against a black background, or light to particularly reflective parts of the object can be restricted by means of shaped slips of black paper inside the funnel. There are many variations of this sort of lighting, and only experimentation will show the best variant for a particular object.

One further type of diffused lighting, suitable for photographing dark but shiny objects such as polished tools of basalt or small highly glazed objects, which can be particularly difficult to light adequately, is to immerse them in a beaker of water or other liquid, and to direct light through the beaker. The liquid acts as a diffuser and baffle and gives the object a surface sheen, revealing its texture, but without strong highlights. The obvious drawback to this method is that few antiquities other than stone can safely be immersed in water or any other liquid. The whole arrangement must of course be absolutely stable, since the slightest movement of the liquid would completely distort the image.

Scales

The making of scales, and the lengths desirable for close-up photography, were mentioned in Chapter 3. It is, obviously, important to include a scale or to print the negatives to a set scale in close-up work, particularly when the image is magnified. It is also important, however, not to include a scale that overwhelms the image of the object, and to make sure that the scale is clean and with accurately cut edges. An enlarged image of a grubby and battered scale can detract from the value of a photograph. It is advisable to have a stock not only of scales of different sizes (e.g. 0.5, 1, 3, 5, 10 cm), but also of scales on different sizes and thicknesses of mount. In particular, some should be printed on the extreme edge of larger pieces of card so that they can lie along the bottom side of a frame.

White scales may appear as too glaring against a black or coloured background, and it is useful to have some printed in reverse (white on black), some on coloured paper and some on film, so that the background can show through. For extreme close-up and photomacrography, from say 3:1 upwards, microscope graticule scales can sometimes be used, but usually it is better and less obtrusive to photograph a scale on to an adjoining frame of the film, and to use this as a guide in printing. The two frames should, of course, never be separated, otherwise the negative is virtually useless for future printing.

Any scale must be in the same plane as the object. If it is not, then, apart from loss of accuracy, it will almost certainly be out of focus because of the restricted depth of field available.

Exposure and resolution

One, sometimes two, adjustments of meter-indicated exposure times are usually necessary in close-up photography.

The first is an allowance for magnification. As magnification is increased, so is the distance between lens and film lengthened, with a consequent falling-off in the amount of light reaching the film. This follows from the optical Inverse Square Law, which states: 'When a surface is illuminated by a point source of light, the intensity of illumination at the surface is inversely proportional to the square of its distance from the light source.'

The application of this law is only approximate, since the lens is not a point source of light, but the approximation is close enough for practical purposes. The fall-off is of no consequence with a camera fitted with a through-the-lens exposure meter, since these measure the amount of light reaching the film plane anyway. With a separate, off-the-camera, meter, however, compensation is necessary, since these are calibrated on the assumption that the lens is at or near a distance of one focal length from the film. There are a number of formulae which will give the compensation factor based on the lens-to-image or the lens-to-object distance and the focal length. Perhaps the simplest to remember and use, however, is based only on the degree of magnification:

$$E = (m + 1)^2 \times e$$

where E is the compensated exposure, e is the meter-indicated exposure, and m is the magnification, expressed as a multiple or fraction of same-size (e.g. 1:2 = 0.5, 1:1 = 1, 2:1 = 2, etc.).

Thus, if the image were the same size as the object, i.e. m = 1, then

$$(m + 1)^2 = (1 + 1)^2 = 4,$$

so the compensated exposure would be the meter exposure multiplied by 4. A list of the more commonly used values is given below:

Magnifications		$E = e \times$	
	1:4		1.56
	1:3		1.77
	1:2		2.25
	1:1		4.00
	2:1		9.00
	3:1		16.00
	4:1		25.00

As can be seen, if this factor is neglected, at the higher magnifications there will be very considerable underexposure. The value of m is easy enough to find on a large-format camera: simply compare a dimension of the object with that of its image in the focussing screen. It is a little less simple with a 35 mm reflex system where the eyepiece image cannot be measured. A way round this is to focus the camera and then lay a ruler in the plane of the object and across the width of the format. A 35 mm film frame is 24 mm wide. If, then, 24 mm of the ruler can be seen in the viewfinder, the camera is focussed at 1:1; if 12 mm can be seen, at 2:1; if 48 mm, at 1:2; and so on. The result is only approximate because few viewfinders show the whole of the frame. Most, however, show about 95%, and the method is close enough to give a reliable magnification factor.

Whatever meter system is used, it is important to measure only the light reflected from the object itself, or from something of a similar tone. It is essential to switch off any back-lighting while the reading is being taken, otherwise too short an exposure will almost certainly be indicated. If the object is more or less of a mid-tone, a reading from a neutral grey card is often more accurate than one from the object itself, or, if the arrangement allows of it, a good method is to slide a grey card between the glass supporting the object the and background light.

In theory, this compensation for magnification can be made either by opening the aperture or by lengthening the exposure. In fact, the aperture size is nearly always dictated by factors of depth of field and resolution, so allowance must be made by multiplying exposure time. This in turn may result in very long exposure times and thus necessitate the second adjustment, that for reciprocity failure. The direct reaction of film emulsion to light, i.e. so much exposure results in so much density, holds good only within certain light levels. Below these levels, that is at the sort of light levels needing long exposures, extra exposure is needed to bring the negative to normal density. The amount of extra exposure, and the point at which it becomes necessary,

Table 3. *Exposure adjusted for reciprocity failure*

Indicated exposure (seconds)	Compensated exposure (seconds)	Development
2	5	–
5	12	–
10	50	– 20%
15	100	– 20%
20	180	– 30%
25	210	– 30%
30	250	– 40%

varies from one film to another (and for that matter from one authority to another; the figures given in the literature differ to a surprising extent. A summary and discussion is given in James (1979)). The figures given in Table 3 for a black and white film of medium speed represent, as it were, a median value which seems to work in practice. For the longer exposures, compensation has also to be made in processing to prevent excessive contrast. Again, the figures represent a middle path.

If much work entailing long exposures is contemplated, it is well worth making a test film, starting from the meter-indicated exposure × the compensation for magnification, and giving a series of exposures of × 2, × 4, × 8 and × 16 of this figure for various degrees of magnification, e.g. 1:1, 2:1, 4:1, 8:1 and 10:1 (if the equipment allows of such a close-up). If only the longest of these exposures yield sufficient density, it may then be necessary to repeat the test, giving different development times, until an acceptable contrast level is reached. James suggests that for very high contrasts better results are obtained if a compensating or low-contrast developer is used.

The same sorts of compensation have to be made with colour film, both positive and negative, with the added complication that very long exposures on colour film may result in a change in the colour rendering of the emulsion. Within limits, this can be compensated for by using colour compensating filters. Very extensive trial-and-error experiments would be necessary to find the correct one, but manufacturers publish recommendations for all tungsten films which can be used as a starting point.

At close distances, and especially at magnifications greater than 1:1, the depth of field becomes a major consideration.

Of the various factors that affect the depth of field – focal length, magnification, aperture, and standard of sharpness – the first is relatively unimportant. It is normally desirable to obtain as large a negative image as possible, and if lenses of different lengths are focussed to give the same size of image, then the depths of field will be the same.

The magnification, however, is of critical importance. As this increases the depth of field is reduced very rapidly. Thus, for a circle of confusion[2] of 0.025 mm, a lens at f8 will give the following total depths of field:

Magnification	1:10	1:4	1:2	1:1	2:1	3:1
Depth of field, mm	44	8	2.4	0.8	0.3	0.178

This circle of confusion is, admittedly, small, and parts of an object immediately outside these limits would appear unsharp only on the most critical examination.

One point of importance should be noted in this connection. When focussing on distant objects, the depth of field extends twice as far behind the point of critical focus as it does in front – hence the common practice of focussing on a point one third of the way back in the visible depth of the object. As magnification is increased, however, the point of critical focus moves towards the centre of the depth of field, being exactly at the mid-point at 1:1 (see chapter 2). It is therefore preferable in close-up photography to focus on a point approximately halfway back in the depth of the object.

With any lens at any magnification, the depth of field increases as the aperture is closed down. Thus the figures given above can be expanded to include different apertures, as shown in Table 4. As an *aide-memoire* it can be noted that, at this particular circle of confusion, the 1:4 column is the same as the aperture scale, and the 1:1 column the same as the scale divided by ten.

In view of the rapid reduction of the depth of field with magnification, it might be thought that the smallest possible aperture should always be used. Unfortunately to do so brings its own penalties. Most lenses work best at about the middle of the aperture range – f5.6 to f11 – small enough to lose the aberrations likely with a wide-open lens, and large enough to avoid too much diffraction from the rim of the diaphragm. As the aperture is decreased, however, diffracted light becomes a greater proportion of the total light reaching the negative, an effect which becomes even more marked at high magnifications. At magnifications above 2:1 or 3:1, the smallest apertures will yield an image markedly inferior, in terms of the resolution of detail, to those obtained with larger apertures. Very often, then, it is necessary to seek a compromise between depth of field and resolution of detail, and a number of formulae and graphs have been published by means of which the best compromise can be reached. (Kodak (1969) gives a comprehensive account of these calculations and of the whole field of photomacrography.) In practice, however, it is usually as quick, and certainly simpler, to make a number of exposures at different apertures and to select the negative that has the best resolution and an adequate depth of field.

If the object to be photographed has considerable visible depth for its size – a bead or a pyramidal gaming piece, for example – it may well be impossible to achieve sufficient depth of field even at the smallest aperture. In such a case

---

[2] The largest disc that to the eye will appear indistinguishable from a point.

Table 4. *Depth of field in close-up photography*

	1 : 10	1 : 4	1 : 2	1 : 1	2 : 1	3 : 1
f2	11	2	0.6	0.2	0.076	0.044
2.8	15.4	2.8	0.84	0.28	0.104	0.062
4	22	4	1.2	0.4	0.154	0.088
5.6	30.8	5.6	1.68	0.56	0.2	0.124
8	44	8	2.4	0.8	0.3	0.178
11	60	11	3.3	1.1	0.42	0.24
16	88	16	4.8	1.6	0.6	0.36
22	120	22	6.6	2.2	0.82	0.48 mm

it may be necessary to decrease the magnification on the negative and to enlarge the print proportionately more. This adjustment should be kept to a minimum, as inevitably it will entail some loss of detail.

Finally, the standard of sharpness – the measure of acceptably sharp focus – is obviously an elastic term. Normally, using the equipment and materials available, the photographer aims for the best resolution possible, and this standard has to serve.

Photomicrography

Photomacrography – the photography of objects using macro lens, reversal ring, and extension tubes or bellows – is satisfactory up to a magnification of about 20:1. At higher magnifications it becomes necessary to use the techniques of photomicrography, that is, to use a camera built into or attached to a microscope. Normally, only the body of the camera is used, the image being formed by the lens system of the microscope. Nearly all modern research microscopes incorporate an automatic, built-in, camera, usually 35 mm, so arranged that the eyepiece image is also focussed at the film plane at the same magnification. Mechanically they are simple enough to operate, although the same problems of contrast, resolution and colour fidelity arise as with any other form of close-up photography.

If there is not such a built-in camera, an SLR 35 mm camera body can be used, attached to the microscope eye-piece by an adaptor collar; or one of the range of cameras specifically designed for use on a microscope can be used. These consist of adaptor tubes topped by 35 mm or larger format film backs, and which incorporate right-angle viewing eyepieces. Their only real advantages over standard 35 mm bodies lie in the facility for using different sizes of film, and in the position of their built-in shutters which, being close to the microscope eyepiece, are optically preferable. It is also possible to use a large-format, bellows, camera centred over the eyepiece.

For anything other than built-in automatic cameras, the centring of the image, adjustment of illumination and allowance for extra magnification involve a fair amount of skill and knowledge of microscopy in order to achieve good, consistent results. Anyone embarking on a programme of photomicrography would be well-advised to study a standard text book such as Lawson (1972) or Duke and Michette (1990), before starting.

So far as the purely photographic considerations are concerned, most microscope lighting systems are balanced for tungsten-type colour film, although colour-correction filters may well be necessary. High-contrast film with fine grain and good resolution is to be preferred, for example the Kodak 35 mm type 2483, which is designed for photomicrography, although unfortunately this still has to be developed by the E4 process which few laboratories now undertake. Any fine-grain, moderately contrasty panchromatic film is suitable for black and white photomicrography. This may involve the use of contrast filters, and it may be necessary to manipulate the film development to increase or decrease contrast, depending on the nature of the run of specimens.

A certain amount of care is needed in printing black and white negatives, both to retain fine differences of tone and to ensure that enlargement does not result in 'empty magnification'. This can occur if the microscope's magnification is at or near the limits of the combined optical system, when further enlargement of the negative will not reveal more detail but will merely result in coarsening of the image; this may well give the false impression that there is no finer detail of the structure present.

Negatives produced by scanning electron microscopy should present fewer problems. Since the image is formed by an electron stream and not by visible light, it is always black and white, although colour can be introduced on the print. The camera forms an integral part of the microscope, and such things as tonal range and contrast (and the amazing depth of field) are functions controlled by the apparatus and not by photographic means.

11

ULTRA-VIOLET AND INFRA-RED PHOTOGRAPHY

The sensitivity of all silver-based emulsions extends into parts of the electro-magnetic spectrum of shorter wavelength than visible light (ultra-violet, UV); and by using specially sensitized emulsions, use can be made of the wave-lengths longer than visible light (infra-red, IR).

The UV ranges from about 1 nm (nanometre; one nm = 10^{-9} m, or one millionth of a millimetre), taken to be the upper limit of the longest X-rays, to about 400 nm, the shortest band of visible light. The UV spectrum is conven-tionally divided into three or four bands, but for the purposes of photography only two are of importance; the long-wave UV band (also known as Near UV or UVA) from about 320 to 400 nm, and the Middle UV or UVB, from 280 to 320 nm.[1] The peak response of silver emulsions is in the region from 350 to 400 nm, and it is with this band that most UV photography is concerned.

The IR is that part of the spectrum longer than about 700 nm; it merges with microwaves at about 300,000 nm, and beyond that with the radar band. Although images can be formed by means of thermal detectors and image intensifiers in the longer IR and beyond, most photography uses the near, or actinic, part of the IR between 700 and 900 nm.

The division between the infra-red, the visible and the ultra-violet parts of the spectrum is of course arbitrary, and one part of the whole spectrum of radiation merges with the next.

Ultra-violet and ultra-violet fluorescence photography

There are two quite distinct ways in which the UV spectrum is used in photography. One is direct UV, or UV reflectance, where what are recorded are the UV rays reflected from a surface; the other is UV fluorescence, where the camera records the rays that reach the surface as UV but are reflected as visible light (Plates 74, 75 and 76).

Direct UV has only a limited value in archaeology and conservation. Its chief use is in such fields as dermatology, where the different UV reflectance of living tissue in different conditions is of great importance. It has been used for the enhancement of contrast between faded or over-written inks and the paper background, and it is sometimes (but not always) of value in the

---

[1] Other systems of subdivision use similar terms to refer to different groupings, and if possible actual wavelengths should be identified, rather than relying on such terms as 'long', 'short', 'medium', 'Near', 'Far', or 'A', 'B', 'C'.

Plate 74

Plate 75

Plate 76

Panchromatic, direct UV and UV fluorescence. Plate 74 shows a lime-encrusted pot with an area of lighter slip. In Plate 75, taken by UV fluorescence, both encrustation and slip fluoresce strongly, while in Plate 76, by direct UV, the encrustation hardly records and the slip can be seen beneath it.

examination of ceramics that are covered by lime incrustations. The incrustation very commonly found on pottery from tombs cut in limestone records clearly in panchromatic, as it does in fluorescence photography, but much less so by direct UV. Decoration or surface coating of a pot masked by such incrustation can thus be more clearly recorded.

With UV fluorescence photography, what is being recorded is not the UV rays reflected from the surface, but visible light *resulting* from UV rays that reach the surface but are reflected as radiation of longer wavelengths. This general phenomenon is known as luminescence (fluorescence if the reflection lasts only as long as the incident ray, known as the 'exciting' ray, is present; phosphorescence if the effect persists after the exciting ray ceases). It is a widespread occurrence both in living organisms such as fireflies and luminous fish (bioluminescence) and in organic materials, e.g. 'whiter than white' detergents. The exciting rays may be X-rays, short or long UV, electron streams or visible light; and the emitted rays may be in the visible spectrum or in the IR.

Fluorescence in the visible spectrum can be of different colours, depending on the substance being excited, and these colour differences, and their intensity, have been used successfully in the non-destructive analysis of minerals and pigments. In conservation photography, however, very often just the presence of a fluorescing area on an artifact is informative. Heavily worn decoration on pots can be revealed in greater detail, overwritten or partly obliterated inscriptions on both parchment and paper can be made clearer, and, particularly useful, patches of old adhesive on previously restored artifacts very often become obvious. In the conservation of paintings, UV fluorescence, like IR photography, has for long been a standard tool for the detection of over-painting, retouching and past restoration. Fluorescence photography is less used in archaeology than in conservation, although attempts have been made to utilise it in the study of cave paintings – not entirely successfully, since the subsequent deposits that may mask the paintings are nearly always of calcium carbonate, which itself fluoresces strongly and further obscures the painting. It has also been used to establish the position of occupation areas in cave deposits that have been subjected to secondary deposition.

Radiation sources and lenses for ultra-violet photography
Both direct and fluorescence UV photography need a radiation source which provides a high output of UV, since the degree of reflectance is usually low in this part of the spectrum and exposures would otherwise be intolerably long. Both sunlight and tungsten light have too low a proportion of UV in their overall output to be of much value. The most convenient sources are mercury vapour lamps and fluorescent tubes. Both can be obtained so filtered as to give peak emissions either in the long UV, at about 360 nm, or in the short, at

about 250 nm. For large objects like paintings, where even, overall illumination is important, tubes are more suitable, while for small objects mercury lamps, which give a spread similar to that of a spotlight, are best. For direct UV photography, a source could be used that emitted visible light as well as UV, since any visible light is filtered out at the camera lens, but for fluorescence photography the source must emit predominantly UV, with as little other radiation as possible. Lamps and tubes for this purpose incorporate an integral filter (a Woods filter), and are coated so as to emit almost entirely UV of a specified wavelength; they usually emit also a little blue light, but not enough to swamp the fluorescence. In order to allow of both sorts of photography, filtered lamps are preferable. Electronic flash can also be used for both types, if the unit is fitted with an appropriate filter.

Most standard camera lenses will transmit radiation down to about 320 nm, although transmission may be only partial in the shorter wavelengths. Direct UV photography is therefore possible over the whole of the long UV range. For shorter wavelengths it is necessary to use a lens with elements fabricated from quartz (though other materials have been used) with an extended transmission range. Such lenses are manufactured by a number of companies, including Pentax, Zeiss and Nikon, with various focal lengths and able to transmit wavelengths down to about 200 nm. They are extremely expensive, and for occasional use, hiring is a better proposition than buying. A few standard lenses, including some Leitz lenses, have built-in filtration that excludes the UV; these obviously cannot be used for direct UV photography.

Direct ultra-violet photography

All that is necessary for direct UV photography is a radiation source rich in UV of the appropriate wavelength and a filter on the lens that will transmit UV but exclude all visible light. Suitable filters are the Wratten 18A, Ilford 828 and Chance OX.1. These filters are available only in glass.

Although, as with IR, the UV wavelengths come to focus at a slightly different point than does visible light, the difference is so slight that the focus will be sharp enough if a stop of f8 or smaller is used. Exposure determination is not easy with direct UV, since ordinary light meters are ineffective. There are UV radiometers that will measure UV intensity, but they have to be re-calibrated to serve as light meters. By far the most effective way of estimating exposure is by experiment. It may be necessary to give a long series of exposures, starting at, say, 1 sec and doubling the exposure up to, say 16 min. A series of this length is necessary, at least for the first attempt, because of the widely different output of UV sources. Once a standard is established, it will serve as a basis for future exposures so long as the lamps are used at a similar distance.

Virtually any black and white film can be used (there is little point in using colour film), but a film with a speed of about 100 ISO is most suitable, giving good resolution with reasonable speed. Processing is normal, although it is often necessary to extend the development time to achieve a reasonable degree of contrast on the negative.

Ultra-violet fluorescence photography

With UV fluorescence photography, the need is to ensure as far as possible that only UV radiation reaches the object, and that only the fluorescence excited in the visible spectrum is recorded. Lamps must therefore be filtered to emit UV, with minimum visible light (there is always a slight spill-over into the blue/violet with integrally filtered lamps and tubes). The operation must take place in a darkened room or cabinet, and the lens must be filtered to exclude residual UV, otherwise the film will record both the fluorescence and the UV reflectance, and the latter may overwhelm the former. A light yellow filter, known as a barrier filter, Wratten 2A or 2B, is usually effective both in filtering out the UV and in reducing the effect of the background blue/violet. Problems may arise if the fluorescence itself is in this part of the spectrum; the filter cannot be expected to admit fluorescence while blocking out background radiation of similar wavelength. The only recourse is to put 18A filters over the lamps, which together with their integral filters should eliminate all but the UV completely, and to use a colourless UV barrier filter, e.g. Wratten 1A, over the lens.

Since what is being recorded is visible light, in theory it is possible to measure the surface reflectance with a light meter, and to work out an exposure in the normal way (cadmium meters are a good deal more effective than selenium meters in low light levels). In practice, reflectance is likely to be so low, and consequently exposures so long, that allowance for reciprocity failure becomes necessary, and first-time accuracy is difficult to achieve. As with direct UV, it is usually easier and quicker to start with a series of test exposures and thus to establish a standard around which future exposures can be bracketed.

For black and white photography, any medium-speed panchromatic film will serve. For colour, daylight-type emulsions are reckoned to give better results than tungsten-type because of their better balanced response to the blue end of the spectrum.

Long exposures with colour film can distort the colour balance, and it is necessary to follow the makers' instructions in using colour-correcting filters to restore this balance. In order to reduce, if not eliminate, the need for additional filtering, it is advisable to use a fast film – 200 ISO or faster – and to use as large an aperture as possible. If extra filters are needed, they should be placed between the barrier filter and the lens. Both positive and negative colour film can be used, and a barrier filter similar to that used for black and white photography is usually effective (with the same proviso about recording fluorescence at the blue end of the visible spectrum). Normal film processing should be all that is necessary.

Infra-red and infra-red fluorescence photography
IR recording is normally used for the following purposes:

(1)   For an increased penetration of atmospheric haze, and also in turbid water;
(2)   To differentiate between materials that have a similar visual appearance but which reflect IR differently;
(3)   To record images without using visible light to illuminate them;
(4)   To record thermal radiation.

Only the first two of these applications are of interest in archaeology and conservation.

In aerial and long-distance photography it is often possible to achieve far better definition of distant land-forms or buildings by using IR rather than panchromatic emulsions. The scattering of light in the atmosphere affects short wavelengths more than long, and yellow, orange and red filters will each give progressively greater definition of distant detail by restricting the section of the spectrum recorded, at the cost of some distortion of tones. Even more penetration is obtained by using only the IR, although there is a limit to what can be achieved. The degree of penetration depends largely on the size and distribution of water droplets in the atmosphere, and in practical terms when visibility drops to one kilometre or less atmospheric saturation will be so high that IR will yield no better results than will visible light photography. A further limitation is that an IR image has an inherently lower resolution than does a visible light image. The advantage of greater penetration may therefore be counterbalanced by the loss of detail in the negative.

The difference in reflectance between IR and visible light has also been used in aerial photography, with both black and white and colour IR emulsions, for recording crop- and soil-marks and for the study of vegetation. Two other techniques may prove to be of value in archaeological aerial photography in the future, although neither has yet been fully developed or exploited. One is multi-band photography whereby, using several cameras simultaneously, records are made of clearly delimited bands of the visible and IR spectrum. Comparison and superimposition of these images, together with computer enhancement, can be of value for both visual and quantitative estimations of natural resources, morphology and settlement. The other technique uses the longer IR wavelengths to measure and plot small temperature differences. As can often be seen at a time of thaw, reflection of heat may vary slightly across buried structures, and by recording these variations by means of an IR thermal detector, it may be possible to build up an image of the buried structure. The chief problem still to be overcome is that thermal differences in the atmosphere – particularly in sunlight – completely blanket the surface differences.

IR photography is a most useful tool, if rather an unpredictable one, in the examination of painted surfaces on canvas or wood, and of textiles, leather and parchment. Many pigments reflect IR and the degree of reflectance differs greatly from one pigment to another, even though visually they may appear very similar. In particular, natural pigments may show a completely different degree of IR reflectance than do modern aniline-based colours. In addition, the penetrative power of IR can be used to record details masked by semi-opaque varnish and to examine under-painting. With canvas-based

Plate 77, Plate 78   Panchromatic and IR images. Plate 72 shows one door of a rather grimy and repainted ikon, taken on panchromatic film (FP4). Plate 78 shows the same door taken with IR film (Kodak 4143) and an IR filter (Wratten 88A).

paintings, or those on thin wooden panels, often the most effective way of recording under-painting is to trans-illuminate the picture, that is, to photograph through the back of the painting with a fairly strong light on the front of it. Either direct or luminescence recording may be used.

Traces of dyes and pigments on textiles, leather, parchment and occasionally on ceramics are often clearly visible by IR photography even though the base-material may have been darkened by age or grime or by partial carbonisation (Plates 77 and 78). The remarkably clear records of the Qumran scrolls were obtained by IR fluorescence photography.

Radiation sources, lenses, filters and materials for IR photography
The factors which affect the choice of IR radiation source, lenses, camera filters and film emulsion are common to both direct and fluorescence IR photography.

Both tungsten bulbs and electronic or expendable flash contain high levels of IR radiation and can be used without difficulty. Daylight is a very variable source for while direct sunshine is rich in IR, in cloudy conditions the proportion of IR to visible light drops considerably, and the exposure indicated by a light meter would probably have to be doubled or trebled.

Normal optical glass will transmit IR through the whole of the actinic range. However, owing to chromatic aberration the IR image is formed a little farther from the lens than is the image formed by visible light. The usual practice with large-format cameras is to focus the image through a red filter and to expose using an aperture of f16 or smaller, relying on the depth of focus to produce an acceptably sharp image. Many 35 mm lenses have a small red bar or spot just to the left of the central distance indicator on the lens barrel. The image is focussed in the normal way and the distance shown against the central indicator then reset to the IR mark. But again it is advisable to use a small aperture. Another method may be used for critical work and for photomicrography. This relies on the assumption that the focus of the IR is about as far from the red focus as the red is from the green. The image is first critically focussed through a green filter and the focussing tube marked at this point; it is then refocussed through a red filter and this point also marked. The focus is then extended by the difference between the two marks.

Panchromatic black and white film emulsion, unfiltered, is sensitive to the ultra-violet and the visible spectrum up to wave-lengths of about 700 nm. By incorporating sensitising dyes into the emulsion, the range can be extended into the IR up to approximately 900 nm, i.e. to cover the actinic section of the IR spectrum. Beyond this, spectrographic plates, which require hypersensitisation before exposure, can record images by wavelengths up to about 1200 nm.

The black and white IR film most readily available is Kodak HS IR film

Type 4143 (5 × 4 in) or 2481 (35 mm). A similar film is produced by Agfa-Gevaert, Scientia 52A86, while Polaroid market an IR print film, Type 413, and both Kodak and Ilford will supply spectrographic IR plates to special order.

All IR films are sensitive also to visible light, in fact more so than they are to the IR wavelength, and it is necessary to use a lens filter to exclude all or part of the visible spectrum. A Wratten filter 87 or 88A will exclude all visible light, and Wratten 25 will filter out all but the red and infra-red (it is often an advantage to include the red end of the spectrum as a background for the IR).

Film speeds are given by the manufacturers to take account of the appropriate filters; thus Kodak recommends ISO 25 to daylight or ISO 64 to tungsten light using an 87 or 88A filter, and double these speeds with a 25 filter. It must be emphasised that these settings are no more than suggestions. Normal exposure meters do not fully measure IR reflection, and the IR may not be proportionate to the reflection of visible light, which is what they do measure; but these settings will usually serve as a starting point.

Black and white IR film is processed in the same way as other black and white film. Kodak recommend D 76 as a standard developer, but it is often necessary to enhance the film's rather low contrast, and for many subjects a rather higher-contrast developer such as Kodak D 19 is preferable.

Kodak manufacture an IR-sensitive colour reversal film (Ektachrome Infrared film 2236, process E4, available only in 35 mm, 36-exposure cassettes) which records visible light plus IR in so-called 'false colour'; green records as blue, red as green and IR as red. The film must be exposed through a yellow filter (Wratten 12) in order to reduce its sensitivity to blue. It is used extensively in aerial photography, particularly for the recording of vegetation, and occasionally in the photography of pigments, but the complete distortion of colours compared with those of the artifact limits its value.

Direct IR photography

For IR reflectance photography it is sufficient to use a light source rich in IR, the appropriate filter, and an IR-sensitive film emulsion. However, some visually opaque materials may transmit IR to some extent, and precautions are necessary to avoid fogging. It is advisable to avoid using wooden cameras or darkslides, or cameras with plastic components, including plastic bellows (leather bellows are usually IR-proof). The plastic shutters of darkslides should also be replaced by metal. Before starting a programme of IR photography, it is as well to test the equipment for IR opacity. This can be done by loading into the camera a sheet, or in the case of a 35 mm camera, a short length, of IR film with a strip of adhesive tape stuck to the emulsion (by the ends only, otherwise the traces of adhesive may be deceiving). With the shutter closed, a bright tungsten light is played over the whole camera, shining it also into the closed lens (the blades of a lens shutter may also be of plastic). The film is developed, and if an image of the strip can be seen on the negative, the camera is not IR-proof. If there is only a slight leak, it should be sufficient to swathe the camera in a double thickness of black cloth with only the lens protruding.

Fogging may also result from the fact that some plastic developing tanks are not IR-proof; and IR may also penetrate thin, unpainted plywood window shutters or darkroom doors, particularly if there is a strong light outside.

One further precaution must be observed. IR emulsions are sensitive to heat, and unexposed film should always be kept in refrigerated storage; the emulsion surface should never be touched with the fingers, and care must be taken not to expose loaded cameras or slides to the heat of the sun or of tungsten lamps.

IR fluorescence photography

It is possible to record the IR luminescence, i.e. the luminescence emitted in the IR but excited by a shorter wavelength, usually blue-green. For this process it is necessary to filter the light source to emit only blue-green (Corning filter 9780) excluding all other visible light, and to use a filter over the lens (Wratten 87 or 88A) admitting only IR. Some pigments and minerals show a strong IR luminescence compared with their IR reflectance.

When taking such a photograph, it is important always to take a comparative photograph using direct IR. Since both direct and fluorescence IR are in a part of the spectrum to which the eye is not sensitive, there is no other way of comparing the two images.

A more extended account of UV and IR photography is given in Arnold, Rolls and Stewart (1971), and of their applications in Kodak (1972) and Kodak (1977b). The use of IR in aerial photography is described in Graham and Read (1986), and in photomicrography in Lawson (1972). The IR luminescence photography of paintings is discussed in Brideman and Gibson (1963).

12

PHOTOGRAPHING FINDS

Once a suitable arrangement of camera and lights has been established and an effective combination of film, exposure and processing decided upon by calculation or by trial runs – and better, by both – the photography of most artifacts can be undertaken with reasonable confidence. Some classes of commonly encountered finds, however, merit special consideration, and for some of them there are conventions of positioning or lighting which help standardise the record and aid comparisons. At the cost of some repetition, some of these are discussed in the following pages.

Pottery and sherds

Pottery is not usually difficult to photograph, but since the criteria of type series can be quite small differences in rim or body shape, ware or decoration, it is important to standardise photographs, and perhaps also to be aware at least to some extent of what the criteria are.

The normal convention is that a single handle should be shown on the right of a pot, from the camera's viewpoint, and a spout or lip on the left (Plate 79).

Plate 79   Conventional viewpoint. The pot is seen from a little above its mid-line, with the spout on the left. Its outline, rim and handles are shown clearly against a white background (see Plate 74 for the same pot against black).

These are not unbreakable rules, however; if, for instance, one side of a pot had been extensively restored, it would be better to show the other side, wherever that put the handle (unless, of course, it was the restoration that was of interest). There is no unanimity about the viewpoint for single pots, some workers preferring to come as close as possible to a profile view, that is, with the lens pointing at exactly the mid-point of the pot, others to take a viewpoint looking down slightly at the pot, so that the rim appears as a shallow elipse. This latter viewpoint has the advantage of showing a little of the interior of the rim, which may or may not be of interest, but, more important, it gives a better impression of the depth of the pot, front to back. Although nearly all pots are circular in plan, there are exceptions; coil-built wares are often not quite circular, which may be an important property, and pilgrim flasks and lamps are far from circular. The depth from front to back – the third dimension – may therefore be important. With a globular pot, or a bowl, the viewpoint should be low enough, and the camera far enough away, for the shape of the base to be visible, and a slight turning away of the pot from a strict profile will often enable the thickness of a strap-handle or the shape of a lip to be seen. Another disadvantage of the profile view is that it may suggest too strongly that the photograph is indeed a true profile. With large vessels especially this can never be the case; from a mid-point the lens must always be looking up slightly at the rim and down slightly at the base. If the profile is all that matters, the pot should be drawn rather than photographed.

As was said in Chapter 9, attention must be paid to arranging the lighting so that the roundness of the pot is apparent, but without too great a range of contrast, so that the texture is emphasised. There are some surfaces that are particularly difficult in this respect, for instance deeply incised wares, and pattern-burnished and glazed wares. The problem with incised wares is not only to avoid too directional and too strong lighting, which could make the incisions appear to be slits, but also to make sure that, because the incisions are distributed around the pot and therefore receive light at different angles, some do not appear to be much deeper or darker than others. Fairly soft, almost overall lighting usually gives the best results. The same method of lighting is normally effective with vessels like face-jars and image-urns and with rusticated wares. Pattern or stripe burnishing can be very subtle indeed, and if the tone of the body is dark, it may be almost impossible to see, let alone record, the pattern or the stripes except by turning the pot under a strong angled light. If the vessel is small, a single fixed spotlight, with a reflector, might reveal the detail; or a moving light may give a better representation, the light being moved in an arc around the front of the pot, at a fixed distance, either immediately above or immediately below the level of the lens.

Burnished wares, and even more glazed wares, present a different problem. Fixed-position light may produce glaring reflections from the surface of the vessel that are not only obtrusive but which can mask important detail. If, on the other hand, the lighting is so overall and bland that there are no reflections at all, the surface may well appear to be matt rather than burnished or glazed. Often the best solution is to illuminate the pot with a single small-diameter lamp, with reflectors, and to position the lamp so that its reflection falls on a part of the body without important detail. In this way the burnish or glaze will be apparent, and if the surface of the pot is touched with plasticine or putty at the point of reflection, its glare can be reduced. As well as individual spots of reflection – 'catch-lights' – glazed and burnished vessels may show areas of more general reflection from windows or white ceilings, or from glancing light. This is often the case with dark-surfaced vessels like red- or black-figure vases. Usually it can be cured by using a polarising filter, but it may also be necessary to restrict with barn-doors the width of beams of light used to illuminate the object.

The use of filters and their characteristics are discussed in the section on filters in Chapter 3. One specific point on their use in the photography of pottery must be made. Polychrome wares normally have no more than two or three colour washes in addition to the body-colour; for example Attic red-figure vases may have only occasional patches of yellow or white on the red figures, against the black background. Such colours may be faded and indistinct, and not at all easy to make out in a black and white photograph. Obviously it is important to distinguish them from each other, and from the background, and for this purpose contrast filters may be necessary; but it is equally important that in a series of photographs of such pots, similar colours should be similarly rendered. If, then, a contrast filter has had to be used to enhance, for instance, the rendering of red detail in one pot, it should also be used to photograph the rest of the series, in order to give a similar range of tones throughout.

Small groups of pottery can be photographed in very much the same way as single pots, except of course that lighting cannot be so individually adjusted. Care has to be taken, however, with the way in which they are arranged. Two, three or even four vessels can usually be placed in an arc so that all are at about the same distance from the lens; but with greater numbers it becomes necessary to rank them in some way, to avoid too strung-out a grouping. Obviously if the pots overlap each other they have to be carefully placed so that no important features are masked, that no pot casts a shadow across another, and that details such as handles and spouts are shown against clear backgrounds. If sizes are very different, for example one jar 40 cm tall and three or four smaller ones 10 or 15 cm high, it is worth arranging a glass or perspex shelf part-way across the frame and about halfway up the height of the jar, so that the smaller vessels are at two levels. With large groups of pottery, the problems become greater. With a tomb group, for instance, of thirty or forty vessels, there can really be no arrangement that will give a similar viewpoint of all the pots and dishes. The best that can be done is to arrange them up a flight of steps or a series of shelves, and to take a viewpoint, with a long lens, focussed at about the middle of the flight. Better, if it can be arranged, is to have a series of glass or perspex shelves, staggered vertically so that each shelf overlaps the one below it by about half its depth, and the whole flight standing in front of a white background. In this way, each row stands sufficiently in front of the row above for lighting to be effective, but the total depth, front to back, should not be so great as to give problems with perspective or depth of field. Since the group is placed well in front of the background, shadows are avoided and the background can be separately lit. Whatever the arrangement, consideration has to be given to the shape of the total photograph; for example, an excessively elongated group, horizontally or vertically, may be too awkward a format to be accepted for publication.

One of the necessary but more uninspiring jobs on many digs is the photography of sherds. Generally the intention is to show the tone and texture of the ware rather than the rim or body shape, which are best shown by drawing. There are a few ground rules which help to ensure a standardised result, and at least speed up what is always a tedious task (Plate 80).

Plate 80 Photographing sherds. The sherds are arranged within a frame, the rims horizontal and in line, and each within a clear rectangle (lower left) so that they can be printed separately.

For black and white photographs, the best background is a fluorescent-tube light-box; for colour work it is either glass over an inclined sheet of white paper, lit by a lamp shielded so as to avoid extraneous light reaching the lens, or else a light-box covered by a sheet of amber-coloured acetate. It may, however, take a deal of trial and error to achieve a neutral white background. If the photographs are to be published, an attempt should be made to determine beforehand the format of the publication and the scale of the published plate. Thus an A4 format publication might specify a maximum print space of 17 × 24 cm per page. For two plates to a page, and allowing for caption space, this would give a plate size of 17 × 10 cm. Assuming it was decided that the sherds were to be published at a magnification of 1:2, each group of sherds should therefore fit into a frame of 34 × 20 cm. If a mask is cut to this size, plus perhaps 0.5 cm all round to allow for trimming, and placed on the light-box, the sherds can be quickly positioned to fit the format. The sherds should be arranged with the rims to the top, and propped up so that the rims are straight when viewed from above (placed flat down on a surface, the rims of most rim sherds will appear to be curved, but this curve is mostly a function of the size of the sherd, not of the diameter of the rim, and can be deceptive). Bases should be aligned base-down, and body sherds placed the correct way up and with the wheel marks horizontal. With hand-built pots, of course, it may not be possible to orientate plain sherds correctly; in fact wiping marks or burnishing may run in any direction and be quite misleading. One final point: if possible, each sherd should occupy a separate rectangular space, not encroached on by any other sherd. This is merely a precaution, in case it is ever decided to print separately one sherd in the group, which will be easier if the sherds are separated in this way.

Lighting should be from the top, and it is nearly always more effective to use a moving light to avoid hard shadows being cast under the rims. The light should be moved in an arc, taking care to avoid directing the light into the lens, from a position pointing down at the rims (since the rims are lying flat, this will be from a position at right angles to the lens axis) up to a position pointing at the flat surface of the sherds.

Coins

Coins, medals, and similar objects of low relief, have one considerable advantage for the photographer; the visible depth is rarely more than a few millimetres. Depth of field is therefore seldom a problem, and an aperture can be used – usually f8 or f11 – which will give maximum resolution. They may be photographed with oblique light, with reflected axial light, or with ring-flash (see Plate 72). Each method is particularly useful for certain types of coins, but unfortunately quite unsuitable for others. Dark coins of medium relief can be photographed by any of the three types of lighting. Oblique light has the advantage of direction, and coin obverses are usually more easily identified if the main light is falling across the profile (if the coin has one). Care must be taken, however, to avoid casting heavy shadows on the side of the relief away from the light. Often it is necessary to use a small reflector to throw light back into the shadows. If the relief is rather deep and close, it may be better to use axial lighting, which will throw light on to the surface of the coin and show the relief as a dark rather than a light line. In either case, it makes for much easier printing if a full exposure is given – a reading from a neutral grey card might give a negtive difficult to print.

If the coin relief is very shallow, and particularly if the coin is much worn and polished, then low oblique lighting is virtually the only method that will produce a reasonable result; any sort of axial lighting would probably give an image like a blank disc. Highly reflective coins are often best photographed with axial lighting, and usually with reflected light rather than with ring-flash. Although oblique lighting may be satisfactory, it would certainly have to be baffled to minimise catch-lights, and the combination of this and low-angle lighting often renders the tone of the coin far too dark. Reflected axial lighting may also give catch-lights, but if a piece of frosted glass is held between the light source and the box, it is usually possible by adjusting its angle and distance to achieve a lighting balance showing both relief and the correct tone. Ring-flash may be satisfactory, or it may give unacceptable reflections, and, being flash, there is really no way of telling without exposing and processing a negative.

The highest resolution in the print would be obtained if coins were photographed at same-size on a large-format camera and the negative contact-printed. However, this would be expensive in film and time if a large number had to be dealt with, and perfectly satisfactory results can be achieved using a 35 mm camera, on a solid, vibration-free stand, and with a good macro lens. If only a few coins are to be photographed, then it will probably be satisfactory to take the obverse and reverse views on adjacent frames and to print and mount them separately. But if it is a question of a whole catalogue, it is more convenient, and certainly quicker, to arrange the coins so that both faces can be printed together. If the coins are light in tone and can be satisfactorily photographed on a black background, the technique is simple; the obverse of the coin is positioned so as to be centred on the left-hand side of the final print (i.e. on the right-hand side of the negative), and the coin is photographed and then turned over so that its reverse is on the right-hand side (Plate 81). With most 35 mm cameras, it is necessary to re-tension the shutter without winding the film on, by operating the wind-on while holding down the rewind button. This will produce quite satisfactory results if the background is solid black. This way of double-exposing a negative on a focal-plane camera is satisfactory so long as, as in this case, exact register is not important. If it is, then a camera with a register clamp mechanism would have to be used. If the camera has a lens shutter, then of course it is only necessary to re-cock the shutter.

a

b

Plate 81   Photographing a coin on black. Plate 81a shows the obverse
positioned in the centre of the left-hand side by means of a mask and flap. In
Plate 81b the obverse is exposed and the shutter re-tensioned. Plates 81c and
81d show the same procedure for the reverse. Plate 81e shows the two sides
together, printed from the same negative.

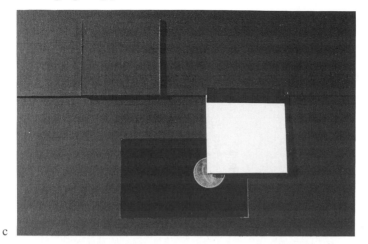

c

d

e

This method of double-exposing on black can also be used for photographing the obverse and reverse of groups of coins, the coins being arranged in rows with the obverse side up, and enough space left between the rows for the coins to be turned over between exposures. Two minor points should be noted. Firstly, if the photograph is to have a scale on it, this must be in only one of the exposures, otherwise it will receive twice the exposure of the rest of the photograph. Secondly, care must be taken to position the coins for the second exposure so that they are directly below their previous positions. This can be done either by laying a straight-edge across the coin before it is moved and centring the coin along it, or by marking the centres of the sites for the turned coins with slide-spots or something similar.

To obtain the obverse and reverse of coins on the same negative using a white background is rather more difficult. The problem, of course, is that the background, including the area into which the coin is to be turned, is exposed, dense, film, and not unexposed, clear, film. It is possible to make two negatives of the coins in their obverse and reverse positions and then to print the two on to the same sheet of bromide paper, in each exposure blocking out with strips of card the area reserved for the other negative. This is quite a fiddly business and one which succeeds only if the background of the prints is completely white. For single coins at least, an easier method can be used with a 35 mm camera. The obverse of one coin and the reverse of the next are exposed in each frame, and the sequence so arranged that an obverse is next to its own reverse in the subsequent frame. When the film is printed, half of one frame and half of the next are positioned in the negative holder. If the background is a dense white, then the clear division between the frames can easily be masked. Obviously it is vital to get the heads-and-tails sequence correct (see Figure 12.1), otherwise the coins cannot be printed together. Again, with this method there can be a problem of lining up the coins correctly, so that the printed views are in line and separated by a set distance. The simplest solution is to cut a rectangular mask as big as the focussed area, or a little bigger. On to this are taped two flaps or pointers, arranged so that their corners fall on the centre points of the two halves of the frame. By arranging the coins with their centres exactly under these points, and then lifting the flaps clear of the photograph, the coins can be aligned reasonably exactly.

The usual convention when photographing coins is to keep the axes of both sides of the coin upright, even though, as is often the case with struck coins, the axes are not aligned.

Glass

Glass, and to a lesser extent polished metal, are notoriously difficult to photograph. A cylindrical, or worse a globular, glass vessel will inevitably reflect any light-toned object around it, including the camera. Often, moreover, any such object is reflected twice, from the exterior and the interior of the glass.

If the overall shape of the vessel is its most important characteristic, it is best photographed against a white background; if the surface detail is more important, against black (Plates 82 and 83). Even for colour photography, black or white is usually the best background, since a coloured background will give a deceiving colour cast to the glass.

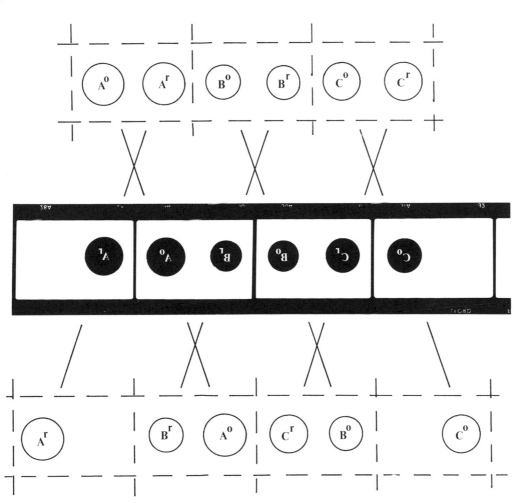

Figure 12.1   Photographing coins on white: the reverse of the first coin (A^r) is positioned on the left-hand side of the first frame (lower left in the figure). This is recorded on the right-hand side of the first negative (centre row). The obverse of this coin (A^o), and the reverse of the next (B^r) are positioned on the right and left-hand sides of the next frame and exposed, and so on. If the right-hand of the first negative and the left-hand side of the next are printed together (top row), with the division between them masked out, obverse and reverse appear together.

In photography against black it is advisable to illuminate the object with only one light, placed behind and to one side of the object and slightly above it. In this way there will at least be only one light to be reflected, and since it comes from behind the object, the frontal reflection is reduced. With completely plain glass it may be preferable to use a large light source, or to use a diffuser, so that the reflection is large but undefined. With decorated glass it is often better to use a very small light source (a slide projector with a slide in its gate, masked above to a circle of about 0.5 cm, does very well), giving a small intense reflection which can be arranged to be on an unimportant area of the object. If there are extraneous reflections from room lights, windows, etc.; the object should be surrounded by black cloth or paper, including the space above it. If a large-format camera is being used, the reflection of the camera itself can be eliminated by using the rising front. Such photographs

Plate 82, Plate 83   Photographing glass against white and black backgrounds.

are of a naturally high subject contrast, and they are usually improved by increasing the exposure and reducing the development time.

For clear glass of simple shape, and for cut glass, it is often effective to photograph against a translucent white background, with no frontal lighting. This can be arranged by placing the object on a light-box, or against a sheet of opal glass or plastic with a light behind it. Another method is to stand the object on a glass shelf in front of a white background, and with a spot behind and below it, shining up through the shelf. These methods are also useful for showing flaws, cracks or repairs in the body of the glass.

It is not easy to determine a correct exposure when photographing in this way, since the main light is coming through the object. A meter can be used from the camera position with a dome over the cell as if to measure incident light, or a reading can be taken from a grey card held so that its surface is roughly in line with the object but tilted back to the light source. In either case it may be necessary to rely finally on a trial exposure.

With glass of complex shape, and with polished or reflective metal, often the only effective type of illumination is overall, diffused lighting. This can be achived in two ways; either by photographing the object in overcast daylight with the sky as a background, or by building round it a 'light tent' with walls and roof of thin white paper or, better, of white translucent acetate, so that lights shone on to the tent from outside will be diffused enough not to give catch-lights on the object's surface. A hole is cut in one wall of the tent, just large enough to admit the lens.

Whichever method of lighting is used, there may be especially bright spots of reflection which would be better subdued. This can be done by dabbing the point with a ball of putty, or a little matt make-up on a brush. With antiquities, it is as well to avoid using aerosol dulling sprays; the spray may penetrate cracks in the surface, or react with repair materials.

Flints

Many archaeologists consider the photography of flint tools to be more or less a waste of time, the results being rarely as accurate and never as informative as those obtained from a good drawing. There are several grounds for this opinion. Against a light background the edges of even slightly translucent flints are lost, while a dark background will cause darker flint to become virtually invisible. No matter how carefully the lighting may be arranged, reflections will cause some faces of the flint to be emphasised – an emphasis having little relationship to natural shape or to working. The colour of the material may be so marked, or so variegated, that the face-intersections are partly or wholly obscured. Another and perhaps subtler drawback is that if a group of tools (or of course of any artifacts) is photographed so as to fill the picture-area of a short focal length of lens, those toward the edges of the frame will not present a strictly plan view, and may indeed suffer distortion of their dimensions, the ratios of which may well be of importance in analysis. Unfortunately, when the objects are of irregular shape the final print will not reveal that there has been this distortion.

It might seem, then, that it would be wiser to abandon flint photography altogether and to trust that the time and skill will be available to draw whatever flints are significant both in the field and in the study of collections. But time is almost always at a premium on an excavation, especially overseas, and skilled draughtsmanship is not always available, the more so as the only hand that many flint specialists trust is their own. This problem becomes critical, of course, in countries that will not allow finds to be exported or even taken out of the country for study.

The first of the above objections is easily dealt with. If the underside of the flint is painted with any dense water-soluble paint it will appear as completely opaque against a white or illuminated background, and the edges will be recorded (Plate 84). The colour of the paint is of little importance unless the photograph is in colour and the flint is very thin, when white or light grey is preferable.

Problems of the unequal emphasis of different surfaces and of variegated colours are more difficult, and sometimes almost impossible, to overcome. This is especially the case with multi-faceted tools. Flake tools with only a few facets are not difficult to light adequately, but hand-axes may have dozens, and not all can be evenly and separately lit. As with other artifacts, if there is directional lighting, it should come from the same direction in every photograph.

Reflections can usually be eliminated by diffusing the light source or by using a polarising filter, or even by means of a dulling spray. Whatever is done in this way, however, may be to some extent self-defeating. If the

Plate 84   Retaining the edge of flint. The back of the lower half of the flint has been painted out with opaque, water-soluble paint. As can be seen, this edge is clearly visible, while the upper edge, untreated, is lost against an illuminated white background.

lighting is so diffused, or the object so treated, that all the surfaces reflect equal amounts of light, then none may be distinguishable at all. It is not uncommon to see published flint photographs where the lighting is so subtle that even the main facets have been lost.

A great improvement in clarity can often be achieved by treating the flint with a thin, opaque, non-reflecting coating. A commonly used method (Weide and Webster (1967)) is to deposit a layer of ammonium chloride over the tool, thin enough not to obscure any three-dimensional detail, but opaque enough to mask the colour of the flint, and to present a uniform white surface. This technique can, however, give rise to other problems (Dorrell (1973)). The process has to be carefully watched and controlled throughout because the bottoms of deeply conchoidal faces are inclined to fill up, while the powder slides off the steeper faces. Although in laboratory terms the apparatus is simple in the extreme – a hot plate, and flasks of ammonia and of hydrochloric acid connected by tubes and a Y-junction to a bell jar or dessicator – even this equipment might not be readily available on an excavation, nor might quantities of the reagents be welcome in a field head-quarters' stores. There are a number of paints, sprays and powders that could

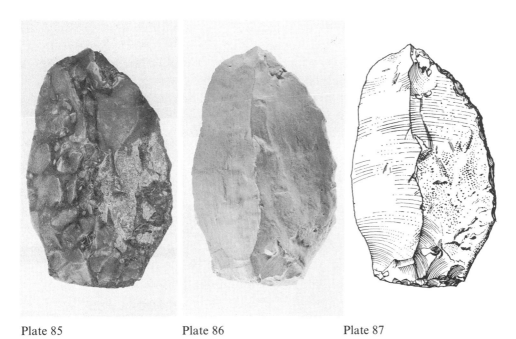

Plate 85 Plate 86 Plate 87

Painting-out and over-drawing a flint tool. Plate 85 shows a scraper made of very variegated flint, photographed with frontal lighting. In Plate 86 the tool has been painted out with flat, water-soluble paint and photographed under the same lighting. Plate 87 shows a drawing made with insoluble ink on the painted-out print, the tone background having then been bleached away.

serve equally well, and in fact ordinary commercial, light grey, poster paint, thinly applied, is as good as any, provided that it is water-soluble and can easily be washed off afterwards. (In the interests of possible later micro-wear analysis, flints should never be scrubbed, especially with a nylon brush.) The worked surfaces of a flint can be reasonably well recorded by this method, although this delineation of surfaces is at the expense of any record of the material itself; in fact the tool appears to be cut from meringue or something similar. The result is not ideal, but at least a page of such flint photographs would give a fairly faithful rendering of shapes and surfaces, and the eye could distinguish and compare the more important features (Plates 85, 86 and 87).

A similar technique has been used successfully (Callahan (1987)) for reducing the glare from flint, obsidian and shiny artifacts by coating them with aluminium powder, brushed on dry.

Based on this method another technique, widely used in technical drawings, suggests itself. If the negative of a painted-out flint is printed on to non-glossy paper (preferably a matt surface rather than a stippled or textured one), to give a rather pale image, it can be used as a guide for drawing in waterproof ink, and the image then bleached away, using a non-staining reducer, to leave a line drawing. The reducer is made up in two stock solutions:

> Solution A: 500 ml of water at 50°C, 15 g thiourea, 700 g sodium thiosulphate, made up with water to 1 litre.
> Solution B: 375 ml of water at 50°C, 150 g potassium ferricyanide, made up with water to 500 ml.

To use, mix two parts of A with one of B, and dilute with water to a pale straw colour. The print is immersed in the mixture until the silver image disappears, rinsed in water, re-fixed and rinsed again.[1]

For a skilled draughtsman all this may seem an unnecessary and complicated procedure, but for anyone less competent it offers advantages of accuracy and time saved. If large quantities of flint tools are found on an excavation it may not be possible to draw them during the season; and if it is for any reason impossible to bring them back to the home laboratory they could be painted and photographed very quickly, and the printing, over-drawing, and bleaching done later. This is not an ideal solution – no draughtsman should be asked to make a drawing without the original object – but the choice may be not between the best and a less good series of drawings, but between a record or no record of the flints.

Distortion of shape due to the oblique viewpoint of objects at the edge of the field can never be completely eliminated, but if no more than a dozen or so

---

[1] I am indebted to Mr Jim Frazer for this formula.

flints are photographed at once, and if a long lens is used to minimise angular differences of view, then such distortion should be minimal.

Details of flint tools, such as retouch, flaking and denticulation, can usually be well recorded even with the simplest equipment. Often drawing will not reveal such detail in full, accurate measurements being very difficult. By arranging one light at right angles to the lens axis, and then holding the flint below the camera and twisting it slightly until the greatest amount of detail is revealed, a reasonably accurate record can usually be achieved. It is often better if the light (which need be no more than a 100 w bulb in a desk lamp) is baffled to cut down reflections along the edge (Plate 88).

One of the most difficult materials to photograph successfully is obsidian, because it combines dark colour, highly reflective surface, and translucency. It is perfectly possible to render the material opaque by painting out its back surface, and to subdue reflection by baffling the lighting and using a polarising filter, but it then ceases to look very much like obsidian and resembles any dull, dark stone. While there may be no single method that will render adequately the texture, the tone, the worked detail and the nature of the material all at once, there are a number of techniques that can be used to show one or other feature. The tool can be placed on a black or a white background – but not on an illuminated white background – and lit by a moving baffled light (Plate 89). This is best achieved by placing a cone of white paper, or better a large translucent plastic funnel with the spout part cut off, over the tool, and during the course of the exposure moving a light around the funnel so that all parts of the tool are evenly illuminated. This method can show the facets very clearly, and the baffle effect of the funnel should prevent undue reflection, although the nature of the material may not be apparent.

Good results have been achieved in the field by using sunlight diffused through a pivoted sheet of opal glass to light one side of the tool, and a pivoted mirror to reflect light to the other (Bireaud (1991)).

One or other of these methods should give reasonable results, although none can be said to be infallible. If the nature of the material is to be recorded,

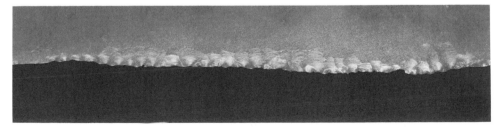

Plate 88   Detail of re-touch. The re-touch (at 2:1) was photographed with a single baffled light at right angles to the lens axis.

rather than the worked surfaces, then light transmitted through the artifact, and not reflected from its surface, should show detail quite adequately.

Tablets and inscriptions

With this sort of artifact, whatever the material, and whether the inscription is in relief, on the surface, or incised, the primary criterion is intelligibility. It is also, of course, highly desirable to achieve a correct balance of tones or colours to show the nature of the material, but the overriding consideration should be that the message, whether on a clay tablet, a wooden panel, or high on a rock face, should be comprehensible.

Nearly always this is a matter of angle and intensity of lighting, and to a lesser extent of exposure, processing, and sometimes the use of filters.

Even more than with other artifacts, it is important that the main light should come from the top, and preferably from the top left. The familiar optical illusion whereby a dome viewed from above can appear to be a hollow, and vice versa, if lit from an unfamiliar direction, can be very apparent with artifacts of this kind. It is all too easy to make a raised inscription appear to be in intaglio, and the other way round. The direction of light is particularly important with cuneiform tablets, which can be quite unreadable with the light coming from any other direction.

One other general point needs to be made. Most inscriptions are on more or less flat surfaces, and given a reasonably good lens they present no problems of distortion or loss of resolution at their edges. Most clay tablets, however, are pillow-shaped, and the inscriptions commonly run slightly over on to the sides. With these, it is important to use a lens of longer-than-standard focal length to reduce the inevitable distortions of the marginal letters. There is obviously a limit to what can be achieved and, on 35 mm, a 1000 mm lens would probably show very little more than would a 200 mm lens; but at all events a wide-angle lens should never be used. Similarly with a rock engraving, the surface may be curved (although not excessively – most such inscriptions after all were meant to be seen from one viewpoint), and a

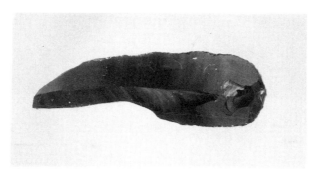

Plate 89   Photographing obsidian. The back of the tool was painted out, and it was then photographed with a single moving light.

long-focus lens should minimise the distortions caused by slightly differing angles of view. By the same token, more of an inscription on a concave surface should be seen using a shorter lens, although the advantage is relatively less.

Tablets

Apart from the curvature, tablets are simple enough to photograph, usually needing only one light from the top left and a reflector at the bottom right. The temptation – and this applies, though less forcibly, with other inscriptions – is to over-dramatise the lighting: to place it at too low an angle, by which means some of the characters will show up very clearly while others, or parts of others, will certainly be masked. Moreover, the impression of the stylus into the clay often pushes up a slight ridge beside the character, and this can also cast a shadow if the lighting angle is too low. The sides, and sometimes the ends, of the tablet are often inscribed as well as the faces, and these may have to be photographed separately. If the faces of the tablet are curved at all strongly, it may be impossible to find an angle for the light which will adequately illuminate the whole face. The best way to deal with this is to use a lamp masked to give a sharp cut-off of light, and to move it during the exposure, following more or less the curve of the face. If the photographer is non-cuneiform-reading, he should make sure from a published text, or from an epigraphist, which way is up for the characters, and check that both faces are the same in this respect, which is not always the case.

Detached inscriptions

Carved or incised inscriptions in stone or other material rarely present such difficulties – or at least not the same difficulties. If the inscription is of any size, say greater than 100 cm across, care must be taken to avoid a perceptible fall-off of light from one side to the other. Ideally, exposure meter readings taken on a grey card on the two sides should show no difference, or no more than half a stop. More than this can, of course, be compensated for during printing, but it adds an unnecessary complication, and in any case such compensation could not be made for a colour slide. Since such fall-off is proportional to the distance away of the light source, it is better to use a strong light source some way off (say a couple of metres) than a weaker source close at hand. Unfortunately, if an ordinary floodlight is being used, the farther away it is the more diffuse the light, and to achieve reasonable crispness it may be preferable to use a spotlight. If the inscription is on dark stone or wood, then a reflector will be necessary to record some detail in the shadowed parts. If, however, it is on white marble, or even ivory, it may act as its own reflector. (The effects of different types of lighting are shown in Plates 90 and 91.)

In fact, the difficulty then is often to record some texture on the uncut

Plate 90   Photographing detached inscriptions. Plate 90a: lit from the top with
no reflector or second light. Although the texture is clear, the heavy shadows
overemphasise the thickness of the letters. Plate 90b: lit from the top with a
reflector at the bottom. The weight of the letters is about right and the detail in
the shadows clearer. Plate 90c: lit from the bottom with no reflector. Again the
letters are too thick and dramatic, and the underlighting makes them appear to
be in relief. Plate 90d: lit by subdued daylight. Although the letters are legible,
the diffused light does not show the sharpness of the cutting, and they appear
spindly.

surfaces and to prevent them finally appearing as blank white. For black and white photographs, it is better to take a rather low-contrast negative with detail in both light and dark areas, and to increase the contrast, if need be, at the printing stage, rather than to aim for a a higher contrast negative in which, given even the slightest over-exposure, the light detail will be difficult to print. (It is difficult, and perhaps may be misleading, to lay down guidelines about negative contrast and density even in general terms. So much depends on the material being used, on the enlarger, and on the use to which the photograph is to be put, that familiarity with the equipment and film-stock, and test exposures, are the safest guides.)

Squeezes

The photography of a squeeze – an impression in latex or papier maché taken from an inscription – should be a good deal easier than photographing the inscription itself.

There are three points to consider: colour/tone, shape, reversal. The colour or tone of a latex squeeze, usually a mottled yellow-brown, bears of course no relationship to the original. If it is reasonably even across the impression, then it can be disregarded; but if, as is sometimes the case, it varies considerably, then the differences should be minimised as far as possible by lighting or by using filters, otherwise a spurious tone or colour change will appear in the final result. Similarly with translucency; most squeezes are more or less translucent, and it is tempting to try to photograph them with back-lighting only. They are never completely even in thickness, however, and again, this variability in degree of light transmission has nothing to do with the original inscription. It is better always to photograph them as three-dimensional

Plate 91   The whole inscription in Plate 90, at 1:2. Lit from the top left, with a reflector.

artifacts. Squeezes are commonly ragged-edged, and beyond making them large enough to cover the whole inscription, attention is rarely paid to their size or shape. There is a natural tendency, though, to assume that if a photograph is published of a squeeze say 10 cm longer and 5 cm wider than the inscription, then this size in some way represents a significant area within which the inscription was cut – perhaps the limit of a building block. If it is at all possible, it will be less deceptive if the photograph is trimmed round the inscription, not showing the edges of the squeeze.

A squeeze is, of course, reversed left to right, and the image has to be reversed again to get back to the original (Plate 92). This is easy enough; the negative is simply turned upside down for a print, or the film is reversed in a slide. If the squeeze has been lit from the top left, then its reversed image will appear to be lit from top right, so, as a matter of standardisation, it is better to illuminate it from top right, resulting in a top-left reversal (at first glance, it might seem necessary to light it from bottom-right i.e. the opposite of top-left, but of course the squeeze is reversed left-to-right, not top-to-bottom). A scale that is reversed left-to-right should be used, otherwise the lettering on it will appear back-to-front on the final print.

Plate 92   Photographing a squeeze. The light came from the top right, and the image was reversed during printing. By lighting from the bottom right it might have been possible to give the impression of the original engraved inscription rather than of relief, but since the tone is of a latex squeeze, and the finest detail shows the fabric backing of the squeeze and not the rock surface, this might have given a false impression.

In situ *inscriptions*
The photography of inscriptions and such things as rock engravings *in situ* is very little different from the photography of other artifacts – often simpler in fact, since such inscriptions are commonly flat and almost two-dimensional, and depth of field is therefore not a problem. As with architectural detail, however, the question of viewpoint needs consideration. Take, for instance, a memorial on the wall of a church, or a Roman dedication stone, or for that matter a Meso-American or Mesopotamian stela; all are meant to be readable, or seeable, from one particular viewpoint, usually from ground level. In this they are unlike such things as Egyptian tomb texts or Paleolithic cave paintings, which were not, presumably, addressed to a human audience. With the first group, it is vital to record the inscriptions from the viewpoint for which they were placed, whatever other photographs are taken. Equally, of course, it is necessary to place the inscription in its setting, whether this is a wall, a floor, a building or a rock face. For a Roman inscription, for example, the minimum setting would be the 'titulus', the panel prepared for the engraving, and the maximum the whole building in which it is set, so far as that has survived. It is possible to think of all sorts of intermediate cases – stained-glass windows in large churches, designed, one assumes, for the edification of the congregation but painted in detail that could not possibly be seen from ground level; hill figures; mosaic pavements that could have been seen in their entirety only after the building above them disintegrated. But at all events, it is always necessary at least to consider the original viewpoint. Similar considerations apply to all sorts of architectural details – a pillar capital is meant to be viewed from below, the repetitive arches of an Umayyad mosque are deliberately designed to be contemplated as a series, a Greek temple frieze was also intended to be viewed from below and in some cases the proportions of the figures were subtly designed for that viewpoint.

As well as the photograph setting the position of the inscription, it is necessary to take a 'square-on' photograph in order not only to show the details but to record the relative proportions of the field. For this it may be necessary to employ scaffolding or a stepladder, but if the distance above or below a convenient viewpoint is not too great, an apparently square-on result can be achieved by using the rising or dropping front of a large-format camera with movements.

Lighting can be a problem. The perfect illumination – hazy sunlight from the top left – may never be achievable. A reasonable photograph can be taken in complete shadow; although the image may be dull and shallow detail lost, this is certainly preferable to one taken in direct frontal sunlight, and infinitely better than one taken half in sunlight and half in shadow. If the object is fairly small – up to a metre or so across – good results can be achieved by using a diffusing sheet, either gauze or pierced aluminium foil, in the path of direct sunlight. It may be, however, that the only way to record shallow relief is to use flash, either as the main light or as a subsidiary, just skimmed across the surface to increase contrast between surface and cutting and to sharpen relief. As when using continuous artificial light, there is a great danger of fall-off between the sides near to and those far from the flash, the more acute as flash is almost a point source of light. It is better always to use a fairly powerful flash a couple of metres away than a small one held close to one edge. The resource of using a small flash several times is rarely possible, unless there is virtually no other light, since exposure to ambient light will certainly result in a negative density far too high to be usable.

Rock engravings

There can be no clear division between cut inscriptions and legends, decorations and depressions incised, scratched or pecked into surfaces. There are all degrees across the spectrum, but the various kinds of graffiti have two things in common: they are not normally deeply incised, and the surface on which they appear is rarely flat. Also, since they were seldom cut on a prepared surface, they may be visible not so much by their incision as by a colour or tone difference between the scratch or peck mark and the stone's natural surface. This is particularly apparent in desert areas where rocks are commonly coated with dark desert varnish, and the slightest incision or fracture shows as a lighter mark. In wetter areas they may be revealed only by the presence of lichens on one or other surface.

Except in very rare cases, the only effective type of illumination is a strong raking light, whether sunlight or flash. If the surface is curved or irregular, however, the shadows cast by such lighting may obscure more than the light reveals. It may be possible to use several flashes in low ambient light (with the attendant problem that there is no way to judge the result until the film is processed, unless there is a Polaroid camera available), or a moving hand-held lamp, also in comparative darkness. The lines can be emphasised by talcum powder brushed or blown across the surface, but this is not a course to be recommended unless all else fails. The result always looks artificial, and the strength and positiveness of the filled lines can easily give a false impression of the original. It is better, particularly with colour film, to use a non-white dust, ideally perhaps a lighter or darker shade of the colour of the rock. If the lettering or design is apparent only because of a colour difference, it is often more effective to take only a colour transparency, and to copy the transparency on to pan film for black and white prints. Since the colour difference is nearly always a matter of lighter or darker shades of the same colour, contrast filters are rarely useful.

Curvature and irregularity of the rock face may be at least partly compensated for by using a long lens and moving further away, thus minimising irregularities; or if this is ineffective, it may be necessary to take a series of negatives from different positions and to mount the final prints together. This is not at all an easy thing to do because, of course, quite slight differences in angle and size will result in unmatchable prints. If the negatives can all be taken from a single camera position – as would be the case, for instance, if the inscriptions were round a concave face – it is reasonably easy. All that is necessary is to set up a tripod at about the centre point of the curve, check through the camera that everything necessary can be seen from this point, and, most important, level the tripod head through a full pan movement with a spirit level so that for each shot the camera is exactly horizontal both along its length and from front to back. If the camera is not levelled then, inevitably, the resultant prints, when joined, will curve either up or down. A series of identical exposures should be taken, allowing an overlap of 40–50% (exactly the same rules apply when making a panoramic series of a distant horizon). If the series cannot be taken in this way – if, for instance, the inscription runs round a convexity – it is difficult to be so precise. The best that can usually be done is to take a series of exposures, again with full overlaps, from viewpoints each the same distance from the rock face and each, so far as can be determined, at right-angles to the face (or rather, if the stretch of convex face in each photograph can be thought of as an arc, at right angles to the centre of a chord of that arc). Again, it is important to make sure that the camera is horizontal for each exposure and, if it can be arranged, to ensure that the successive positions of the camera are in a horizontal line, otherwise the series will be stepped. If there is any sort of level or theodolite available, this is easy enough. If not, it may be possible to lay out a horizontal string between a series of sticks, using a spirit level, and to line the camera up with the strings. This technique resembles that of rectified photography described in Chapter 6.

A similar problem is presented by such things as Roman milestones, often small pillars with inscriptions running round more than 100° of their circumference. A completely accurate 'rolled-out' image is impossible, but a reasonable approximation can be achieved by taking a series of photographs from around the circumference of an imaginary circle drawn from the centre point of the pillar. If some small object can be placed on top of the pillar, this can be centred in the viewfinder in each shot (and removed before the exposure), ensuring that the camera is square-on to the inscription.

Such joined-together or mosaiced photographs can, obviously, be accomplished only in black and white; it is not possible to join together fragments of colour transparencies. If a colour transparency is vital, the only resource is to expose colour negative film, print and join it, and re-photograph the result on to colour positive stock.

Organic Materials

Materials of animal or vegetable origin are often fragile and subject to damage by heat, and sometimes by strong light and ultra-violet rays. They

Woven materials

Textiles are often best regarded as flat copy: evenly spread and lit and, for black and white photographs, the contrast balanced and the maximum detail revealed with filters, if necessary, or by the manipulation of film and developer. However, textiles often have texture of two or three kinds; the texture of the material itself – the weave and the twist of the thread – and, in some cases, the texture of the made-up piece (Plates 96 and 97). Quilted and seamed pieces, for instance, have a second, superimposed texture. With ordinary weaves a moderately raking light at an angle of 25° or 30° to the surface should show the texture well enough without over-coarsening it. Often it is better to have the light diagonally to the direction of the threads, to avoid emphasising one or other direction too strongly. However, there are some fabrics, like twills, where the bias threads are the most important and should be shown clearly; and others, like watered silk, where light from different directions may show completely different colours or tones. All that can really be done with these is to choose the direction which best shows the colour or tonal differences. Quilted textures or the like usually need no more than a slightly directional illumination; often, in fact, frontal lighting is enough to show their bumps and declivities. A polarising filter is often useful if the material has a shiny surface.

Baskets and objects of split cane should present no particular problems in photography, the lighting and viewpoint being very much the same as is used for pottery. Fragments of basketry, or of coarse cloth, however, can be difficult, particularly if they are light in tone. Against a white or illuminated

Plates 96 and Plate 97   Multiple textures. Plate 96, lit from the left, shows the weave of the basketry well enough, but Plate 97, lit from the top, also shows the second texture of horizontal ridges and the diagonal fold.

background, the edges of the strips may disappear, while against black the interweaving may be so dark as to need frontal lighting, in which case the texture disappears. There is a way of dealing with this, at least for small and fairly flat pieces (this is also effective for such things as filigree work). The piece of basketry is placed flat on a sheet of glass which is held a metre or so above the ground. Black velvet is spread on the floor beneath it and two lights positioned at either side of the velvet, directed up at the basketry at an angle of about 45°. Enough top lighting is then brought in to show the texture of the material. By this means the edges of the strips are clearly rimmed against a black background and the top lights can be at an angle low enough to show the interweaving.

Wood

Ancient wood may be either dark and friable, with a rather dusty appearance, or bleached. In either case it can be quite difficult to make the material look like wood, and very careful lighting is necessary to show the pattern of the grain. Unfortunately, it is one of the materials least able to withstand heat; quite substantial pieces can warp if lit – and therefore heated – on one side only. When photographing polished wood, and particularly dark polished wood like mahogany or rosewood, it is often necessary to use a polarising filter to reduce reflections, and sometimes an orange contrast filter (also known as a 'furniture filter') to enhance the difference between the light and dark, often almost black, areas of the grain.

Other organic materials

The only special problems which may arise with *shell* and *ivory* are the rendering of the nacreous sheen along the lip of shells, and the gloss of ivory. Bright reflective areas can usually be softened by steering the lights or by using a polarising filter, but it may be difficult to record the difference between the glossy areas and the body of the object, particularly if the object is light in tone overall. It is most important not to over-expose the negative, since this will cause the lightest tones to coalesce. With soft overall lighting and minimal exposure, any necessary increase of contrast between the lighter tones can usually be achieved at the printing stage. This refers to black and white photographs; the contrast balance is not so critical in colour work since there is usually a slight but sufficient colour difference between such areas.

Things like ivory plaques do need directional light from the top left to show their orientation. Usually one light is sufficient unless the cutting is very deep, or unless the object is strongly three-dimensional, for instance a carved tusk, or inlay *in situ* in furniture. Burnt ivory is not so easy to deal with; the surface can become very dark – almost black – and highly reflective. A light tent may be necessary, or soft, diffused frontal lighting with a low-power directional light falling across the surface and a polarising filter on the lens.

Ivory, like thin wood, can be badly distorted if it is subjected to heat.

Bone tools are much like ivory or shell as far as the surface goes, but there may also be polished areas resulting from use. Weaving tools in particular show this feature, and the extent of these areas of polish may be important. If they occur on a flat part of the tool they should be apparent with ordinary diffused lighting. On a rounded surface however it may be necessary to move the light across the area, following the curve, to make them clear.

Something has been said in the chapter on site photography about recording skeletons and bones *in situ*. Most bones can be readily photographed with two lights, or with one light and a reflector, placed low enough to give some roundness to the bones. Skulls are best photographed with a moving light, however, to avoid having hard shadows within the orbits or behind the cheekbones, and the same may be true of pelvises. When bones are photographed separately there are a few conventions, mostly of orientation, that should be followed. Human bones should always be photographed as if in their natural alignment to a skeleton the head of which is at the top of the frame, with fingers and toes pointing downwards. Long bones are normally recorded from the front and back (anterior and posterior views) and from the side (lateral view). It is important that the anterior view should be exactly from the front and the lateral and posterior views exactly at 90° and 180° to this. If, for instance, a lateral view is not taken exactly from the side but from slightly above or below it, the various parts of the joints may not appear in their correct proportions and may mask one another. Bones of the shoulder and hip girdles are usually – though not always – orientated in their normal position in the skeleton, and again anterior, posterior and lateral views may be called for.

Animal bones are photographed in approximately the same way as human except that with four-footed animals the backbone rather than the head is assumed to be at the top of the frame. If several long bones are photographed together, for the lateral view they should be placed approximately in their positions as if articulated; for instance, the femur and tibia of a horse meet at a marked angle when articulated, and should be photographed in this position.

Human skulls should always be orientated on the so-called 'Frankfurt Plane' or 'Frankfurt Horizon', with the upper margins of the two earholes and the lowest point of one orbit aligned to form a horizontal plane (owing to slight asymmetry it is often not possible to bring both ear and both orbit margins to the same plane). With this plane maintained in the horizontal, five standard views are normally taken: from the left side (*norma lateralis sin.*), from the top (*norma verticalis*), from the front (*norma facilis*), from the back (*norma occipitalis*) and from below (*norma basilis*). The mandible is usually photographed from the side and from the top, with the biting surface of the teeth horizontal (the occlusal view). Animal skulls should be photographed either on the Frankfurt plane or on the upper occlusal plane, i.e. with the upper grinding teeth horizontal. Apparently the Frankfurt Plane places the skull roughly in the position in which, in humans, it is carried in life, which is not the attitude in which most animals carry their heads.

A few other organic materials may be encountered from time to time: horn, feathers, various sorts of fibre, dessicated body tissues and so on. All can usually be dealt with in much the same way as those described above, paying particular attention to their textures, and with thin and fragile materials, to their edges against the background. And again, such delicate materials should not be subjected to heat or rough handling.

13

FLAT COPY

The photography of such things as wall and easel paintings, drawings, plans and even stained-glass windows, has much in common with that of inscriptions, except that the depth of field is rarely of concern, and evenness of illumination, flatness of field, and the recording of subtle tonal differences, becomes of more importance.

Camera lenses, whether for 35 mm or for larger formats, are normally constructed to give an optimum image in terms of sharpness of detail and evenness of resolution and illumination when focussed at or near infinity. For any sort of copying, however, the focussed distance is very much less than this, and many taking lenses will not give an even image of a flat copy at such short distances. Usually the quality is improved if the lens is stopped down to f16 or less, at the cost of long exposures and some loss of overall resolution. Lenses specially designed for photo-mechanical reproduction (*process lenses*) are of relatively long focal length, small aperture (often they have a focussing aperture of about f11 but a maximum taking aperture of f22 or less) and are highly corrected for distortion and curvature of the field. Those designed for colour reproduction (*apochromatic*) are also corrected to give a minimal difference in the points of focus of the spectral colours. Such lenses are expensive, and work within a limited range of magnification, and they could hardly be justified unless a great deal of flat-copy work were to be undertaken. *Copying lenses* are less completely corrected, especially for colour, and are often, in fact, enlarging lenses in different mounts. For occasional photographs of flat-copy material, however, standard lenses or, better, moderately long-focus lenses will give reasonable results.

Two considerations are of prime importance in this kind of photography, evenness of illumination and squareness to the camera.

Originals of up to about A3 in size can be adequately lit with two flood-lamps set at 45° to the surface. For larger sizes, four lamps – one for each corner – are essential, and each must be maintained at the same output. It is best to start work with four new bulbs. When one bulb ceases to work, all four should be replaced, keeping the partly used ones. From then on, when a bulb fails, it should be replaced by one of the original three until all are used, and the cycle started again. In this way differences in output will be minimised.

In the field, shadowed sunlight will serve very well, but it is often necessary to place a reflector on the side away from the sun. A quick way to check the evenness of illumination is to point a pencil or something similar at the centre of the original, compare the direction and weight of the two or four shadows cast, and adjust the position of the light until all the shadows are equal. For a more accurate assessment, take a series of light-meter readings on a piece of white paper held at the four corners and at the centre of the original. In general the aim is to obtain even light right across the original; nevertheless if an ordinary, non-process, lens is being used, the amount of light transmitted through the lens may fall off slightly at the edges, and it is therefore advantageous to have slightly more light around the edges of the original than in the middle.

The second consideration is squareness (or square-on-ness – there is no wholly suitable word). Unless the camera is fairly exactly arranged so that the lens axis is at right-angles to the original at its central point, it is virtually impossible to record an image in true proportion. Gallery cameras, and some copy cameras, are built on rails or tracks with this relationship mechanically fixed; for occasional use, ordinary cameras on tripods can be so arranged, at least within limits. If the camera is pointed downwards at the copy, the problem is easily solved simply by using a spirit level along and across the copy and the camera-back to make sure that they are parallel; the geometry will then be correct. If the camera is being used horizontally, however, levelling is more difficult. By using a spirit level with a cross bubble, the copy and the camera can be made vertically parallel to each other. To line the camera up horizontally, however, cannot be done in this way; but if the camera is arranged with the centre of the focussing screen aligned with the centre of the copy, and the operator then stands back three or four metres behind the camera and looks across the top of it, it is, for some reason, immediately obvious whether or not the lens axis is at right angles to the copy. A more accurate method, certainly at close range, is to stick a small mirror in the centre of the copy and focus the image of the lens in it; this image is made to coincide with the central disc of the screen, ensuring squareness. (In fact, this is more difficult than it sounds, since the focussing position of a mirror reflection is not on the surface of the copy.) A third method, which is much to be recommended if a purely temporary set-up is being arranged in the field, is to draw an accurate rectangle of approximately the same size as the sheets to be copied and of the same proportions as the camera format (for 35 mm, 1.5:1 is close enough). This rectangle is focussed so that its sides are exactly parallel with the sides of the viewfinder and then, without disturbing the camera, the originals to be copied are substituted for the test sheet.

If there is to be a semi-permanent arrangement for making copy-negatives, with the copy-holder always in the same position on a wall, it is worth laying out a line on the floor, marked by tape or a line of tacks, exactly at right-angles to the centre of the copy-holder. The camera can then be positioned over the line by plumb-bob and the centre of the focussing screen be aligned with a point marked in the centre of the copy-holder. This will ensure squareness every time.

If the original is flat and on an opaque base, it can simply be pinned on a suitable wall or laid flat on a box or on the floor. If the original is at all valuable, of course, it should not be pinned; it should either be stuck in position with double-sided tape or held with drawing pins along the edges, with only their heads overlapping the original; or a metal baseboard with magnetic corners can be used, if one is available. If it is curled or cracked, however, it is best photographed covered by a sheet of glass wedged or weighted down to flatten the original, unless the original is so brittle or fragile that pressure might damage it. It is particularly necessary to flatten drawings on tracing paper or linen, under glass. These are nearly always slightly bubbled, and lines, or even worse transferred tints and hatchings, may stand off the surface slightly and cast a shadow masking their own edges. Great care must always be taken to avoid both reflections from the surface of the cover-glass (which should be checked by looking at the copy from the lens position rather than relying on seeing such reflections through the focussing screen – they are often quite difficult to spot) and flare resulting from peripheral light reaching the lens (a lens hood should always be used), from a dusty lens, or from reflections within the camera. Process cameras normally have large square bellows, ensuring that any stray light is absorbed. Little can be done with a normal camera beyond making sure that there are no sources of possible reflection within it; the back of the lens mounts, for example, are often of bright reflective metal.

There are three main types of original, line, tone and colour, with several intermediate types, and each requires slightly different treatment.

Line originals

The commonest type of archaeological originals, whether plans, sections, or drawings of pots or small finds, are drawn as black lines on a white background, and are intended for publication in the same form. Very often the base is not white paper but tracing linen or tracing paper, which must always be flattened onto white paper.

The prime requirement is to produce a negative, and from this a print, with absolute black and white, and with the sharpest possible division between the two, so that the edges of lines are hard and without gradation; and to reproduce cleanly both fine black detail, e.g. a thin black line, and fine white detail, e.g. a thin line of white paper remaining between two black lines.

With any ordinary film, even if developed to a high contrast, this is almost impossible to achieve. It is necessary to use a type of film known as lithographic film, (usually shortened to 'lith'), which when processed with the correct lith developer gives extreme contrast and extreme edge gradations. The film can be obtained in a wide variety of sheet sizes, 5×4 in or larger, and as 35 mm stock. The most commonly used type is orthochromatic, which can be handled under a red safe-light, and is satisfactory for black or red lines on a white or blue base. For other coloured line originals, it may be necessary to use a panchromatic type of the same film. The film's speed is very slow – perhaps 6 or 8 ISO – but it so depends on the type of equipment and the method of processing that an exposure must be determined by experiment. As an indication, an exposure of 8 sec at f16, using four 500 w lamps set at a distance of about 1.5 m produces a satisfactory negative.

As might be expected, far better results can be achieved on a large-format camera than on 35 mm, the more so as the most effective method of development (unless a machine is available) is in a dish and by inspection. This process, although not especially difficult, does require a certain amount of practice; the image develops slowly at first, and then, once it starts to blacken, very quickly. By holding it up to a red safe-light and inspecting it with a magnifying glass, the moment is chosen when the lines are hard but the finer details have not begun to block in. Fixing and washing are the same as with any other film. This type of developing is naturally not possible with 35 mm film, nor with panchromatic lith film, so the usual method is to work with a non-lith, high-contrast developer which will not give the same edge-contrast but which is not so critical in time.

Because of its high contrast, lith film is apt to record, as pin-holes, any tiny marks on the original, and any dust on the film. It is nearly always necessary to spot out such marks on the negative, using a water-based opaque paint.

A special problem is posed by sections, object drawings, or indeed graphs, drawn on graph paper. Usually with sections or drawings it is desirable to lose the lines of the graph paper altogether in the final print, while sometimes with graphs the intention is to retain them. Whether they can be lost or retained depends very much on the colour in which the graph lines are printed, and this may be black, red, blue, green, brown or grey.

Black graph lines are, obviously, going to appear on the negative and print no matter how they are exposed or processed. Unfortunately – and the same applies to other colours – such lines on cheap graph paper are often not very dense or hard, and it may be difficult to record them sharply even on lith film.

Red lines will appear as black on orthochromatic lith film, or as grey on panchromatic lith. They can be eliminated by using a red filter on panchromatic lith (see section on filters in Chapter 3), but a red filter cannot be used with orthochromatic emulsions; since orthochromatic film is not sensitive to red light, the film when processed would be completely clear.

Blue graph lines will usually disappear on orthochromatic lith film without a filter, but if the blue is dark a blue contrast filter may be necessary. It may be possible to retain blue lines by using a red filter on panchromatic lith, but they rarely record as a really solid line.

Green lines are difficult to lose altogether, even with a green contrast filter; they can be retained with a red filter on panchromatic lith, and sometimes with a blue filter on orthochromatic lith. Brown and grey lines are impossible either to eliminate or to retain completely.

If there is an opportunity, it should be suggested to the draughtsman that, if the final result desired is a black drawn line on a white background, then only light blue graph paper should be used; or if what is wanted is a black drawn line on a background with black graph lines, then well-printed black- or red-lined paper should be used. Apart from other considerations, any other alternative involves stocking and using panchromatic lith film, which is not easy to dish-process. Brown- and grey-lined paper should be avoided at all costs.

Line negatives can be printed by contact or by enlarger. It is important not to over-expose the print, otherwise there can be a certain amount of creep of penumbral light along the edges of the lines, giving a halo which destroys the hardness of lines; nor to under-develop, otherwise the lines, while quite visible, may not be completely black.

Tone copying

Unless the original consists of hard-edged, opaque lines or areas against a background of strongly contrasting tone, it must be treated as a tone, not a line, copy. For example, a line drawing of a section, traced on to linen with a good drawing pen, using opaque ink, can be reproduced successfully as a line negative. If, however, the original drawings were in pencil, they could never be so reproduced. At best the thicker lines would be recorded but the detail lost.

The usual aim in tone copying is to reproduce on the print the same range of tones as in the original, although with, for example, a stained and faded photograph, it might be desirable to increase the contrast, as it might be also with an indistinct wall-painting. Indeed, if something like a crumpled, stained and faded manuscript were being photographed, a conscious choice might have to be made between regarding the original as an artifact, and therefore trying to make a facsimile record of it; or aiming for maximum legibility of the writing and suppressing, as far as possible, any imperfections in the background that might detract from its comprehensibility. Ideally, both aspects should be recorded (Plates 98, 99 and 100). As with line copying, large-format cameras have a distinct advantage over small.

As well as easily avoidable faults like reflection in the cover-glass, another problem has to be considered. Because of the tendency for the combination of lens, film and processing to shorten the range of tones, there is always a

ERRATUM   0 521 455340 / 455545

DORRELL:Photography in archaeology and conservation

Page 243

Plate 100 in the printed book (currently a duplicate of Plate 99) should be <u>replaced</u> with this photograph.

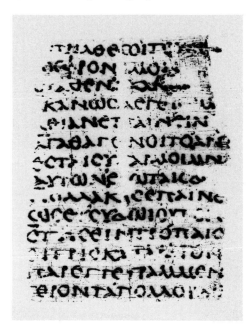

Plate 98

Plate 99   Plate 100

Tone and legibility, Plate 98 shows a fragment of papyrus with a black
inscription, taken on panchromatic film (FP4) without a filter. In Plate 99 a
yellow contrast filter (Wratten 15) was used, lightening the tone of the papyrus
while retaining its texture. Plate 100 was taken on lithographic film. Only the
letters remain, and the gain in legibility is slight.

danger of increasing unacceptably the contrast of the copy negative. In particular, the detail in the darkest tones is liable to be lost, and all the dark tones merge as solid black. If, in addition, there is any lens flare, or the slightest fog on the film, these tones will not be black but a dark muddy grey. Ideally, therefore, a film with a large tonal range should be used, developed to give a printable variation of tones in the shadows and no more. Copy films for black and white tone originals are blue-sensitive only and developed by inspection, which, as in developing lith film, takes a certain amount of practice. Failing a specialist film being available, a fine-grain general-purpose emulsion should be used, a grey-card reading or an incident-light reading should be taken, and the film should be over-exposed by about 25% (to register all the darkest tones) then underdeveloped by a similar amount (to prevent excessive contrast).

Perhaps the most difficult originals to deal with incorporate both line and tone: photographs with captions are examples. If the shape is simple, perhaps a rectangular illustration with a line of type beneath it, it is not difficult to make two negatives, one line and one tone, and print them separately on the same piece of paper, for each exposure masking out the area taken by the other negative. For anything more complicated than this, for instance inserting numbers or lines on to tone originals, it is sometimes possible, though time-consuming, to mask different parts of the copy, or to overprint a line negative of the same size, as the print on to the exposed tone print on the enlarger; but the sort of complex line/tone combinations that can be achieved by computer graphics overlay are best not attempted by simple photography.

Colour
Copying coloured originals in black and white requires no different techniques, except that panchromatic film must be used, and it is occasionally necessary to use contrast filters to enhance colour differences when these are translated into black and white tones. Exposure through a blue light filter (Wratten 38) used to be recommended as standard, in order to compensate for the extended red sensitivity of panchromatic film used under tungsten light, but this seems to be less necessary with modern films, and it is as well not to use filters if avoidable. When an oil painting is to be photographed, there may well be problems caused by reflections from brush marks, and a decision may have to be made whether these should be eliminated, by adjusting the lighting and/or by using a polarizing filter; or, if a study of the impasto is in question, retained by using shallow-angle lighting. If the picture is generally dark, then the reflections are likely to stand out far too brilliantly, completely masking all else. Sometimes this problem can be overcome by using a polarizer adjusted, through the viewfinder, to give partial elimination.

Copying a coloured original on to either negative or positive colour film is easy enough, but to reach a facsimile result is very difficult indeed, and perhaps best left to the professional. The main problem lies in obtaining a true colour balance among the variables of lighting, exposure, processing and the variations in film stock from one batch to another. If absolutely necessary, it is better to work from test exposures, rigidly controlling the processing, and adjusting the balance with colour-correcting filters.

A comprehensive account of the photography and reproduction of drawings and paintings is given in Lewis and Smith (1969) and in Keefe and Inch (1990).

14

PREPARATION OF MATERIAL FOR PUBLICATION

The end result of all excavations and surveys is – or should be – publication, whether as a monograph, article, microfiche or on disc. Similarly, although the prime objective of conservation is the conserved and stable artifact, publication of results and methods should never be neglected. Unfortunately it is even more difficult to raise money to publish a site than it is to obtain the funds to dig it (and, it must be confessed, working on publication is commonly much less interesting and enjoyable than digging). In addition, the involvement of more and more scientific disciplines in the analysis and elucidation of sites and artifacts makes the tasks of editorship and co-ordination of reports more demanding.

All this is very well known to anyone working in the field, and certain guidelines on publication have been laid down (Council for British Archaeology (1991)). At the same time as the demands of adequate publication have become more exacting, the costs of printing, blockmaking and binding have risen until conventional hardback publication has become out of the question for most sites. The gap has been filled to some extent by the advent of such techniques as computer typesetting, small-scale litho printing and desk-top publishing, and through the sometimes heroic cost-cutting efforts of learned journals and such concerns as British Archaeological Reports. However laudable the attempt to maintain the flow of publication, one effect has been that the standard of reproduction of photographs, and to a lesser extent of line drawings, has fallen. This is unfortunate, to say the least, since a page of type that is poorly printed retains its legibility, but a photograph reproduced with blocked-in shadows, or muddy highlights, or badly defined detail, has lost much of its value. There are, of course, even now publications with well-produced illustrations, but they are becoming sufficiently rare to be a matter for comment. Undoubtedly the standards of small-scale, short-run publications will rise in the future as the techniques are refined and better understood, but meanwhile the most the photographer can do is to produce work for publication in a form, and of a style, best suited to present reproduction and printing techniques.

Of the methods of photo-mechanical reproduction most widely used – process engraving (or letter-press), photogravure, and photo-litho (or offset lithography) – photogravure has never been important for short-run publications, nor is it likely to become so. It can produce superb results, especially with reproduction of dark detail, but the time, cost and skill involved, and the cost of the presses, more or less confine its use to long runs of such things as weekly journals of wide circulation, and to postage stamps.

Process engraving and letterpress printing were at one time the workhorse of the printing industry, handling everything from newspapers to leaflets, as well as nearly all books. Over the last decade or so, however, the publishers of nearly all books and journals have switched to photo-litho, and it is by this process that most reports will be published at least for some time to come.

The usual method now employed for publication by photo-litho is for prints of the text material and line illustrations to be positioned in the page-format, either by pasting-up or electronically, to form a sheet of camera-ready copy. This is photographed to make a photo-mechanical transfer (PMT) with the screened tone originals inserted in position, having been photographed either with the rest or separately by laser-scanning (which gives greater control over contrast).

Fortunately the requirements of process engraving and photo-litho, so far as the photographer is concerned, are much the same. Both processes involve scanning or re-photographing tone originals through a screen, so that tones are translated into a pattern of dots; and with both processes, the fineness of detail that can be recorded depends on the fineness of the screen used. This in turn is controlled at least partly by the quality of the paper used for the print-run. The best quality of reproduction is achieved by either process on opaque, heavyweight, coated paper, but, other things being equal, photo-litho will give the better results on poorer quality paper. At their best, both will reproduce detail in dark, mid-tone and light areas of a photograph, and both will give a reasonably full range of tones, although neither can produce a result to match the range possible in a bromide print. There is always some compression of the range, since printing ink will not yield as intense a black as will bromide paper, nor as white a white; in addition, the pattern of dots extends, however finely, into both the darkest and the lightest areas, further reducing the range.

All too often, however, with short-run, low-cost publication, the processes are not at all at their best. With photo-litho the result is often that dark areas block in, losing detail in the shadows, and giving a dull and oppressive appearance to the whole page. With poor-quality process engraving – rare in this country, but common enough in a number of Departments of Antiquities' journals elsewhere – the faults lead to the opposite result. A combination of badly made blocks, poor printing and poor-quality paper, results in grey-looking illustrations with washed-out highlights and without detail. The very worst of both extremes is rare – although there are examples to be seen – but quite a lot of publications show a tendency one way or the other. The only advice that can be given is that the photographer should ensure that important detail is kept in the middle tones, that large areas of black are avoided and that, so far as possible, tones are well separated. Subtle gradations of tone which can give a bromide print depth and shape and impart an almost tactile quality to the image of an artifact, can be lost entirely in reproduction and printing, resulting in an image which is little more than a flat grey shape.

Black and white tone prints for reproduction should be on glossy paper, preferably glazed. Depending on the process, the publisher may ask for prints to be supplied at the size at which they will appear on the page, or at one-and-a-half times or twice this size. Very often the most important consideration is that, whatever the magnification, it should be common to all the prints, so that they can be dealt with in batches, and that photographs that are to be printed together on a page should be mounted together in position, and in the correct proportion. Prints should be clean and unmarked – the impression of writing on the back of the print, or of a paper clip on its edge, can persist right through to the printed page. If a picture is to be cropped, the cropping lines should either be marked on the back of the print, very lightly, in pencil (ink from writing on the back of a print in ball-point or fibre-tip pen can only too easily get smudged on to the face of the next print in the pile), or on its face in a light blue wax pencil of the 'chinagraph' type; or, best of all, marked on a tracing-paper flap covering the face of the prints.

Sections, plans, pottery drawings and other line originals often have to be presented in 'camera-ready' form, that is, to their final size and proportion and with the numbers and captions that will appear with them mounted in position. As was said earlier, this usually means copying original drawings on lith film and printing them on glossy glazed paper. If possible, numbers and lettering should be added at the drawing stage rather than on the print. If transfer lettering is used it is altogether too likely to peel off the print, particularly if the print is rolled. It should be noted that although fold-outs and separate loose plans and so on are sometimes unavoidable, especially with architectural reports, they should be kept to a minimum. Fold-outs add greatly to the cost of binding, as do separate sheets if they are in wallets at the back of the publication. Separate sheets are also extremely unpopular with librarians, because they can so easily go astray.

By definition, the responsibility for producing a finished drawing ready for photography and subsequent reproduction lies with the draughtsman and not the photographer – although they may be the same person. It behoves the photographer, however, to point out whenever possible that any line in a drawing must be of solid black, and thick enough to survive when reduced to size. The same applies with even more force to transferred tints and hatchings. Line drawings of artifacts should always include a scale, whether or not they are drawn or printed to a set reduction, since they may later be reproduced from the publication to some other size.

If a large number of drawings are to be published, it is well worth while producing a camera-ready bromide print from the first available, and consulting with a publisher about its suitability. Unfortunately the traditional boast of blockmakers and printers, 'If you can see it, we can print it', no longer holds good for some processes, and to have plans or sections returned for redrawing after all the copy has gone to the printers is a time-wasting and expensive business.

The cost of colour reproduction more or less precludes its use in most archaeological and conservation reports, apart from the occasional frontispiece or an illustration of a particularly important artifact. This situation seems likely to continue in the foreseeable future, even though the cost of colour printing has risen less than that of other forms of printing in recent years, due largely to the widespread use of colour-separation by scanners. Books aimed at a wider audience than the professional archaeologist and conservator, however – guidebooks and regional and historical surveys, and the whole field of large-format picture books of one sort or another – rely heavily on high-quality colour illustration. The taking of such photographs is very much the province of professionals, and of a fairly small group of professionals at that. This is not to say that other people are not capable of this type of photography, but rather that for such a book the photography has to be planned meticulously, and the pictures taken with the book in mind, all in the same style and to the same standard. The rather piecemeal accumulation of transparencies taken during the seasons of a dig, or during a conservation programme, is formed with other ends in mind, and cannot be expected to show the same consistency nor, perhaps, the same aesthetic qualities. Colour photographs taken on digs or of objects have, of course, been published on many occasions outside the covers of site reports, because of their intrinsic interest, but only rarely have they formed the whole framework of a book.

Publishers normally prefer a larger size of positive than 35 mm for colour reproduction, but if 35 mm transparencies are all that is available they can be used, provided they are correctly exposed, have no noticeable colour bias and are of pin-point sharpness. The results of working with transparencies are often disappointing to the layman's eye because the extreme luminosity of a transparency viewed by transmitted light can never be matched in a reproduction printed in inks on paper. Colour prints, rather than transparencies, can also be used as originals, although most publishers prefer transparencies because of their purer colours and because there are more ways of dealing with them. If colour prints are used they should be unmounted.

The basis of the colour printing of tone originals is the separation of four colour plates, one for each of the complementary colours: cyan, magenta and yellow, and one for black. Each plate is screened to give tones as dots, and they are printed one over the top of the other but with the differently coloured dots separated, so that any colour can be reproduced using different proportions of the complementaries.

If a number of transparencies are being selected with a view to publication, they should always be viewed as a group. Quite minor differences in colour balance, which are hardly noticeable when transparencies are looked at one by one, and which may be inoffensive when they are shown singly as slides on a screen, can show up strongly if they are reproduced side by side on a page. It is even more necessary with colour originals than it is with line originals that the publisher, plate-maker or printer should be consulted on the suitability of transparencies before an ambitious programme is embarked upon.

Quite clearly this has been no more than a passing glance at the essentials of photo-mechanical reproduction and printing. Any archaeologist or conservator embarking for the first time on producing graphic material for publication would be well advised to learn something of the techniques and processes discussed and illustrated in, for instance, Craig (1974), Ballinger (1977), Sanders (1983) and Bann (1986).

15

THE FUTURE

As long as archaeological excavation continues, and as long as artifacts are studied and conserved, there will be a need for accurate visual records. How far such records will continue to be based on optical–chemical systems, or how far they will in future rely on electronic imaging in one form or another, cannot yet be predicted. New processes and new types of equipment are constantly being promoted, each apparently surpassing and superseding its predecessor. Because of this, great care has to be taken in setting up or re-equipping a project or laboratory, to ensure not so much that everything is the latest or the quickest – which hardly matters – but that apparatus and methods are not of a type that might become obsolete and therefore difficult to service or to supply with materials.

There are a number of fields in which developments of great potential interest are taking place. Two in particular seem likely to affect archaeological and conservation recording within a few years. These are the use of video and the introduction of digitalization in image capture and storage.

Video
At present, the resolution of detail and the recording of colour are considerably better with silver-based conventional photography than they are with video-recording, and the apparatus needed is simpler and cheaper. However, the use of video cameras on excavations, usually as a secondary visual record, is becoming more widespread (Hanson and Ratz (1988), Grace (1988) (but see also Hanson (1988)) and Locock (1990)), and there have in fact been suggestions that in the future video could serve as the primary record.

There can be no doubt of the usefulness of video-tape as a sort of visual diary of an excavation, especially during the writing-up and post-excavation period, when it can serve to recall the relationships of structures and phases quickly and easily. Similarly, the context of a find could perhaps be seen and understood more completely by means of a video sequence panning or zooming from the background to the artifact than it could from a series of still photographs. For this sort of use, unedited tapes, or tapes edited only to the extent of linking together the sequences from the same areas, should suffice, and any ordinary camcorder, preferably used on a tripod, should give reasonable results. Those unfamiliar with using camcorders, however, would do well to consult an introductory manual on the subject e.g. Brookes (1985)

251

or Davison (1993). There are several mistakes that nearly everyone makes when first using such cameras, especially over-enthusiastic panning and zooming, which can detract from the result.

Because of its immediate availability, such a record can also be of advantage during the course of an excavation, given a player and monitor. For instance, supervisors can discuss and review work going on in the different areas, and visiting specialists can be given an overview of the excavation.

In the same way, video could be of great value in conservation, not so much for recording aspects of the artifact being conserved as in showing the stages and processes of its treatment for later discussion, demonstration or monitoring.

Beyond this use as a visual diary or as a simple unmodified record, there are a number of fields in which video-tapes and discs are playing an increasing role, often combining still and moving images, text and graphics, usually with a spoken commentary or other audio component. The main fields are in teaching, in the introduction and explanation of sites to visitors, and in the compilation and analysis of data.

Although the use of such multi-media presentations is well established as a highly effective way of conveying fairly complex information, the methods available for recording and combining images, text and commentary are constantly changing and developing, and it would be rash to try to predict what methods and equipment might be in use in five or ten years' time. (For a survey of present and potential methods in the field of archaeology, see Lock and Dallas (1990) and Martlew (1992).) It is worthwhile nevertheless to say more about present uses and techniques, and to form some idea, however tentative, of probable future developments.

In the first place it is necessary to emphasise that the filming, production and editing of video to a high standard (the sort of standard which audiences have become accustomed to on television) is a highly skilled and professional business, calling for the talents and experience of a range of specialists. It is not likely to be achieved by a field archaeologist or a conservator in the intervals of doing other work.

Secondly, the cost of equipment, beyond a simple camcorder, is considerable and beyond the reach of most digs, although a university department or an archaeology unit might think it worthwhile.

Thirdly, at present and probably for a good many years to come, the publication of sites and artifacts will be overwhelmingly by way of monographs and journals, and single images taken by a video camera – even to broadcast quality – are not yet of a high enough resolution to allow of their reproduction in printed works. So competent photographs on film will still be necessary.

A final caveat concerns archival quality. Any information held on magnetic tape is subject to deterioration with time, and the useful life of a video-tape is probably of the order of ten to fifteen years. Tapes can, of course, be easily copied, and their lives thereby renewed, but each copying entails a loss of picture quality and colour balance, even if the organization exists for such long-term monitoring and treatment of the archive.

So far as equipment is concerned there is a considerable gap both in cost and in the level of skill needed between ordinary camcorders, designed and manufactured for the home video market, and professional equipment giving broadcast-quality results. The same sort of gap, of course, exists between mass-market and professional equipment for still photography, but here, commonly, a competent photographer can produce good results using simple equipment, which is often not the case with video work. There are, it is true, cameras and recorders which stand midway between professional and amateur level, for example VHS-S and 8 mm formats, but unfortunately neither of these can be edited or played using ordinary VHS equipment.

The next ten years or so will probably see the introduction of another major development in video presentation: high-definition television. This, of course, will be a worldwide phenomenon with great commercial and financial implications, and may finally resolve the anomalies of the different TV formats of America, Asia and Europe, but a small offshoot of the development should be that video-generated images will become of a quality good enough for printing reproduction.

As well as video-tapes or video-discs which can best be considered as narrative or expository, i.e. starting at the beginning and following a single path to the end, the last few years have seen the introduction of multi-media, interactive discs: discs incorporating a great deal of ordered, stored visual information through which the user can choose different predetermined paths. At the moment such discs function only as computer peripherals, the paths chosen or changed by means of a mouse or touch-screen, but it is expected that within a few years the necessary programmes will be built into the discs themselves, and they could then be used in video-disc players. In this country, the exemplar of such discs in the field of archaeology is the 'Leicester Archaeology Disc' (Martlew (1991, 1992)) which incorporates, among other things, images and details of all the stone circles in Britain. Undoubtedly in the future similar discs will become a powerful tool in teaching and research. Each can incorporate an immense collection of data; the discs themselves are almost impervious to deterioration, although not to damage; many different arrangements of the data can be presented, depending on the computing power available; and two or more audio channels can be incorporated, giving commentaries at different levels, or in different languages. All these advantages mean that the disc, once assembled, can serve several different purposes. It can act as a straightforward catalogue, assembling images of all the objects or structures from a site, a region or a period, or from a museum collection, together with relevant information for each image. For research purposes a wide range of characteristics can be quickly compared and selected, while for teaching, images, text and commentaries can be assembled at different degrees of complexity for different levels of teaching, with the added advantage that students are able to change direction into more detailed examination of particular aspects if they so choose.

The chief drawback is, as usual, cost. The assembly and production of such a disc obviously calls for a great deal of initial research and expertise – akin to that needed for a major printed publication – although, once produced, the cost per disc is low. Moreover, the market is ill-defined. No doubt some librarians would be willing to buy a definitive catalogue of sites or collections, even though the cost would have to cover a proportion of the production expenses, just as they would be willing to buy a book covering the same ground, but some might be deterred by the need for accessible computer equipment, while the triple function of reference, research and teaching might prove to be a deterrent: one or other function might be of interest, but not all three. In addition, there remains the problem of resolution of the image. As was said earlier, video-generated images are not so far of sufficiently high resolution to allow of their retrieval from the tape or disc for close study, let alone publication; and while they are reasonable when seen from ordinary television-viewing distances – two or three metres – they are not so satisfactory seen from the distance convenient for using a mouse or touch-screen.

Within the next few years this problem also may be overcome with the introduction of digitally recorded video, although to judge by the now well-established process of digitally recording still pictures, at the cost of curtailing the number of images that can be recorded on a disc or tape.

Digital recording

The process of digitally recording images, storing them on compact video discs, and retrieving them either on the screen or as hard copy, has become, within the last few years, relatively widespread in commercial photography, and in the long term it offers a solution to the enduring problem of the storage and management of pictorial archives in many fields, including archaeology. Several large corporations are developing or manufacturing systems – supposedly compatible one with another – and at the moment Kodak's Photo CD system seems the most viable. The original may be the direct input from a digital camera, although these are expensive, of relatively low resolution, not easy to use, and unlikely to be suitable for archaeological work for some years, if ever. Alternatively, a colour or black and white negative or positive can be scanned, and tones and colours recorded as an array of digital values. The image can be stored in this form and retrieved at different levels of resolution. Various programmes exist, or are being developed, for this retrieval, so that the image can appear at relatively low resolution suitable for reference and selection either singly on the screen or as icons (postage-stamp-size images in predetermined groupings) or at high resolutions suitable for off-printing. At the highest resolution the system can deliver a 10×8 in print indistinguishable from a silver-based colour print. The degree of resolution determines the total number of images that can be preserved on the disc. In concert with this and similar systems, a number of programmes have been developed whereby the stored image can be manipulated; tones, colours, contrasts and proportions changed; parts of the picture rearranged or eliminated, or parts of other images inserted. To an extent the same sort of thing can, of course, be done by physical retouching of any print, but with computer retouching the process is quite undetectable; unless a back-up of the original image is retained, the new image would completely replace the old. It is difficult to imagine circumstances in which such manipulation of an image would be of concern in everyday archaeology or conservation, but it might become so in cases where photographs are evidence in the illegal traffic in antiquities.

This rather paranoid reservation apart, it can be envisaged that in the future a combination of digitalised image storage and text and graphic discs could provide an excavation archive encompassing all the records, including even site notebooks and working drawings, in an accessible and permanent form.

It is only in recent years that this aspect of archaeological and conservation photography – the assembly and management of archives – has been seen to be of major importance. Few would disagree that the records of even minor excavations and surveys, and of the artifacts recovered, should be preserved, but rarely is provision made, either in budgets or in space and storage equipment, for reliable archival preservation. In this country there are major accessible archives such as that held by the Archaeological Records Section of the Royal Commission for Historical Monuments; but there are many small excavations the records of which have been lost and, more important, numbers of excavations abroad of which the drawings and photographs are uneasily divided between museums or university departments, Departments of Antiquities in the countries concerned, and the excavators' (or their executors') private files. It is, of course, a difficult and thankless task to try to assemble the records of past excavations, especially those for which no particular body now feels responsible, and to rehouse and if necessary conserve them is expensive and unlikely to attract funds. At least, however, the need to ensure the preservation of the records of present work should always be acknowledged. Archaeologists and conservators must recognise a duty not only to preserve the past, but to conserve the record of its preservation.

Instrumental analysis
There are a number of other techniques now being used, or being introduced, in archaeology and conservation, for example scanning electron microscopy, in which the results are being recorded on film, and all that is required photo-

graphically is an absolutely reliable and standardized way of processing and printing these results. With others, such as flint surface analysis and remote sensing, a combination of computer and photographic means is used to enhance, quantify, and distinguish differences across surfaces, whether these surfaces are the facets of a hand-axe, an assemblage of pollen grains, or an aerial photograph of a stretch of country. The output of many types of instrumental analysis, however, is in the form of computer-generated and printed graphs or cluster-diagrams; fast, accurate, and to the specialist at least wonderfully informative. Too often, though, such print-outs are used for publication just as they are, and the results on the page are grey and spidery, with attendant legends and figures appearing in type-faces unsuited to the printed page and clashing with the text. At worst they can be almost illegible. Re-drawing or re-photographing such figures to camera-ready standards may involve extra time and expense, but the gain in legibility is well worth while.

Conventional equipment

Some more immediate developments in conventional photography also give promise of improved technical results. For example, medium-format cameras, although still expensive, are becoming more common and accessible, and their wider use should result in a general improvement in black and white negative quality compared with that obtained by the ubiquitous 35 mm format. Both colour and black and white films, also, have been improved considerably in recent years as far as the resolution of detail is concerned, as has the accuracy of colour reproduction in colour positive films.

There is one aspect of present-day archaeological and conservation photography that must give rise to some anxiety. The widespread use of 35 mm cameras has undoubtedly led to a degree of carelessness in their use on excavations. There are published reports (though a small minority) in which the photographs have obviously been taken with little thought; the excavator has simply picked up his or her camera at some convenient pause in the work, pointed it more or less in the right direction, and taken a snap, relying on the camera to decide on exposure and aperture.

Another cause for concern is lack of standardisation and consistency. It is often not appreciated – or perhaps not appreciated in time – how much more comprehensible an illustrated report can be if successive photographs of artifacts under study or conservation, or of objects and structures *in situ*, are taken from the same angles, under similar lighting and against similar backgrounds.

Whatever the new techniques available to archaeology and conservation in the coming years, the goals of photography will remain the same: maximum clarity, a comprehensive and comprehensible record of the site or the artifact, and an enduring archive.

REFERENCES

Arnold, C. R., Rolls, P. J. and Stewart, J. C. J. 1971. *Applied Photography*. Focal Press, London and New York.

Badekas, J. (ed.). 1975. *Photogrammetric Surveys of Monuments and Sites*. North-Holland Publishing Co., Amsterdam and Oxford.

Ballinger, R. A. 1977. *Art and Reproduction*. Van Nostrand Reinhold Co., New York.

Bann, D. 1986. *The Print Production Handbook*. Macdonald and Co., Ltd, London and Sydney.

Barker, P. 1982. *Techniques of Archaeological Excavation*. Batsford, London.

Bircaud, B. 1991. 'Note sur un procédé de photographie des objets en obsidienne', *Cahiers de l'Euphrate*, 5–6, 127–129.

Blaker, A. A. 1976. *Field Photography*. W. H. Freeman and Co., San Francisco.

Bridgman, C. F. and Gibson, H. L. 1963. 'Infrared luminescence in the photographic examination of paintings and other art objects', *Studies in Conservation*, 8/3, 77–83.

British Journal of Photography. 1986. 39, Photokina report, 1110.

Brookes, K. 1985. *Video Film Making*. Argus Books, Hemel Hempstead.

Buchanan, T. 1983. *Photographing Historic Buildings*. HMSO, London.

  1986. 'Peripheral lighting', *British Journal of Photography*, 40, 1136.

Callahan, E. 1987. 'Metallic powder as an aid to stone tool photography', *American Antiquity*, 52 (4), 768–772.

Chéné, A. and Réveillac, G. 1975. 'La photographie en archéologie', *Les Dossiers de l'Archéologie*, 3, Nov.–Dec.

Collins, S. 1992. *How to Photograph Works of Art*. Amphoto, New York.

Conlon, V. M. 1973. *Camera Techniques in Archaeology*. John Baker, London.

Conze, A., Hunser, A. and Benndorf, O. 1880. *Neue Archaeologische Untersuchungen auf Samothrake*. Carl Gerolds Sohn, Wein, (Taf XXII).

Cooke, F. B. M. and Wacher, J. S. 1970. 'Photogrammetric Surveying at Wanborough, Wilts.', *Antiquity*, 44, 214–216.

Cookson, M. B. 1954. *Photography for Archaeologists*. Max Parrish, London.

Council for British Archaeology. 1991. *Signposts for Archaeological Publication*, 3rd edition. London.

Craig, J. 1974. *Publication for the Graphic Designer*. Watson-Guptill Publications, New York.

Crone, D. R. 1963. *Elementary Photogrammetry*. Edward Arnold Ltd, London.

Dallas, R. 1980. 'Surveying with a camera, rectified photography', *Architectural Journal*, 20 Feb., 395–399.

  1983. 'Plumb-bob to plotter; developments in architectural photogrammetry in the United Kingdom', *The Photogrammetric Record*, 11 (61) (April).

Daniel, G. 1967. *The Origins and Growth of Archaeology*. Penguin Books, London, 143.

Davison, P. 1993. *The Camcorder User's Video Handbook*. Boxtree, London.

Dean, J. 1981. *Architectural Photography: Techniques for Architects, Preservationists, Historians, Photographers and Urban Planners*. American Association for State and Local History, Nashville.

Dever, W. G. and Lance, H. D. (eds). 1978. *A Manual of Field Excavation*. Hebrew Union College and Jewish Institute of Religion, Cincinnati and Jerusalem.

257

Di Peso, C. C. 1975. 'Problems of site photography', in Harp (ed.), 1975.

Dorrell, P. G. 1973. The photography of flints', in Strong, D. E. (ed.), *Archaeological Theory and Practice: Essays Presented to W. F. Grimes*. Academic Press, London and New York.

Duke, P. J. and Michette, A. G. 1990. *Modern Microscopics*. Plenum Press, New York and London.

Evans, J. 1984. *Photographic Lighting in Practice*. David and Charles, Newton Abbot and London.

Evans, Joan 1956. *A History of the Society of Antiquaries*. Oxford University Press, Oxford, 290–292.

Feyler, G. 1987. 'Contribution à l'histoire des origines de la photographie archéologique, 1839–1880', *Mélanges de l'Ecole Française de Rome*, 99 (2).

Fleming, D. 1978. 'A simple wooden tripod for vertical photography', *Institute of Archaeology Bulletin*, 15, 131–148.

Grace, A. 1988. 'Archaeology through the viewfinder: an assessment of the potential application of video in archaeology', *Scottish Archaeological Review*, 5, 12–18.

Graham, R. and Read, R. 1986. *Manual of Aerial Photography*. Butterworth and Co., London.

Graham, W. A. 1981. 'Overhead site photography; how to build and use the monopod', *CEDAC Carthage Bulletin* 4, 53–55.

Hanson, W. S. 1988. 'Every picture tells a story: comment on archaeology through the viewfinder', *Scottish Archaeological Review*, 5, 15–16.

Hanson, W. S. and Rahtz, P. A. 1988. 'Video recording on excavations', *Antiquity*, 62, 100–111.

Harp, E. (ed.). 1975. *Photography in Archaeological Research*. University of New Mexico Press, Albuquerque.

Houlder, E. 1980. 'Scales in photography', *Archaeolog*, 13, 6.

Howell, C. and Blanc, W. 1992. *A Practical Guide to Archaeological Photography*. UCLA Press, California.

Jacobson, C. I. and Jacobson, R. E. 1978. *Developing*. Focal Press, London.

James, D. I. 1979. 'The effects of low-intensity reciprocity law failure in macrophotography', *The British Journal of Photography*, 48, 1163.

Jeffrey, I. 1981. *Photography. A Concise History*. Thames and Hudson, London.

John, D. H. O. 1965. *Photography on Expeditions*. Focal Press, London and New York.

Joukowsky, M. 1980. *A Complete Manual of Field Archaeology*. Prentice-Hall Inc., New Jersey.

Keefe, L. E. and Inch, D. 1990. *The Life of a Photograph*. Focal Press, Boston and London.

Kenworthy, M. A. *et al.* 1985. *Preserving Field Records*. University Press, University of Pennsylvania.

Kodak. 1969. *Photomacrography*. Technical Publication N–12B.

  1970. *Kodak Filters for Scientific and Technical Uses*. Kodak Publication B–3.

  1972. *Ultraviolet and Fluorescence Photography*. Kodak Publication M–27.

  1977a. *Handbook for the Professional Photographer, Vol. 1*.

  1977b. *Applied Infrared Photography*. Kodak Publication M–28.

  1978. *Professional Photographic Illustration Techniques*. Kodak Publication 0–16.

  1985a. *Prevention and Removal of Fungus on Prints and Films*. Kodak Customer Service Bulletin AE–22.

  1985b. *Storage and Care of Kodak Films and Papers*. Kodak Reference E–30.

  n.d. *Photography in the Tropics*. Kodak Data Booklet GN–5.

Langford, M. J. 1974. *Professional Photography*. Focal Press, London and New York.

  1986. *Basic Photography*. Focal Press, London and Boston.

  1989. *Advanced Photography*, 5th Edition. Focal Press, Oxford.

Lawson, D. 1972. *Photomicrography*. Academic Press, London and New York.

Layard, A. H. 1849. *Nineveh and its Remains* (2 vols). Murray, London.

Levin, A. M. 1986. 'Excavation Photography. A day on a dig', *Archaeology*, 39(1), 34–39.

Lewis, J. and Smith, E. 1969. *The Graphic Reproduction and Photography of Works of Art.* W. S. Cowell Ltd, London.

Lock, G. R. and Dallas, C. J. 1990. 'Compact Disc – interactive; a new technology for archaeology?', *Science and Archaeology*, 32, 5–14.

Locock, H. 1990. 'The use of the video camera for archaeological recording. A practical evaluation at Dudley Castle, West Midlands', *Scottish Archaeological Review*, 7, 146–149.

Martlew, R. 1991. 'Every picture tells a story: the Archaeological Disc and its implications', in Lockyear, K. and Rahtz, S. (eds), *Computer Applications and Quantitative Methods in Archaeology*. BAR International Series 565, Oxford.

———— 1992. 'The implications of large scale image storage for primary archaeological research', in Reilly, P. and Rahtz, S. (eds), *Archaeology and the Information Age*. Routledge, London.

Matthews, S. K. 1968. *Photography in Archaeology and Art*. John Baker, London.

Muir, R. 1983. *History from the Air*. Michael Joseph, London.

Myers, J. W. 1978. 'Balloon Field Survey, 1977', *Journal of Field Archaeology*, 5, 145–159.

Myers, J. W. and Myers, E. E. 1980. 'The Art of Flying: Balloon Archaeology', *Archaeology*, 33/6, 33–40.

Nassau, W. E. 1976. *Practical Photography for the Field Archaeologist*. Wilfred Laurier University, Ontario.

Newton, C. T. 1862. *A History of Discoveries at Halicarnassus, Cnidus and Branchidae*. London. (Plate LXI).

Nylén, E. 1964. 'A turret for vertical photography', *Antivariski Arkiv*. 24. Stockholm.

———— 1978. 'The recording of unexcavated finds: X-ray photography and photogrammetry', *World Archaeology*, 10(1), 88–93.

Parr, P. J., Atkinson, K. B. and Wickens, E. H. 1975. 'Photogrammetric work at Petra, 1965–68', *Annual of the Department of Antiquities of Jordan*, 20, 31–45.

Pattison, S. R. 1872. 'On a bronze vessel from the province of Huelva, Spain', *Archaeologia*, 43. (Plate xxxix).

Philibert, P-Y. 1975. in Chéné, A. and Réveillac, G., 1975.

Pillet, M. 1962. 'Un pionnier de l'Assyriologie: Victor Place', *Cahiers de la Societe Asiatique*, XVI. Paris.

Place, V. 1867. *Ninive et l'Assyrie* (3 vols). Paris.

Reiss, F. 1990. 'An improved technique for photography of artefacts in the field', *Mediterranean Archaeology*, 3, 47–54.

Riley, D. N. 1987. *Air Photography and Archaeology*. Duckworth, London.

Sanders, N. 1983. *Photographing for Publication*. R. R. Bowker Co., New York and London.

Schulman, J. 1977. *The Photography of Architecture and Design*. Billboard Publications Inc., New York, and the Architectural Press, London.

Simmons, H. C. 1969. *Archaeological Photography*. New York University Press, New York.

Smithsonian Institute. 1951. *Smithsonian Meteorological Tables*. Washington.

Spence, C. (ed.) 1990. *Archaeological Site Manual*, 2nd edition. Dept of Urban Archaeology, Museum of London.

Sterud, E. L. and Pratt, P. P. 1975. 'Archaeological intra-site recording with photography', *Journal of Field Archaeology*, 2, 151–167.

Stewart, H. M. 1973. 'Photogrammetry in archaeology', in D. E. Strong (ed.), *Archaeological Theory and Practice*. Academic Press, London and New York.

Stroebel, L. 1986. *View Camera Technique*. Focal Press, London and Boston.

Weide, D. L. and Webster, G. D. 1967. 'Ammonium chloride powder used in the photography of artifacts', *American Antiquity*, 32, 104–105.

Whittlesey, J. H. 1974. 'Aerial archaeology; a personal account', *Journal of Field Archaeology*, 1, 206–208.

　　1975. 'Elevated and airborne photogrammetry and sterophotography', in Harp (ed.), 1975.

Williams, J. C. C. 1969. *Simple Photogrammetry*. Academic Press, London and New York.

Wilson, D. R. 1982. *Airphoto Interpretation for Archaeologists*. Batsford, London.

Wright, R. B. 1978. 'Photography', in Dever, W. G. and Lance, H. D. (eds), 1978.

Zayadine, F. and Hottier, P. 1976. 'Relevé photogrammétrique a Petra', *Annual of the Department of Antiquities of Jordan*, 21, 93–104.

INDEX